The twelfth-century renaissance

MANCHESTER
UNIVERSITY PRESS

The twelfth-century renaissance

R. N. SWANSON

MANCHESTER UNIVERSITY PRESS

MANCHESTER AND NEW YORK

distributed exclusively in the USA by St. Martin's Press

The right of R. N. Swanson to be identified as the author of this work has been
asserted by him in accordance with the Copyright, Designs and Patents Act 1988

Published by Manchester University Press
Oxford Road, Manchester M13 9NR, UK
and Room 400, 175 Fifth Avenue, New York, NY 10010, USA
http://www.man.ac.uk/mup

Distributed exclusively in the USA
by St. Martin's Press, Inc., 175 Fifth Avenue, New York,
NY 10010, USA

Distributed exclusively in Canada
by UBC Press, University of British Columbia, 6344 Memorial Road,
Vancouver, BC, Canada V6T 1Z2

British Library Cataloguing-in-Publication Data
A catalogue record for this book is available from the British Library

Library of Congress Cataloging-in-Publication Data applied for

ISBN 0 7190 4255 0 *hardback*
       0 7190 4256 9 *paperback*

First published 1999

06   05   04   03   02   01   00   99   10   9   8   7   6   5   4   3   2   1

Typeset in Dante
by Koinonia, Manchester

Printed in Great Britain
by Biddles Ltd, Guildford and King's Lynn

Contents

List of figures

Preface

Although it remains a staple feature of undergraduate courses in medieval history, and generates considerable interest, students usually find the 'twelfth-century renaissance' difficult to deal with. While there is an ever-expanding flow of specialist literature on particular aspects, the range of survey texts is surprisingly limited. The basic introductions have remained unchanged for too long: the main outlines are still those which I myself used as an undergraduate far too many years ago.

One consequence of this is that students often find work on the twelfth-century renaissance appealing, but infuriating. Dependence on older texts for the basics frequently means that their detailed work requires amendment in the light of research which is more recent, more specialised, but frequently less accessible. That, and conflicts between authors, cause confusion.

Not much can be done about disputes between authors: they are usually signs of the healthy debate which surrounds many of the sub-themes brought under the subject's broad umbrella. Something can be done, however, to give a more up-to-date introduction, which is the aim and function of the present book: it makes no claims to be anything more. A full restatement of the material and debates on the subject would require a truly massive tome. My own interest in it was stimulated as a student, and has been maintained as a teacher, but I do not come to the task as someone deeply immersed in research on the period. That non-involvement has its benefits. I have taught an Optional Unit on the subject at Birmingham, given the appropriate lectures in survey undergraduate courses, and dealt with several generations of student essays on it; but as a non-participant in the debates among researchers, and unaffected by their personal priorities, what follows aims to provide a fair summary of current approaches and views.

The more work that is done on the twelfth century, the more critical the century appears in all spheres of human activity. Concurrently, expanding research produces greater incoherence. Nowhere, perhaps, is that more evident than in the debates about 'the renaissance of the twelfth century'.

One of the greatest debates concerns the very validity of the label of 'renaissance' for the cultural and intellectual changes of the period. It would be easy to prejudge the issues and assume either that the label applies, or that it does not, and offer a book based on one or other of those propositions. I have tried to avoid that. The first chapter offers a brief survey of the development of the subject, and of the debates it has generated (including that about 'renaissance' itself); but the others deliberately leave the options open, or at least try to. They treat aspects of the changes which took place roughly between 1050 and 1250 – a 'long twelfth century' – as the framework and basis for the debates among historians. But they deliberately try to avoid a partisan conclusion. It is for the reader to decide, ultimately, whether the concept of a 'twelfth-century renaissance' is acceptable and tenable. Yet, to stay astride the fence throughout would be both tiresome and a dereliction of duty. The last chapter therefore returns to the debates, providing the opportunity for me to offer my own verdict. As a personal and avowedly subjective judgement it may or may not convince; that does not really matter. The conclusion chiefly serves as a departure point, something to attack or defend in another context, a statement – perhaps a temporary anchor – to be tested (maybe completely rejected) by subsequent deeper reading. If it does that, the book is justified.

Looming over any attempt to deal with the momentous changes of the years 1050–1250 is Hugh of St Victor's stark injunction: 'Learn everything; you will see afterwards that nothing is superfluous. A skimpy knowledge is not a pleasing thing.'[1] Daunting as that comment may have been to Hugh's contemporaries, it is even more unnerving to a historian now. I have not read everything, and could not; indeed, the more I did read, the more I was aware of what I had not read. I can only fall back on another quotation from Hugh: 'The wise student ... considers not how much he knows, but of how much he is ignorant.'[2] For gaps, errors, confusions, and failures to pick up the latest changes in dating or ascriptions, I can only apologise, admit guilt, and plead the mitigating circumstances of current university life. The work has relied mainly on the resources of Birmingham University Library, supplemented by occasional Inter-Library Loans, and raids on Cambridge University Library. The torrent of relevant material shows no signs of abating; but only so much can be assimilated and confined within the word limit assigned by a publisher (a limit which has none the less been broken).

1 *The Didascalicon of Hugh of St Victor*, trans. Jerome Taylor (New York, 1961), p. 137.
2 *Ibid.*, p. 95.

No book is written in isolation, every textbook ransacks the work of others. This one is based on debts accumulated over a period perhaps longer than is usual, which it is harder than normal to personalise. My prime obligation is to all those authors whose work has stimulated, annoyed, and intrigued me over the years: but for them, indeed, this book would never have been attempted. A major debt is to students at Birmingham. Since 1979, successive intakes of first-years have traipsed through the debates, been appalled by the booklists, and constantly forced me to refine ideas. More recently, those who took the Option course pushed some of the ideas to the limits, challenged interpretations, and made me think and rethink. Of course, none of them is responsible for what follows; but it is certainly true that, without them, it would not have been written.

As always, my family has lived with this book in all its episodic progress from idea to reality. They told me off for spending too long on the computer, dragged me away to be sociable, and generally tried to make me get my priorities right. They did not always succeed; but their victories were worthwhile.

The last stages of preparing the text for the press were even more hectic than usual. I am grateful to Louise Edwards at Manchester University Press for her patience, and to Monica Kendall for conscientious and perceptive copy-editing. I am especially grateful to Suzanne Reynolds and Christopher Wilson for their last-minute help in dealing with illustrations.

I

Debates and contexts

ALTHOUGH the existence of a 'twelfth-century renaissance' was postulated by French scholars as early as 1840, the idea acquired coherent identity in the English-speaking world only in 1927, with the publication of Charles Homer Haskins' *The Renaissance of the Twelfth Century*. It remains a focus of debate, yet seems ever-changing, constantly perplexing. This book attempts to answer the question: Just what is this 'twelfth-century renaissance'?

The search for an answer requires that other fundamental questions must also be posed as preliminaries: questions of content, time, and location, of what, when, and where? These intermingle, but are distinct. They cannot be tackled in order; nor can precise answers be promised. This chapter aims to establish the bases of any attempt to define what the twelfth-century renaissance might be. Subsequent chapters will offer partial solutions to the substantive questions, with the last giving my own view, intentionally personal but intentionally not exclusive or definitive.

All three of the fundamental issues tend to be sucked into a black hole of trying to identify 'what' the twelfth-century renaissance might be, particularly when discussion turns to the concept of 'renaissance' itself. Debates on historical definitions may sometimes seem little more than dreary semantic exercises; but the problem of definition is a real one. In this respect Haskins had the advantage of writing when the issue did not need to be met head-on: he was merely suggesting that the twelfth century might be accorded a status commensurate with that normally allowed for the later Renaissance of the fifteenth and sixteenth centuries – *The* Renaissance – which was already a secure feature of historical enquiry. Nevertheless, to claim that the twelfth century was a time of renaissance automatically elicits comparison with the later event, and runs the significant risk of deforming historical perceptions.

When asked to articulate their idea of 'renaissance', most people would probably respond with a mixture of Italy, art, and classicism. The weight of the later Renaissance, with its associations with Michelangelo and Leonardo, and perhaps Petrarch at a pinch, inevitably imposes presuppositions about what any other 'renaissance' should contain. More refined analysis might wish to include 'humanism', a weasel word which proves elusive in definition, but is nevertheless considered a 'Renaissance characteristic'. There might be a more explicit insistence on the sense of the past, of a new age which was consciously building on classical founda-tions (and, in the fifteenth century, equally consciously abandoning the medievalism of intervening centuries).

The emphasis on Italy and on art for the late medieval phenomenon raises real questions about how a 'renaissance' label might be applied in earlier centuries. How far can it be applied to other manifestations of cultural change and development? Must all transitions which have been called 'renaissances' be tested against the late medieval version, or can they instead be taken on their own terms, using the word merely in an indicative rather than definitive sense?

Such questions are not mere sophistry, for the twelfth century has been the victim of precisely such quibbling. In 1948 and 1951 the pages of *Speculum* accommodated a series of short articles on the nature and identity of the twelfth-century phenomenon. Nothing concrete came of that brief flurry, even though the articles drew attention to the spectre of historical – and historians' – uncertainty, which still affects approaches to the issues. Indeed, the challenge to historians inherent in the debate about the meaning of the term was effectively swept under the carpet. For R.W. Southern, writing in 1960, the label of twelfth-century renaissance was 'a mere term of convenience which can mean almost anything we choose to make it mean ... It achieves ... the sort of sublime meaninglessness which is required in words of high but uncertain import.'[1] In 1969, Christopher Brooke concurred. The label 'carries overtones ... But it is vain to search for a definition.'[2]

Yet it is impossible not to search for a definition. Meaninglessness, no matter how sublime, is still without meaning. It is hardly surprising that, in 1977, the conference organised to commemorate the fiftieth anniversary of the appearance of Haskins' survey felt obliged to ask

---

1 R.W. Southern, 'The place of England in the twelfth-century renaissance',
   History, 45 (1960), p. 201. These comments are omitted from the revised version
   of the essay included in his *Medieval Humanism and Other Studies* (Oxford, 1970).
2 Christopher Brooke, *The Twelfth Century Renaissance* (London, 1969), p. 13.

questions to construct, if not a definition, at least 'a conceptual framework for ... reflection'. The first of six sheaves of questions posed with this aim sought to clarify the 'defining characteristics of the renaissance':

> What is meant by the term renaissance? Can it be said to have had a beginning or an end? In what areas of learning and knowledge was its impact primarily felt? Can it be understood exclusively in terms of a revival of classicism? Did it involve broad changes in point of view, such as attitudes toward God, the world, and the self? Was it associated with a new view of history? a new sense of change and progress? a willingness to accept innovation? Did these in turn contribute to the emergence of new secular values?[3]

Part of the 'conceptual framework' has to be chronological, with the very term 'renaissance' invoking comparison across time. Just how validly that can actually be done is an important issue, here made even more complex by the fact that 'The Renaissance' is in reality no more than a historians' construct, and its own identity is now insecure. As has been pointed out,[4] to combine the earliest date at which that renaissance allegedly begins with the latest date at which it ends gives a period of over 400 years; yet a combination of latest starting date and earliest finishing date reduces it to a mere twenty-seven. Such disparities make it virtually impossible to establish a consistent yardstick against which the twelfth century can be measured; always assuming that it has to be measured against any such standard in the first place. Moreover, the great Renaissance has itself fragmented, or at least acquired offspring: the amoebic tendency of academic specialisation and analysis means that what once seemed a reasonably coherent and identifiable template against which to test other claimants to renaissance status has now virtually dissolved.

Yet there is no shortage of candidates for that status. The nineteenth-century French scholars who argued for a twelfth-century renaissance also suggested that another occurred even earlier, under the Carolingians in the ninth century. That Carolingian renaissance remains well-entrenched, although not without its own problems of definition and

---

3 Robert L. Benson and Giles Constable, 'Introduction', in *Renaissance and Renewal in the Twelfth Century*, ed. Robert L. Benson and Giles Constable (with Carol D. Lanham) (Oxford, 1982; reprinted Toronto, Buffalo, and London, 1991), p. xx.

4 Paul Oskar Kristeller, 'The Renaissance in the history of philosophical thought', in *The Renaissance: Essays in Interpretation* (London and New York, 1982), p. 128.

identity.[5] Now, however, the search for renaissances has become so contagious that virtually every medieval century has acquired one (even if not always as a continent-wide phenomenon). Several have been squeezed in between the Carolingians and the twelfth century; and even though the traditional historiography did not leave much room between the end of the twelfth-century movement and Petrarch's role as midwife to The Renaissance, at least one more has been detected in the crack, located in the Spain of Alfonso X.

This proliferation of medieval renaissances intensifies the problems of identification and distinction. Any attempt to establish whether there was a twelfth-century renaissance must set fairly precise boundaries, in time, space, and content. Their formal definition can be left for later; their creation merits some discussion here.

Time is obviously important: must any twelfth-century renaissance be restricted precisely to the years from 1100–1200? Few would be so pedantic, and Haskins extended his own coverage to a period beginning c. 1050 and extending not quite to 1250. However, once the chrono-logical edges start to fray, how much fraying can be accepted before the definition becomes meaningless? For the years before 1100 the issue is perhaps not too insistent; although as more work is done on the eleventh century it is becoming more so, with emerging hints that the eleventh century deserves a more positive assessment than it has often received. It can now be claimed that 'The eleventh century has gained a reputation for innovation and imagination; the twelfth for normalization and secure growth.'[6] While this remark chiefly relates to economic changes, its perspective is echoed in considerations of other aspects of the time. For one commentator, 'The humanists of the twelfth century wrote out of nostalgia, not out of the vaunting self-confidence of an age of Renaissance. Their works are shoring to stave off the inevitable collapse of a culture passing out of existence.'[7]

Turning the spotlight to the eleventh century highlights the problem of seeking the origins and impetus for the twelfth-century changes. Questions of continuity and contexts arise, without which what is labelled the 'twelfth-century renaissance' becomes merely an episode.

5 See e.g. Rosamond McKitterick, *The Frankish Church and the Carolingian Reforms, 789–895* (London, 1977), pp. xvi–xvii.

6 S.P. Bensch, *Barcelona and its Rulers, 1096–1291*, Cambridge studies in medieval life and thought, 4th ser., 26 (Cambridge, 1995), p. 399.

7 C. Stephen Jaeger, *The Envy of Angels: Cathedral Schools and Social Ideals in Medieval Europe, 950–1200* (Philadelphia, PA, 1995), p. 9.

The question of boundaries also reappears. Arguably, for instance, a consideration of intellectual evolution must take in the debate generated by the eucharistic speculations of Berengar of Tours (d. 1088), which means going back to the middle of the eleventh century. Lanfranc and Anselm of Canterbury have always been considered honorary (and actual) participants in the twelfth-century movement; their teaching activities at Bec justify giving the abbey's school a mention in the academic changes of the time. The significant boost to canon law during the so-called 'Investiture Contest' of *c.* 1073–1122, when bishops, kings (and would-be emperors), and popes locked horns over their relative theoretical (and, consequently, practical) powers, similarly pushes the frontier backwards. Other developments also date back before 1100; but for these the world of shadows is less penetrable.

While the extension of boundaries into the later eleventh century is relatively unproblematic, at the other extreme things become more difficult. As the twelfth century gradually fades out, into scholasticism, the twelfth-century renaissance whimpers off stage. The difficulty of identifying the later terminal point may owe something to undergraduate syllabi: the twelfth-century renaissance suddenly confronts the pontificate of Innocent III, with the Fourth Lateran Council of 1215 providing a convenient if arbitrary end. Yet there is also something of a tradition, based on the link between the twelfth-century renaissance and the spread of Aristotelianism, which sees the appearance of the Latin translation of Aristotle's *Politics* in the 1260s as the signal for the end. Once the full Aristotelian corpus was available, the twelfth-century renaissance could end, and Aquinas could really get going. The problem here is one of ambivalence. From another viewpoint, the translation of the *Politics* provides the green light for the start of the *real* Renaissance. While a single date can be both an end and a beginning, here the role of Janus seems decidedly artificial, perhaps unsustainable. The translation of the *Politics* seems to link, rather than separate, the two movements. The search for other roots of 'the' Renaissance produces other collisions. The identification of someone like Lovato Lovati (1241–1309) as an early Renaissance humanist leaves very little (if any) gap between the two movements, while making the chronological boundaries very precise, and apparently arbitrary.

The question of the geographical limits for a 'twelfth-century renaissance' is equally insistent. In some ways 'where' is harder to resolve than 'when' or 'what'. 'Europe' (which silently excludes the Byzantine empire and other Orthodox territories, and the non-Christian territories of Spain until their conquest) is too imprecise: it may be necessary to allocate specific strands to different areas, while admitting that the immediate impact on others was relatively minimal. Regionalisation is another form of fragmentation; but the 'where' of renaissance also extends to specific social, economic, and cultural contexts which provided not merely opportunity, but encouragement. Those contexts which were actually disincentives must also be acknowledged. The focus here will be on France, Italy, and England, with excursions to Spain and Germany. The question of how far these areas can be treated as a solid and single geographical unit is something to be considered as discussion advances.

With the insouciance of a pioneer, Haskins could blithely sketch out an expansive map of the cultural changes in the twelfth century: the chapter headings of his book – focusing on topics like 'Intellectual centres', 'The revival of the Latin classics', 'The revival of science', and 'The beginnings of universities' – catalogue virtually everything which was happening in the cultural arena in those years. On that model, the fruit of the 1977 conference to mark the fiftieth anniversary of the publication of Haskins' opus, the volume of essays entitled *Renaissance and Renewal in the Twelfth Century* (edited by Robert L. Benson and Giles Constable, and published in 1982) was equally inclusive. Yet its ambitious coverage also shows the cracks which had appeared in the concept's unity since 1927, and so revives the fundamental question of the coherence of any 'twelfth-century renaissance'. How much of a unit is it? How much attention needs to be paid to differing regional inputs in the cultural changes, to the different disciplines which are represented, to the differing demands, and the abilities to satisfy those demands? Can discussion of twelfth-century art and architecture, let alone the rise of the troubadours and vernacular poetry on courtly love, legitimately be treated of a piece with transformations in attitudes to law, the emergence of a theological science, and the origins of the universities? Do we have to start looking not at a European phenomenon, but at a series of regional phenomena, each distinct even if linked? Does it then follow that we have to construct a hierarchy of regions, of places which had 'more of a renaissance' than elsewhere?

Depending on the answers offered to these questions, further questions may follow. The process of working out what is to be included also entails exclusion, consigning certain cultural activities to a 'non-renaissance' shadow-land, because they do not fit. The need to make such choices may, however, suggest that the time has come to discard the notion of a single, all-embracing twelfth-century renaissance, whose impact is assumed to be Europe-wide. The unitary phenomenon may need to be replaced by a series of more closely defined movements which more accurately reflect the way in which understanding of the twelfth-century world has changed since 1927. This would not denigrate or undermine the significance of Haskins' work; it would, though, subject it to the processes which in due course affect all pioneering histories, as their analyses become increasingly divorced from the reality perceived by their readers.

Before turning to the cultural and intellectual transitions of the period c. 1050 to c. 1250, the broad European background requires some comment. No twelfth-century renaissance could occur in splendid isolation. Its components must be set against the background of their time, of the conditions which facilitated the changes, and which allowed their development. That backdrop is a complex one, often raising issues of causality and coincidence: questions of chickens and eggs are never far from the surface.

Without falling into a determinist trap, perhaps the key feature in the general European context between 1050 and 1250 was the massive economic transformation. This was a period of continued and almost unrelenting expansion, a lift-off which was perhaps too drawn-out to merit being called a revolution, but none the less had revolutionary results. There are, indeed, good grounds for integrating the economic and technological transformations into a renaissance. Such, however, are the effects of academic ring-fencing and the constraints of word limits that that cannot be done here. The possibility should not, however, be forgotten.

In these years, agricultural production grew as population increased and colonisation and reclamation liberated more land for exploitation. Trade expanded as the Mediterranean became increasingly a Christian lake, and the North Sea and the rivers which fed it developed their own economic coherence. There was a fundamental transformation, perhaps best summarised as commercialisation. The increasing role of money within the economy was a means of liberation and a cause for concern. Commercialisation offered increased opportunities for trade, and an expansion of the market; including an extension of the trading community within which Europeans could operate. Not only were the northern and southern economies developing, but the two were united by the lynchpin of the Champagne trade fairs. Cash – and with cash, credit – became an increasingly important factor in the economy, something both movable and exploitable. Cash also challenged received wisdom: money did not rot, could be accumulated and hoarded, exacerbated differences between rich and poor, and raised ethical problems when lent at interest. It is symptomatic of the scale of money's cultural impact that avarice and usury became, alongside pride, the great sins of the long twelfth century. Cash also provided opportunities: it was portable, and could therefore be transported; it snapped ties between land and landholder, allowing a rent-paying tenant or farmer to be set between them, transforming land for some into a source of revenue at a distance, rather than produce; it meant skills of all sorts could be hired; it made life generally more mercenary.

This commercialisation was not universally welcomed, and commercialisation alone would have been insufficient background or stimulus for the twelfth century's cultural and intellectual changes. The problems raised by this new economy did not have to be confronted; they could be shunned. Attacks on usurers in many ways ignored economic potentialities and realities; many sought to evade rather than resolve the emerging tensions by a radical rejection of 'the world'. This is a particular characteristic of religious movements in the period, ranging from the hermits and early Cistercians of the late eleventh century, through the poverty movement of people like Waldes in the twelfth, to the apostolic poverty of St Francis and his followers in the early thirteenth. There had to be a moral accommodation to money, a redefinition of the ethics of *nouveaux riches* and poor, which took some time to evolve.

Closely linked to the commercialisation of the economy, and an important element in the overall context of the period, was Europe's growing urbanisation. Towns were becoming increasingly important and distinctive, as the combination of trade and money reduced the intimacy of their ties with the countryside. As relatively large centres of population, sucking in produce (and people), centres for the exchange of goods and services, centres of administration and government, they did not have to produce wealth to survive. To some extent parasitic, they could support cohorts of students and their teachers (even if those cohorts were numerically fairly small), providing accommodation and services, especially for independent schools and scholars who were now less tied to the institutional structures of monastic and cathedral schools. This proved particularly important at Paris, at the heart of an area where economic growth was particularly notable; but it also has more general application.

Significant also was the relative peace of twelfth-century Europe, especially at its core in that broad band running from Italy through France into England. It was, of course, only relative peace, and the disruption caused by outbreaks of civil war (as in England in the reign of Stephen, 1135–54), or by the incursions of the emperor Frederick I into Italy in the second half of the century cannot be overlooked; but it still provided a more stable background for change with the reconstruction of government. Perhaps most importantly, peace reduced fear, and thereby encouraged freedom of movement. This was especially significant for those operating within the Church, the Latinate clerics (not necessarily priests) who provide the backbone of many of the major developments of the period. A striking feature of these years is the sheer mobility of individuals: Italian canon lawyers like Vacarius were active in England; English clerics participated in the government of the Kingdom of Sicily. Some people were clearly willing and, more important, able to move around. They moved voluntarily, not through coercion.

Peace both grew from, and contributed to, political stability. The enhancement of Capetian authority around Paris, the enforcement of government in Angevin England and the Norman kingdom of Sicily, even (despite a seeming contradiction) the emergence of communal institutions in northern Italy, all contributed to this process, guaranteeing peace and providing employment. Although governmental and admini- strative developments will be considered more specifically in due course,[8] they deserve mention here as a facilitating feature. The new governmental structures (enhanced by the general cultural shift 'from memory to written record', which encouraged administrative develop- ment at all levels of the society) created a demand for administrators and clerks, provided employment opportunities for those with the requisite skills. Enhanced prospects encouraged people to take advantage of the novel developments which characterise the period. The circle completed itself, and developed into a spiral.

One other 'internal' element must be integrated into this contextual framework. It may be represented as a 'new mentality', one which gave greater attention to the laity, especially those below the ranks of nobility. A widening range of historical sources brings much more of the Euro- pean population into the historical picture, making 'ordinary laypeople' much more visible. Society was becoming appreciably more complex. Even if the model society of the Three Orders (those who prayed – the clergy, those who fought – the knights, and those who worked – the peasants) had never existed in reality, those who did not fit into it were becoming increasingly obvious. Merchants and townspeople, for instance, were not peasants, but neither were they knights or priests.

8 Below, pp. 98–102.

New social complexities for laypeople had to be acknowledged, and addressed. Moreover, the world of the Three Orders was overtly male; yet women now appear to challenge its formulations.

The laity become particularly visible when dealing with religious developments and spirituality, indicating that Church leaders were increasingly aware of their concerns, and felt obliged to address them. Here the problem of the 'twelfth-century renaissance' merges into that of the 'twelfth-century reformation'.[9] It is clear that worries about the changing contexts of the twelfth century were shared by many of the laity, and were not confined to clerics. The laity sought answers to some of the fundamental questions raised by Christianity in the period's new social contexts, on problems of evil, of human relationships and responsibilities. There are signs of considerable lay dissatisfaction with existing ecclesiastical and spiritual structures, in the laity's support for aspects of the Gregorian reform movement, their participation in the poverty movements, their openness to heretical ideas. Laypeople were as much affected by the social and economic changes of the period as the clergy, and worried about their souls accordingly; yet it was for the clergy to resolve those worries. While groups of both clergy and laity fled the challenge, there are signs of growing awareness of lay spiritual and moral needs, and with this greater concern about the Church's pastoral responsibilities during the twelfth century. This concern appears, for example, in the way that Augustinian canons assumed duties as preachers and parish priests. After the Fourth Lateran Council of 1215 it would burgeon into what has been labelled a pastoral revolution. This awareness of a lay perspective provides yet another undercurrent to some of the intellectual concerns of these years, particularly relevant in the emergence of a specifically pastoral theology concerned with the nature of sin and the possibilities for redemption.

One final aspect of the broad context remains to be mentioned. After 1050, no longer threatened by the attacks of Vikings, Saracens, and Avars, Latin Christendom took the offensive. The response to Pope Urban II's call to crusade, issued at Clermont in November 1095, was the most dramatic and potent demonstration of this shift, even if presaged by the Norman encroachments in central and southern Italy, and their assault on Muslim-held Sicily. It was also foreshadowed in Spain, where papal involvement in the anti-Muslim campaigns from the 1060s used to be

---

9 On this see the useful summary by Brenda Bolton, *The Medieval Reformation* (London, 1983), or the magisterial survey by Giles Constable, *The Twelfth-Century Reformation* (Cambridge, 1997).

considered prototype crusades, and where the frontier stunningly jerked southwards with the conquest of Toledo in 1085. Although the advance in Spain was obviously led by the local Castilians, Catalans, and Aragonese, there was considerable French involvement. This derived from the colonising activities of the French religious orders (especially the Cluniacs and Cistercians), from the involvement of French knights in the fighting, and from dynastic changes which brought Capetians to the throne of Portugal and Burgundians to that of Castile.

The southward and eastward advances had massive cultural implications, bringing western Europeans into immediate and long-term contact with different civilisations. Particularly important here was the specifically French character of much of the expansion in these areas: the Levant, southern Italy, and Spain. In all three areas, moreover, access to a locally cosmopolitan culture offered opportunities for outsiders. The crusader states provided contacts with Arabic culture, and through Constantinople and the native Christians of the Middle East (whose presence and importance are too easily overlooked) access to Greek as well. In southern Italy, the establishment of a Latin veneer over Lombard, Greek, and Muslim cultures – with, for a while, strong contacts with North Africa – created a zone of cultural exchange which, given southern Italy's role as a transit territory attracting many north Europeans, must have assisted the spread of new ideas. Finally there was Spain, which is a case all of its own. There the survival of a Mozarabic culture (albeit marginalised by the newly imported papalist Latinity of Gregory VII and his successors, establishing a Church which required trans-Pyrenean clerics for its implantation) offered the possibility of extensive cultural interchange. The continuity of Muslim settlement in newly conquered areas, the presence of a significant (and active) Jewish population, and the constant dribble of cultured émigrés from southern Spain, provided a rich context for cultural exchange. Geographical expansion accordingly created conditions for a flow of ideas and texts into northern Europe, a flow which had massive implications for intellectual life.

To integrate all the intellectual and cultural transitions of the long twelfth century into these varied contexts in detail requires much more space than is available here. The contexts must often be assumed, rather than analysed. But they cannot be ignored. The changes associated with the 'twelfth-century renaissance' did not occur in isolation, no matter how isolated they may sometimes appear.

2

Educational structures

IN the whirl of changes associated with the 'twelfth-century renaissance', one idea which is often grasped as a lifeline of comprehensible evolution, uncluttered by unfamiliar names and inaccessibly Latinate ideas, is that the period saw 'the beginnings of universities'. So Haskins entitled his twelfth chapter, commenting that

> The twelfth century ... was an age of new creation ... most of all in the institutions of higher education. It begins with the monastic and cathedral schools, it ends with the earliest universities. We may say that it institutionalized higher learning or at least determined that process ... The university is a mediaeval contribution to civilization, and more specifically a contribution of the twelfth century.[1]

Haskins concluded his survey with these educational changes, as something of a culmination. To place them at the start of this overview may, then, seem deliberately perverse. Yet the educational transitions are a key factor which give some overall coherence to the period as one of 'renaissance' (or, more precisely, of my own view of what that 'renaissance' might be). Reflecting, producing, and consolidating several other changes of the time, the educational transitions appear central to any attempt to give coherence and comprehensibility to the many evolutions (particularly the intellectual evolutions) which are crowded together as aspects of the twelfth-century renaissance. The new educational structures generated during the long twelfth century amounted to a fundamental institutional change, whose long-term impact is still felt.

While 'universities' did emerge over these years, to highlight 'the beginnings of universities' is too specific. It is now accepted that

---

1 Charles Homer Haskins, *The Renaissance of the Twelfth Century* (Cambridge, MA, 1927), pp. 368–9.

universities did not actually emerge during the twelfth century itself. Embryos developed, but their future growth could not be predicted or assumed. Yet 'universities' do become visible by 1250 – few in number and differing in character and structure – making the label then applicable, but only with hindsight. There are no signs of contemporary awareness that new formal structures were being created – and apparently no real desire to create them – until the last years of the twelfth century. There was, however, a perceptible shift in emphasis which contemporaries could not have missed: a shift from an educational structure dominated by monastic needs, to one where cathedral (and other non-monastic) schools were the main influence.

Before 1100 the scholarly system was characterised by the existence of a dual pattern of monastic and cathedral schools, with differing purposes. The monasteries emphasised their role as repositories of knowledge which contributed to a spiritual continuum. The education they provided was very much focused on monastic needs, founded on a desire that monks should be intellectually replicated across generations, that their education should assist the meditative and liturgical features of their lives, and be an education for life. It was, in a real sense, a process of formation. This task was greatly eased by the practice of monastic oblation, whereby parents offered their children to the house while still very young, to embark on a life which they would never leave. Nurtured in an enclosed environment, the oblates were trained for a particular way of life which stressed obedience and their role as part of a tradition – in the technical sense of 'a handing on' – of both the way of life and its intellectual inheritance. The system was accordingly based on acceptance and assimilation of the known rather than investigation of the unknown or uncertain. Questions might well arise, but the answers were assumed to be already available, if the right authorities were consulted. If answers did prove elusive, God was expected to provide them through intuition and revelation. In a sense, this was an educational system in which real theology – as a dissective process to comprehend divinity – had little place, despite the emphasis on devotion and spirituality which gave an important place to meditation and communion with the divine. It may also be important that these educational arrangements were essentially local. Although most monastic houses before 1100 were 'Benedictine', they were not part of an integrated order, but autonomous institutions, living their own interpretations of the Rule. Self-contained and self-replicating, the houses functioned over time by their inmates becoming habituated to the thought patterns and intellectual norms of the particular place. Books and texts did circulate, and there were real attempts to create libraries, but the distribution and copying of texts remained haphazard. There was little sense of a 'need' for particular works, little obvious concern for gap-filling or multiplication of copies, because the texts themselves were not the bases for discussion and debate, but stimuli to meditation and rumination.

Non-monastic educational activity before 1100 remains something of an ill-considered quantity. Schools, masters, and pupils obviously did exist. Nevertheless, continuity, context, and activity are rather uncertain, across all of western Europe. Despite valiant attempts at investigation, and to fit them into a broader cultural pattern, cathedral schools before 1100 are relatively dark horses. Although some teachers and students rose to fame (like Gerbert, master at Rheims in the tenth century, who gained the papal throne as Sylvester II in 999 and was renowned for his extensive learning, or Fulbert of Chartres, who gained his reputation as a teacher at Chartres in the early eleventh century), most are obscure. The basic function, and size, of the cathedral schools are often unclear. Even their distribution and catchment areas are uncertain. There is scattered evidence from northern France (for instance, Chartres, Laon, and Rheims) and the Rhineland (as at Cologne, Speyer, and Liège); but from elsewhere in Germany material is scarce. Schools were certainly operating in Italy: there non-monastic schools may not have been solely tied to cathedrals. Although educational texts survive from pre-Conquest England, concrete evidence on the location and contexts of non-monastic schools is almost non-existent. Yet, paradoxically, precisely something like the monastic process of habituation has recently been advanced as the key characteristic of northern cathedral schools in the tenth and eleventh centuries, although perhaps with insufficient justification. The cathedral schools, because they took in children only on a temporary basis, lacked the traditional component of the monastic system. Based more firmly within the world – a world where clerical marriage and clerical dynasties were not uncommon, and where patronage was vital to career prospects – the cathedral schools were arguably more vibrant and vital than many monastic establishments. Because they offered some sort of career training, for boys who would become administrators, and who were hoping to catch the eye of a patron (although patronage may also have been needed to gain access to the schools in the first place), there was perhaps greater keenness in some aspects of their work. To distinguish them from the monastic schools, these non-monastic schools are also labelled as secular, a term which reflects their links with the surrounding world without distancing them from an ecclesiastical or spiritual role (ordinary parish clergy were called secular clerics for the same reason).

The cathedral schools perhaps served primarily to provide a relatively basic education, teaching literacy and some rhetoric, perhaps to enhance documentary skills. These were certainly useful for priests and prospective administrators. But the teaching practices and formal educational arrangements remain obscure. Like the monastic schools, the cathedral schools perhaps had a replicative function: it has been claimed that their main function was instruction in *mores*, teaching the pupil to model himself on the master in behaviour and personal deportment, as well as transmitting the intellectual inheritance. A similar pattern appeared in private tutoring: recollecting his own education in the late eleventh century, Guibert of Nogent (*c*. 1068–*c*. 1125), contrasted the attempted inculcation of learning (which was unsuccessful) with the process of civilisation (which, he said, worked). The notion of the cathedral school as a sort of finishing institution may have some validity, but it is unlikely to have been the prime consideration in their organisation.

Detailed information on how these schools operated is only rarely available; sometimes in letters, sometimes in chance recollections, sometimes in the career of a dominant individual. Characteristic of such citations are the letter of the schoolmaster Goswin of Mainz to his pupil Walcher, written *c*. 1065, or John of Salisbury's description of the teaching practices of Bernard of Chartres, which he reports in his *Metalogicon* (completed in 1159, but referring back to *c*. 1115). The influence of a dominant individual is exemplified by the circle around Archbishop Bruno of Cologne in the late tenth century. This, however, may reflect a household rather than a school: where a bishop was particularly dominant, it is difficult to separate cathedral and household. In any event, a household could offer a third venue for learning. Parents might employ a private tutor (as happened for Guibert of Nogent); more important would be the attraction exercised by a magnatial, royal, or episcopal court, which could lead to the creation of a short-lived quasi-school. This would be especially important as a social phenomenon, providing a context for an explicitly 'courtly' education. It might also erode the barrier between laity and clergy based on assumptions of almost universal lay illiteracy.

Within the cathedral schools (and probably the monastic schools as well), instruction seems to have been directed primarily at the relatively young, in a process of rote learning which aimed to develop and inculcate grammatical and stylistic skills. Using a limited number of texts surviving from the Roman and sub-Roman period, rules would be learnt and applied. The surviving letters and memoirs suggest that this basic education might be literally beaten in: in medieval illustrations the bunch of twigs used to administer beatings was the identifying attribute of the schoolmaster. Uncertainty hangs over knowing when the beating stopped. Perhaps it was when enough seemed to have been drummed in, and the pupil was ready to pass from the basic skills to more advanced matters, including theology. Little is known of theological education before c. 1100. Some was offered outside the monasteries; but its content is unclear, although it probably centred on a basic analysis and explication of the Bible. There were theological debates: Berengar of Tours, who discussed the eucharist in the 1060s, had gained his knowledge somewhere, and as he had pupils and defenders was himself a teacher. Just how far back that tradition went, and how many people received instruction which was recognisably theological, are unknown. Much of the known written production of the early cathedral schools – surprisingly limited in amount – consists of letters, written in an extraordinarily embellished style which seems (despite the anachronism) almost rococo in its superfluous adornment. That very adornment reflects a concern with a practical education, one aiming to instruct diplomats, priests, and administrators, for whom rhetorical flourishes had to come easily.

This cathedral system, like its monastic counterpart, appears relatively static. Investigation and an inquisitive approach were unnecessary; the practical and utilitarian focus eliminated any need to ask questions, or, at least, questions of any radical significance.

This traditional picture of non-monastic education may hold good for most of Europe, but perhaps is more valid north of the Alps than in Italy. There, different cultural traditions possibly generated additional structures. Literacy appears more widespread there at an earlier period than elsewhere. Even in a degenerate form, retention of written Roman law encouraged contact with and dependence on the written word. The recording tradition, based on the notariate, helped to create a society in which writing, and therefore contact with documents, was relatively widespread. It is no surprise that the first manuals for letter writing, codifications of the *ars dictaminis*, appear in Italy in the early twelfth century.

Despite the Italian tradition of access to the written, the local educational system remains obscure. There are few references to schools, possibly because few were under clerical control. If educational provision was mainly lay, and perhaps more informal than elsewhere, there would be little chance of its being recorded. There were presumably some church schools, and almost certainly monastic schools, whose educational tradition probably did not differ significantly from that in the north. However, the difference in church organisation, especially the small size of cathedral chapters and the poverty of many episcopal sees, probably meant that few Italian cathedrals could afford to maintain their own schools. If the later history of ecclesiastical archives offers a guide, the Italian church fitted itself into the notarial (and thus lay) tradition, rather than educating its own corps of administrators. Italy's educational system may therefore have focused on practical literate production, essentially utilitarian in purpose, rather than the more eloquent and orally based education of the northern schools. Yet some 'academic' instruction must have been available, if only to ensure continuity in the ecclesiastical structures. Although Lanfranc and Anselm are usually associated with the northern evolution, they were both Italian, and each had received initial education in Italian city schools. Indeed, Lanfranc's case may be particularly revealing. He had been educated to a high standard (presumably at Pavia) in the liberal arts and (according to Orderic Vitalis, writing several years after his death) in 'civil law'.

Hints of change in the traditional northern pattern of education appear from the mid-eleventh century. Bec in Normandy offers vital evidence, although it may well be a unique case. The emergence of the cash economy meant that monastic education could be provided as a service, for fee-paying pupils without any aspirations to become monks. Here may lie the distinction between 'internal' and 'external' monastic schools, which presumably ended with the erosion of the internal schools as child oblation withered away in the twelfth century. Under Lanfranc, Bec's external school provided precisely such an educational service, for those seeking relatively advanced learning as well as for beginners. That, at least, explains why Anselm, having left Italy, stopped off at Bec, and after a short time decided to enter the house. He eventually took charge of the school, and for a while Bec became one of the leading schools in northern Europe. Perhaps only briefly, though: in this respect it was no different from the cathedral schools, with fame resting solely on the reputation of a single master, providing a fleeting period of prominence before sinking back into relative obscurity. Bec may, however, have remained a school of some importance until around 1140. Although its detailed curriculum is unknown, it produced numerous influential alumni, many of whom became abbots and prelates. There was also a strong contingent who did not enter ecclesiastical careers.

It is still unclear how differences between the internal and external schools affected the monastic tradition, or how widespread the existence of two schools actually was. Perhaps the real distinction was between an external school which emphasised linguistic skills, providing a form of 'vocational training', and an internal tradition which advocated training in meditative practices and awareness of the demands of spiritual life. The ambiguity is evident in Anselm's own intellectual progression. Although widely read, and concerned to explain his arguments, his dependence on inspiration for the resolution of theological uncertainties places him in a very distinct intellectual category, which might justly be called monastic. Texts might provide foundations for his thought, but the resolution of doubts was not explicitly based on textual authority. It is hard to see that approach being transferred to other areas of investigation, whereas a tradition of magisterial authority might be.

The decline in oblation meant the ending of the replicative tradition in which children became habituated to the monastic intellectual culture. Only a few generations after Anselm, Abbot Samson of Bury St Edmunds epitomised the transformation. He had been educated in a school run by a non-monastic master, Walter of Diss (whose son he duly rewarded with a benefice), and had spent some time at Paris. Samson's chronicler, Jocelin of Brakelond, portrays a man very different from Anselm: much more the down-to-earth administrator, and less imbued with a sense of monastic tradition.

While the evolution of 'monastic' education was affected by the decline of child oblation, perhaps more significant was the emergence of new definitions of the religious life in the early twelfth century, and the rise of the Augustinian canons. Their vocation was more pastoral than that of traditional monks, perhaps leading them to adopt a more outward-looking approach to education, stressing pastoral instruction, although their learning remained essentially monastic in focus. The one Augustinian school which was certainly active and outward-looking (at least for a time), at St Victor in Paris, may be as atypical of the canons as Bec was of the Benedictines.

The school at St Victor was established in 1109, when William of Champeaux (c. 1069–c. 1122) resigned his archdeaconry of Paris (and with it his teaching post in the cathedral) to retire to the left bank of the Seine. He offered free teaching to all comers, a policy continued until around mid-century. St Victor rapidly became a leading school, combining a contemplative approach to theology (especially to biblical studies) with a focus on pastoral and sacramental teaching, and laying the foundations for the concern with pastoral care prominent in thirteenth-century ecclesiastical policies. St Victor's early history is dominated successively by Hugh (d. 1141), Richard (d. 1173), and Andrew (although he was absent in 1147–c. 1154/5, and again after 1161/3).

The education offered at St Victor differed from that available elsewhere in Paris. It was certainly more controlled: Hugh reportedly checked his pupils' lecture notes weekly, to ensure that his instruction was being correctly received. As exemplified in Hugh's *Didascalicon*, the school offered a coherent and structured approach to learning, seeking personal improvement rather than acquisition of knowledge for its own sake, or for its future financial rewards. To that extent, the tradition at St Victor was essentially monastic in aspiration; to that extent, also, its relevance and practicality for non-monastic students decreased as time passed. The anachronism is exemplified in Richard of St Victor's *Liber exceptionum*, compiled between 1153 and 1160, a last fling of the all-encompassing encyclopedic texts which had appeared in the first half of the century. Like other monastic centres of learning, St Victor by 1160 was becoming a place for retreat from the schools. That change is embodied in its last leading master, Godfrey of St Victor, who ruled a school primarily concerned to instruct members of the community, rather than teaching others. More importantly, Godfrey was himself a product of the secular schools, entering St Victor after becoming dissatisfied with the learning offered by the Paris schools. But even St Victor could not provide a haven. In 1173 the appointment of an anti-intellectual prior, Walter, sounded the death knell. His *Contra quatuor labyrinthos Franciae* (*Against the Four Labyrinths of France*) was a vitriolic denunciation of recent secular theological teaching, and an abrupt repudiation of St Victor's educational tradition.

Although the monastic schools declined, religious houses remained centres of learning. They still maintained their libraries; they still received new inmates. Now, however, the newcomers were grown men rather than boys; several already had some education, with completion of studies in the 'arts' being seen by some as the point when the choice had to be made between continued progress in the secular schools, or a transition to the very different higher learning offered by the monastic life. The monasteries certainly needed to train their new monks, and to maintain an educational tradition. More significantly, they provided havens for world-weary former scholars. Monasticism's contribution to European intellectual history shifted its focus, but did not disappear. If anything, the emphasis on learning increased into the thirteenth century, as the regular orders evolved an educational compromise with the secular schools, and monks and canons began to attend the nascent universities. The foundation of the orders of friars – especially the Franciscans and Dominicans – proved even more significant. With their specific concern for mission and preaching, the friars created their own educational centres (*studia*), which also taught non-members. They also established major schools, *studia generalia*, at the leading centres, among them Bologna, Paris, and Oxford. Prominent Parisian theologians (for example, John of St Giles and Alexander of Hales (*c.* 1185–1248)) joined these orders but retained their teaching functions. The friars claimed to appoint the successors to their chairs. This, and the fact that the friars often continued teaching when the secular masters suspended their classes because of local disputes (as happened at Paris in 1229–30), contributed to the origins of a major conflict between secular and mendicant masters which festered from 1250 onwards.

The tentative changes in the monastic system of education in the late eleventh century were accompanied by signs of change in the non-monastic schools which would duly lead to their overriding prominence in northern Europe. These are presaged by the dispute over eucharistic theology between Lanfranc of Bec and Berengar of Tours, which began in the 1060s and lingered until Berengar retracted his views at a Lateran synod in 1079. Although this can be portrayed as a personal conflict between Berengar and Lanfranc, it contains elements of the clash of secular (that is, worldly) and monastic traditions, and indeed of the clash of schools of thought based on different concepts of reason. (Other nuances can also be discerned, if the conflict is seen as one between mind-sets: Lanfranc's response to Berengar has been likened to that of a lawyer rather than philosopher or dialectician or, for that matter, a theologian.) Behind both men also stood groups, even parties, composed as much of students and heirs-presumptive as other adherents. Berengar was a teacher; his opponents feared that his teachings would take root and become a tradition. Berengar also reflected a new approach to argument, where the initial direction controlled and dictated the route to the conclusions. Knowledge was no longer a given, the known end of the monastic system whose affirmation was the goal of the arguments and the test of their validity. Now the argument was used to test the validity of a conclusion, and became itself a bone of contention.

The debate surrounding Berengar was not about a novelty. For centuries the nature of what happened at the moment of consecration in the mass had been debated. Berengar, using logic and grammar to dissect the material anew, asserted that Christ could not be physically present in the consecrated host (although this did not prevent some form of 'real presence'). Philosophy precluded any possibility of the essential nature of the bread, its 'substance', being replaced by another substance (Christ) without the simultaneous annihilation of all the attributes (or 'accidents') of bread: its taste, smell, feel, colour, and so on. Lanfranc led the opposing camp, adopting an essentially authoritarian stance, rather than real argument. For him, Christ was physically present in the host, which lost its substance as bread whilst retaining the accidents. Authority – essentially papal authority – forced Berengar to retract his views, and Lanfranc emerged triumphant. But this was a knock-down, not a knock-out. Although philosophical language had been used in the debates, the meaning of the outcome was uncertain: Berengar still asserted a real presence in the sacrament, even if his understanding of what that meant differed from Lanfranc's. His defeat was no clear affirmation of 'transubstantiation', a word virtually unknown before 1180. Even at the Fourth Lateran Council in 1215, which adopted Lanfranc's position as dogma, the definition lacked precision, so that several interpretations were seemingly acceptable, at least during the thirteenth century.

Berengar's case marks a stage in the intellectual shift, setting a pattern repeated elsewhere. In the 1080s Roscelin, teaching at secular schools in northern France, used logical deduction to dissect the Trinity and discomfort Anselm. In turn, he was himself challenged for his application of mere human reason to the accepted truths of Christianity, producing unorthodox solutions which were simply unacceptable, and for which he was condemned in 1092. Roscelin, too, had disciples – for a time Peter Abelard was one of them – but so concerted was the condemnation of his Trinitarian theology that he did not manage to establish a lasting school, and sank into obscurity. So effective was the attack on him that, despite his central position in the debates, he remains a somewhat shadowy figure.

Although the debates circling around the theologies of Berengar and Roscelin (and perhaps, also, of Anselm) elevate the roles of individuals, the schools themselves were also becoming more prominent and gaining reputations, at least in northern France. Rheims maintained a powerful tradition until around 1120. Chartres under Bernard (d. *c.* 1130) was flourishing at the start of the twelfth century, primarily as a centre of grammar and basic linguistic skills. John of Salisbury's description of teaching methods leaves open the possibility that it was essentially a school for youngsters. Laon was also prominent, known for its theological tradition, which suggests a more mature clientele. Laon's reputation, like that of other schools, owed much to the influence of individual masters, in this case Anselm of Laon (d. 1117) and his brother Ralph (d. 1134/5), who taught there from around 1100. The early twelfth century also witnessed the first stirrings of the Parisian schools in their rise to prominence. The city was already a magnet before Abelard (*c.* 1079– *c.* 1142), appeared on the scene around 1100: his great aspiration was to teach there, and much of the early part of his *Historia calamitatum* shows him circling around the city, like a predator around its prey, seeking an opportunity to break into the charmed circle. The chief difference between Paris and other places with major schools at this point was the number of masters Paris could sustain, reflecting the city's economic and political advantages as the emerging capital of the Capetian lands. Whereas normally a town would support only one or two masters, Paris had the official school at the cathedral, schools on the Mont Ste Geneviève – technically outside the city but within walking distance of Notre Dame – and, after 1109, the school at St Victor. It was from the Mont that Abelard planned his break into the city. In addition, masters set up their own independent schools, like that established by Master Adam of Balsham at the Petit Pont. Paris sustained more masters than elsewhere, and more continuously. The city's continued attraction, for both students and masters, was an essential element in Paris's rise to pre-eminence among the schools of northern Europe.

The main problem concerning these early signs of educational change is the context within which they must be set. The schools' later institutional prominence, especially the transformation of some of them into universities, can skew the reality. A hunt for institutional development also deflects attention from individual scholars. Yet in the early stages it was precisely the prominence of individuals which gave some places their academic reputations. Without Lanfranc and Anselm, Bec would not receive much attention, for instance. Other schools are often analysed through the writings left by their leading teachers. This remains the case throughout the period: a school's historical reputation often rests on the writings of only a few people. (This, of course, is a major consideration when assessing the schools, as their culture was primarily oral, not written.) That schools existed in certain places may be recorded, but what they did, or why they arose, can only be guessed through the writings. Institutions cannot be investigated much before 1200. 'Universities' developed only later, as the masters (at least in Paris) saw a real benefit in the shift from the free market to a more regulated teaching structure. The search for the roots of institutions in this pre-university stage may distribute prominence unfairly, and push some places into an ill-deserved obscurity. In England, for instance, the intellectual activity at Northampton, Hereford, Lincoln, and York, in the twelfth century is as impressive as anything recorded for Oxford; yet their schools did not become universities. Why some places did not become universities in the period is just as intriguing as the search for reasons why others did.

In such circumstances, the continued importance of 'non-university' cathedral schools throughout the twelfth century, and probably later, needs to be emphasised. Indeed, Church legislation tried to buttress the educational function of cathedral schools as a medieval form of seminary. The Third Lateran Council, in 1179, decreed the maintenance of a grammar master at every cathedral. This was repeated (with an acknowledgement, admittedly, that the plan had not worked effectively) at Lateran IV in 1215, being then extended to other major churches. Lateran IV also required every metropolitan church to maintain a theology master, mainly to instruct the local clergy. Evidence of this scheme being implemented is scant; but the plan reveals assumptions of the continuing importance of the local cathedral schools.

Emphasis on the 'higher' education at cathedral and proto-university level also hides the equally significant increase in educational provision lower down the scale. Although leaving little evidence, basic educational provision must also have expanded to feed into the expanding network of advanced schools. Whether provided by household tutors (as with Guibert of Nogent), by maintenance in an episcopal or magnatial household, by a form of apprenticeship (as John of Salisbury was instructed by his local priest), or even by local priests taking in groups of pupils as an elementary school, the cumulative effect was to increase the numbers of literates, who could then join the emerging ecclesiastical and administrative career structures. Such people did not need to go to 'the schools', and lacked the resources to do so: beneath the scholarly elite existed a group of unknown size, some of whom may have resented their exclusion from the opportunities created by these educational changes.

As the schools evolved, so the curriculum and academic methods also changed, with a snowball effect as academic questions produced answers which in turn produced more questions. Each stage generated material for scholars to debate, for masters to teach about, and opportunities for students to compare and contrast solutions. As this happened, tensions appeared, orthodoxies were established or overthrown, and dangerous questions broached and then pushed under the carpet, or condemned as heresy. New rules of academic argument, notably the disputation (which required a formal partisan battle of wits), stimulated intellectual agility, inquisitiveness, and daring. 'Handing on', tradition, was discarded as analysis, argument, and debate took its place.

Despite the rearguard attempts to defend the monastic educational pattern, the balance tilted inexorably towards the secular schools. Their proliferation in Paris indeed suggests that the schools need not even be centred on a cathedral. This is confirmed from England, where Oxford, Northampton, and Cambridge were not cathedral towns, but were the sites for major Church courts, and therefore prominent legal centres. Similarly, at Regensburg, it seems likely that a major school (led for a time by the elusive Honorius Augustodunensis) was located at the *alte Kapelle*. Abelard's career hints at other possibilities, with his period of retreat at the Paraclete, when he continued to attract students outside an urban setting. This may have been repeated by other masters; they certainly wandered more in the early years than later on, and students might well follow them.

While a picture which emphasises the rise of the schools holds for northern France and England – and possibly also for the Rhineland – the situation in Italy, and in southern France, was different. The schools in these areas (apart from Bologna) have as yet received relatively little attention, but it is inconceivable that Italy was unaffected by the twelfth century's educational changes. Although the characteristic fruit of the northern schools, scholasticism, did not set deep roots in Italian schools (although it did among Italian scholars, to produce Bonaventure and Aquinas), it does not follow that Italian schools were insignificant. The tradition of scholarly activity had not died out: Milan cathedral certainly maintained schools in the late eleventh century; Bologna did not rise from nowhere. However, Italian education seems much less ecclesiastically (and clerically) focused than it was in the north. In the twelfth century, although there were prominent Italian scholars (like Peter Lombard), it is notable that they sought philosophical and theological learning outside Italy; there was no native tradition of such higher studies, and it seems not to have developed. The more literate laity, the stronger documentary and notarial tradition, perhaps gave Italian education a greater lay and practical influence, generating structures whose curriculum was less focused on ecclesiastical matters, and accordingly avoided ecclesiastical notice. Italian education may have been more like the 'business training' which emerged in thirteenth-century Oxford, providing practical commercial and administrative skills for people not destined for the Church. With rare exceptions, contemporaries recorded the existence of the northern schools (outside Paris) because of their legal and theological activities; instruction in grammar and philosophy drew little attention. Likewise, Italian schools are generally recorded because they taught law; but other subjects must also have been available, for how otherwise did the lawyers acquire their Latin, or the clergy the knowledge needed for their posts? Thirteenth-century Italian Cathar heretics were credited with running schools, some of them allegedly open to the public; there must have been equivalent Catholic structures.

The pitfalls surrounding analysis of the schools become concrete in the debate about the School of Chartres and recent comment on the School of Laon. Until the 1960s, Paris was acknowledged as a centre of teaching, but Chartres was accorded a leading role as a centre of learning (mainly in philosophy). Indeed, the 'School of Chartres' was generally treated as the most important and dynamic source of ideas in Europe in the first half of the twelfth century, beginning with the activities of Bernard, and then continued under his brother Thierry, William of Conches, and several others. The prominence and presumed attractiveness of these men and their ideas meant that Chartres was treated as an intellectual magnet: somewhat circular arguments exploited gaps in the biographies of other prominent thinkers and writers, and ambiguities in the sources, to associate them with Chartres if at all possible. The presumption that Chartres was important encouraged a search for evidence to confirm that presumption, no matter how flimsy it might be. Attempts to fill one remaining gap in John of Salisbury's account of his own education still reflect this tendency: was he actually at Chartres in the late 1130s or not?

The fragile edifice of the 'School of Chartres' was crushingly exposed by Sir Richard Southern; generations of historical speculation and local pride were demolished, as Chartres was relegated to being just another cathedral school. The great names formerly linked to Chartres were transferred elsewhere, usually to Paris, whose standing was accordingly enhanced. Attempted counter-attacks are not fully convincing; nor can much be made of a semantic distinction between the School *at* Chartres (meaning an undistinguished school located at the cathedral) and a School *of* Chartres characterised by a philosophy which can be labelled 'Chartrian'. The former certainly did exist; the latter is essentially a construct based on wishful thinking and hindsight. It is most unlikely that those whom historians identify as 'Chartrians' were consciously so, especially if the label carries connotations of self-identification. Nevertheless, the 'School of Chartres' still has supporters, on the basis primarily of 'a detectable family resemblance among the thinkers committed to the Chartrain project, despite their individual differences, and irrespective of whether they themselves studied or taught at Chartres'.[2]

---

2 Marcia L. Colish, *Peter Lombard*, Brill's studies in intellectual history, 41, 2 vols (Leiden, New York, and Köln, 1994), 1, p. 254.

The prominence ascribed to the 'School of Laon' has likewise been scrutinised, and found wanting. Here, however, historians had built differently: numerous anonymous texts offering theological exegesis whose provenance rested on questionable assumptions were amalgamated to demonstrate the intellectual vitality of Laon and of the exegetical tradition established by Anselm early in the twelfth century. Again, the School *at* Laon survives and, as with Chartres, the School *of* Laon still has defenders; but it appears that several of the texts ascribed to the School actually offer material for the world outside the schools, with several in fact, originating in south-western Germany.

Changes in the schools also affected the masters' careers. Peter Abelard's early life shows the possibilities well enough. He appears first as a student, a cleric but not overtly a priest. He aspired to teach at Paris: there were the students, there the rewards. But teaching might be offered on a private basis (in his case, to a woman), as much as to a 'school'. Once he became a teacher, Abelard operated in a world of competition, of rivalry with other masters to secure students: established masters had to watch their backs. Abelard's trouncing of William of Champeaux, even if not as complete as he proclaimed it, demonstrates the intensity of the competition. William retreated to St Victor, but could still at a distance prevent Abelard from taking his place. Anselm of Laon countered Abelard's attempt to challenge his position at Laon by securing his expulsion from the city, a conflict matched at Rheims, where Alberic drove out Walter of Mortagne after he established a rival school. (This probably happened in the 1120s, although the evidence on the date is not sound.) In the battle between masters to attract and retain students, whose fees provided their incomes, teachers had to offer quality or flair. Just what a teacher–pupil relationship should be remained uncertain; but there was a sense that, ideally, it would be based on a shared love of knowledge. Reality intruded: masters might be driven by a desire for popularity or wealth; pupils by the need to secure their own futures. John of Salisbury's record of the masters whose schools he attended (entered in the autobiographical section of his *Metalogicon*, a key passage for information on the Parisian schools in the 1130s) shows how pupils would construct the course they wanted, picking and choosing among masters as they thought appropriate; in the end voting with their feet, and with their money. (They could also vote with their poverty or stinginess. A major attraction of St Victor at Paris was that the school charged no fees; at the start of the thirteenth century Alexander of Canons Ashby ruefully recalled the lack of free teaching in his student days, in contrast to the several masters teaching without fees when he was writing.)

Largely unknown in all this is the real cost of attending the schools. Masters and students appear in the sources, but often in contexts which leave them detached from the mundane concerns of the surrounding economy and society. However, masters needed incomes; students needed funds. A major change in the twelfth century was a transformation in academic mobility. The masters who had initially wandered around, sometimes attracting pupils even though not formally attached to any establishment, became more stabilised. From the student perspective, the 'catchment area' for a school increased considerably, so that Paris could attract students from Italy, England, and Germany, as well as from France itself. (International attractiveness was not confined to Paris, as Bologna's appeal also shows.) Although a local cathedral school probably drew mainly from its own region, something fundamental had changed, to facilitate this mobility. High-quality education was now available for those who could travel to acquire it.

That travel had a prerequisite: the mobility of money as well as people. The internationalisation of non-monastic education in the twelfth century was possible only through the growth of the money economy. This applies especially to education at the advanced levels. Patrons could now fund students at a distance. Moreover, with the mobility of money (even if with the inconvenience of having to transport money), beneficed clerics could farm out their posts, receiving the fruits whilst far away. Regions where money's integration into the benefice system was relatively underdeveloped accordingly sent fewer people to distant schools. Such has been argued for some German cathedrals, where the maintenance of a common fund in kind, rather than its division into personal prebends with revenues convertible into cash, prevented chapter members from leaving the cathedrals for foreign schools. Students also earned money to cover their costs while learning. Here a 'trickle-down' effect operated: an advanced student would offer private tuition to less advanced pupils, using the payment to meet his own costs. John of Salisbury reports that poverty at one point forced him to such an expedient.

The integration of money into the evolving system caused some moral qualms. Among the uncertainties generated by growing reliance on a medium which increased social divisions and exploitation, one particularly relevant to academic life questioned the morality of masters demanding fees in exchange for their teaching. If the knowledge they were conveying was a divine gift, provided for the general advancement of humanity, how could restricting its spread by demanding payment be justified? Knowledge should be free. Perhaps that moral debate affected some of the masters who joined the mendicant orders in the thirteenth century; there is no sign that it restricted the activities of twelfth-century masters (as some students complained). Teaching was after all labour, and the acquisition of knowledge prior to its transmission a laborious process. In this case, surely, the labourer was worthy of his hire? There are, nevertheless, signs that Church authorities took the debate on board, in papal decrees banning charges for the *licencia docendi* (for formal licence to teach, usually granted by an ecclesiastical official), and in the provisions of the Third and Fourth Lateran Councils which sought to establish a network of gratuitous education.

The accumulating changes transformed the educational process into a tactical process, affecting both masters and students: tactics used by masters to acquire and retain pupils; by pupils to ensure their own education. With no defined system of courses or qualifications – the title of 'master' became more common during the twelfth century, but had no formal standing – there was no sense of working 'towards a degree'. Learning might thus be done in short bursts; doubtless many absentee incumbents only had an odd year at the schools. Learning involved wandering, intermissions, and a programme very much of the pupil's own devising, until he thought that he had done enough, and wanted to try something different. That certainly is the picture to be derived from John of Salisbury's experiences.

The insecurity of these arrangements, for both masters and pupils, is self-evident. Despite the tendency to ignore their surroundings, the twelfth-century schools were not ivory towers. The masters, lacking job security, were in fierce competition. Students who attended purely for the love of learning must have been in a minority, a small minority. Education was job-oriented. Even if the knowledge itself had little immediate utility (although its emphasis on verbal and intellectual skills was highly utilitarian), to have been through the schools gave, at first, a certain status. For the first generations, novelty and scarcity would be a bonus; over time competition for posts among those with similar experience would begin to emerge as numbers increased. Other factors could then affect the hunt for employment.

The priority for most pupils was probably to exploit their scholarly experience to secure employment. Their education was primarily voca-tional, with the stress seemingly on opportunities in law, medicine, and administration. Some would want to go further, to become theologians, and perhaps remain as teachers; but for most experience of the schools was transitory. This did not make the students mere sponges for learning: they could exploit (indeed, create) the competitiveness among the masters. The students' appreciation of the schools could also be warped by their expectations. The schools were certainly the place to acquire knowledge, but only as much as was needed for pump-priming. John of Salisbury complains vehemently about those who gained a smattering of knowledge of law or medicine, enough to dupe the customers, and then went off to earn the money (a complaint echoed elsewhere). Schools also provided opportunities to make contacts: perhaps one key function for students (and for some masters) was to provide networks, where would-be protégés could establish links with people who might have sufficient influence – immediately or later – to secure their employment. The forging of links, the creation of friendship networks (which had to be worked on continuously to ensure that they remained effective) was part of the experience.

Most schools did not offer high-level specialisation. The core of education was 'the (liberal) arts', seven in number, and divided into two groups. More expansive and formal schemes for education were rare, although Hugh of St Victor's *Didascalicon* proposed a complex and demandingly comprehensive scheme which included three further 'practical arts', covering ethics, economics, and politics, and an additional seven 'mechanical arts' which included commerce, agriculture, medicine, and hunting.

The dominant element in the curriculum was the *trivium*, comprising grammar, rhetoric, and dialectic (logic). Grammar and logic became the central subjects, rhetoric receiving much less attention. These three disciplines, the sciences of words, cultivated verbal and argumentative skills. Their interconnection was neatly summarised by Adam of Perseigne: 'rhetoric adorns the discourse that grammar constructs from words, and ... dialectic sharpens it by distinguishing truth from falsity'.[3] Grammar gave instruction in the Latin language, acquired very much as a foreign language, but the fundamental skill needed before all others.[4] (As levels of education became more differentiated, advanced grammar became a component of the first year of a university arts course.) Dialectic, the art of persuasion through reasoned argument, was a mainstay of philosophy and theology;[5] but some of the argumentative

---

3 Quoted in Stephen C. Ferruolo, *The Origins of the University: the Schools of Paris and their Critics, 1100–1215* (Stanford, CA, 1985), pp. 84–5.
4 Below, pp. 108–9.
5 See below, pp. 42–3, 108–9.

techniques it imparted were learned even at the elementary stages of education.

Rhetoric, the third trivial art, which persuaded through eloquence and emotional appeal, proved less resilient than the other two. This was partly due to its uncertain status: the borderline separating it from grammar was imprecise, so that rhetorical instruction was often subsumed under the other art. Rhetoric also suffered from being primarily practical. Although a revived interest in classical ideas of eloquence produced a rash of twelfth-century French commentaries on Cicero's *De inventione* and the pseudo-Ciceronian *Ad Herennium*, including works by Thierry of Chartres and William of Champeaux, rhetoric was mainly seen as a functional skill for the practical worlds of law and administration. One commentator explicitly labelled it a part of 'civic science', equating it with legal pleading and placing it alongside architecture, military science ... and cobbling![6] The stress on practicality generated a range of subsidiary arts derived from rhetoric. The *ars dictaminis*, dealing mainly with letter-writing and the rules of documentary production, went back at least into the eleventh century. It emerged as a formal scholarly discipline at the turn of the eleventh and twelfth centuries in Italy, also acquiring a strong foothold in southwestern Germany (a separate French tradition also arose in the twelfth century). Dictaminal skills were clearly important in Italy's notarial culture; there were close links between the *ars dictaminis* and centres of legal study (Bologna and Orleans), and with the evolving papal curia (where Transmundus produced the first version of his *Introductiones dictandi c.* 1180). Rhetoric also generated other verbal specialisms, including poetic analyses (culminating in Geoffrey of Vinsauf's *Poetria nova* of *c.* 1210, later recast in prose as the *Documentum de arte versificandi*), and instruction manuals on the composition of sermons, the *artes predicandi*. The unstable boundary between grammar and rhetoric perhaps appeared even at elementary levels; aspects of the *ars dictaminis* may have been treated as grammar in some of the northern cathedral schools.

Beyond the *trivium* in the seven liberal arts lay the *quadrivium*, the four sciences of number: geometry, arithmetic, music, and astronomy. Each of these changed during the period, but their academic history is obscure. Evidence for quadrivial teaching in the schools is limited, but it

---

6 J.O. Ward, 'From antiquity to the Renaissance: glosses and commentaries on Cicero's *Rhetorica*', in *Medieval Eloquence: Studies in the Theory and Practice of Medieval Rhetoric*, ed. J.J. Murphy (Berkeley, Los Angeles, and London, 1978), p. 49 n.66.

did occur. Occasional 'quadrivial' references are scattered through texts in other disciplines (like the use of the mathematical formulation 1 x 1 x 1 = 1 as an aid to explaining the Trinity), and suggest an awareness of quadrivial concerns, even if not at any great depth. Usually, however, on all counts a school's curriculum, and indeed its very existence, are known only from occasional citations, with the consequent risk of making too much of too little. Many English schools remain shadowy, and their vitality cannot really be tested. Moreover, the fact of teaching guaranteed neither quality nor modernity. If Salisbury cathedral's extant collection of early twelfth-century texts illuminates interests there, and those interests were translated into teaching, the curriculum offered would have lagged a generation or so behind the teaching of Paris.

For most students, an 'arts' education was sufficient, usually restricted to the *trivium*. The next academic step would be into law or theology, although neither could as yet be considered a 'higher faculty'. Not many pupils made the transition. Most had a spell at the schools, and then reverted to a normal routine, even if not that of their pre-school days. (There was, of course, no bar on a later return to the schools; some ex-students might go back for 'refresher courses'. Such students may have been the intended recipients of the theological education demanded in major churches after 1215.) In general, appearances are affected by perspective: knowledge of how the twelfth-century educational system operated derives primarily from famous individuals; but they are of necessity extraordinary, the people whose use of their education (or other factors) took them beyond the norm, and out of anonymity. Most students remain unknown.

The same problem applies to the masters. The lack of institution-alisation, and of the administrative records which accompany it, and dependence on the evidence of texts, means that we know more of people and their mature (or maturing) ideas than of where and what they actually taught. Such uncertainties, compounded by doubtful ascriptions of particular works, and by the many texts lacking authors and locations, often mean that discussions of the twelfth-century schools and their impact have to be constructed on extremely shaky and insecure foundations.

While the rise of the non-monastic schools was the main educational transition, the twelfth century is usually cited as marking the beginnings of the universities. This concern for university origins is a bit perverse: what few there were cohered mainly in the thirteenth century. Most twelfth-century schools remained just schools. Yet if they were not yet universities, some twelfth-century schools had reputations as centres for particular types of study. Paris was acknowledged as the prime location for philosophical and theological studies (Laon's reputation as a theological centre had rapidly declined after 1130). Medicine was the main subject at Montpellier and Salerno. By mid-century Bologna was the centre for legal studies, especially of Roman law. Canon law also emerged there after the appearance of Gratian's *Decretum* in the 1140s. Franco-centrism, or a distaste for law as a learned and applied subject, may explain a tendency to marginalise Bologna in the twelfth-century changes: the same thing happens with some of the German schools. Cologne, for instance, had an important law school, but attracts little notice. The lawyers these schools produced were, nevertheless, in great demand in the emerging governmental structures of Church and realms. The link between the practice and teaching of law may in part explain the growth of some schools, and their transition into universities. That has been suggested as a key aspect of the emergence of Oxford and Cambridge, as both towns accommodated ecclesiastical law courts.

The increasing complexity of education, especially at the major centres, bred the first signs of institutionalisation. Structures necessarily evolved, although the evolution was not preordained. Two different types eventually predominated, based on the models of Paris and Bologna. Each reflected a different resolution of the difficulties created by the influx of students and masters.

The Parisian system became the most widely applied. In this, the masters were the dominant force. The strong ecclesiastical basis to the Parisian schools – centred on Notre Dame, on St Victor, and on Ste Geneviève – gave the Church an immediate hold over the teaching, as the chancellors of Notre Dame and Ste Geneviève licensed teachers as part of their monopoly on teaching within their jurisdictions (in this respect, proto-universities were no different from other schools). Meanwhile, self-interest urged the masters to reduce their rivalry, limit the volatile habits of their pupils, and share out the benefits of being masters more equitably. The emergence of a 'university' – a word with no specifically educational connotations – was basically the establishment of a closed shop for the masters. The 'university' was a grouping of masters, a professional guild, concerned to protect its own interests by limiting the number of teachers, and establishing and maintaining additional privileges (usually relating to jurisdiction over themselves and their pupils, against the claims of ecclesiastical, royal, or urban officials). Set up as a guild of masters, with a hierarchy which made completion of the arts course the entrée to higher studies (of which the highest was theology), the university could begin the proliferation of officials, structures, and fees which characterised its later existence. This process came to fruition in the first decades of the thirteenth century. In 1215 the papal legate, Robert de Courson, issued the first set of statutes, and papal recognition as a corporation was confirmed in the bull, *Parens scientiarum*, of 1227.

The Bologna model was different. There, although the city lay within territory later claimed as part of the papal states, in practice it was self-governing, under an emerging commune. Much remains obscure about the appearance of a model university in an Italian town which was somewhat off the beaten track, and had no obvious attractions. The acquisition of a reputation as a centre of legal studies seems to have been the initial spur. Students flocked there, but perhaps masters were equally mobile. (Who wanted to remain a teacher when lucrative careers were available through legal practice?) In such circumstances, the students seemingly seized the initiative, possibly in association with the nascent urban authorities. (The latter certainly appreciated the value of the presence of so many students and masters, both for the city's economy and for its prestige. Both facets combined on the city's coinage, which bore the legend *Bononia docet*: 'Bologna teaches'.) The commune sought to tie the masters down, from the 1180s onwards imposing oaths to ensure that they stayed within the city. For a while in the thirteenth century, the commune also guaranteed the teachers' salaries, but this did not last. Meanwhile the students (or, more precisely, the non-Bolognese students) were forming their own associations, or 'universities'. Established in parallel to the emerging urban *popolo*, these bodies used their collective power to gain greater control over the masters and regulate their activities. The student organisations at Bologna, organised by 'foreigners', were as much concerned to defend their chances of learning (and, presumably, subsequent earning) as the closed shop at Paris was to protect the interests of the masters.

In 1200, the only French schools close to becoming universities were those at Paris, although Orleans was not far behind. Both crystallised as universities in the early thirteenth century, by a process of evolution rather than deliberate foundation. (No further French universities appeared until mid-century, and then as formal foundations.) Oxford was taking shape by 1215, with Cambridge originating in a secession in 1209. In Italy, apart from Bologna, only a few places had universities before 1250. Most were short-lived, like those at Arezzo (*c.* 1215 to *c.* 1255) or Siena (1246–52). Padua, founded in 1222, only took off after 1260. Naples was a special case, deliberately created by Frederick II in 1224 to provide jurists and administrators for the southern kingdom. Spain's first university, at Palencia, grew out of the cathedral school in the early thirteenth century (but disappeared c. 1250). Salamanca was reputedly founded in 1218/19, but formal recognition and the grant of appropriate privileges was delayed until the 1250s. Germany, meanwhile, was unaffected by such growths: the formal establishment of universities there was delayed until the mid-fourteenth century.

The precondition for the emergence of a university was, perhaps self-evidently, the presence of a large number of masters with a large number of students. 'A large number' is still vague: in most contexts, a group of teaching masters which achieved double figures was exceptional. Paris had the largest number, but most remain anonymous. Only forty-seven masters are identifiable in the period 1179–1215, a disproportionate number of them theologians. Student numbers are quite unknown: without formal administrative and institutional structures, and with many transient students, there was no need or means to maintain records. It has been estimated that the number of scholars at Paris c. 1200 was about 3–4,000, roughly ten per cent of the population, and that there were then something like 150 masters. Presumably a master dependent on fees needed enough students to enable him to live, but there was no set master:pupil ratio. When Gilbert of Poitiers moved from Chartres to Paris, his audience reportedly increased from four to almost three hundred. At Oxford, the grammar teacher Theobald of Étampes reportedly taught between sixty and a hundred pupils at once early in the twelfth century.

Changing patterns of education generated changes in learning and teaching methods. While initially the schools were centres of a particular type of oral culture, even if awareness of it now depends on written texts, by 1200 the academic culture was becoming much more dependent on a written record. This applied to all disciplines, including the newly emerged higher studies.

Throughout, the lecture – reading a text with commentary – remained the basic format of teaching. However, the masters rarely recorded their thoughts at this stage of their careers. Knowledge of lecture content therefore depends primarily on the notes (*reportationes*) written up by their hearers, records prone to the distortions which still afflict lecture notes. Early in the period masters, particularly theologians, might collect authoritative statements or 'sentences' to settle difficult issues. This culminated in the *Liber sententiarum* (*Book of Sentences*) compiled by Peter Lombard (c. 1095–1160) in mid-century; but the sentence tradition thereafter subsided as a speculative approach took over.[7]

Despite its oral delivery, most teaching consisted of textual analysis and commentary. For this the long-established method was the gloss. These explanations and annotations to a text were frequently recorded, some of them becoming traditional even before the twelfth century, so that text and glosses might be transmitted as a single unit. Glosses retain a modern counterpart, in the commentary and editorial apparatus provided in critical editions of literary texts. Used at all levels of teaching, from relatively elementary instruction in grammar (as when glossing the works of Horace) to analyses of canon law, Roman law, and theology, the gloss was ubiquitous, a technique applicable to any text. Some glosses were extremely simple, providing straightforward explanations of a word's meaning or clarifications of syntax; others were complex, offering lengthy analysis and commentary. Most are anonymous, but several (especially in law and theology) were ascribed to particular masters. In due course the glosses were themselves collected, as authoritative compilations. The *glossa ordinaria* to the Bible is associated with Anselm of Laon (although others were also involved, and it took some time for the gloss to acquire authoritative status); the task of collating the glosses on Roman law was undertaken by Accursius (d. 1263); while the ordinary gloss to the main canon law text, Gratian's *Decretum*, was compiled by Johannes Teutonicus before 1245 (being revised and augmented shortly after by Bartholomew of Brescia).

A major aim of the schools was to resolve uncertainty by reconciling contradictory texts and authorities. The *questio* emerged as a key tool in this process: contradictory statements were set against each other, followed by an attempt at reconciliation. This is the format adopted by Abelard in his *Sic et non* (although without providing the reconciliations); it also underlies Gratian's *Decretum*, seeking to establish (in its full title) a *Concordance of Discordant Canons*. The *questio* was also much used in philosophy and theology. It could be delivered orally, such speeches becoming set pieces in the thirteenth-century universities as 'quodlibets', discussions of 'whatever-you-like', on random topics chosen by the speaker.

The *questio* was a format mainly for the masters; students had their own oral academic exercises. In the twelfth century (but perhaps emerging from older roots) the disputation became their characteristic academic exercise. Disputations allowed for debate between pupils, to hone argumentative skills in a formal battle of logical argument and

7   See below, pp. 113–28.

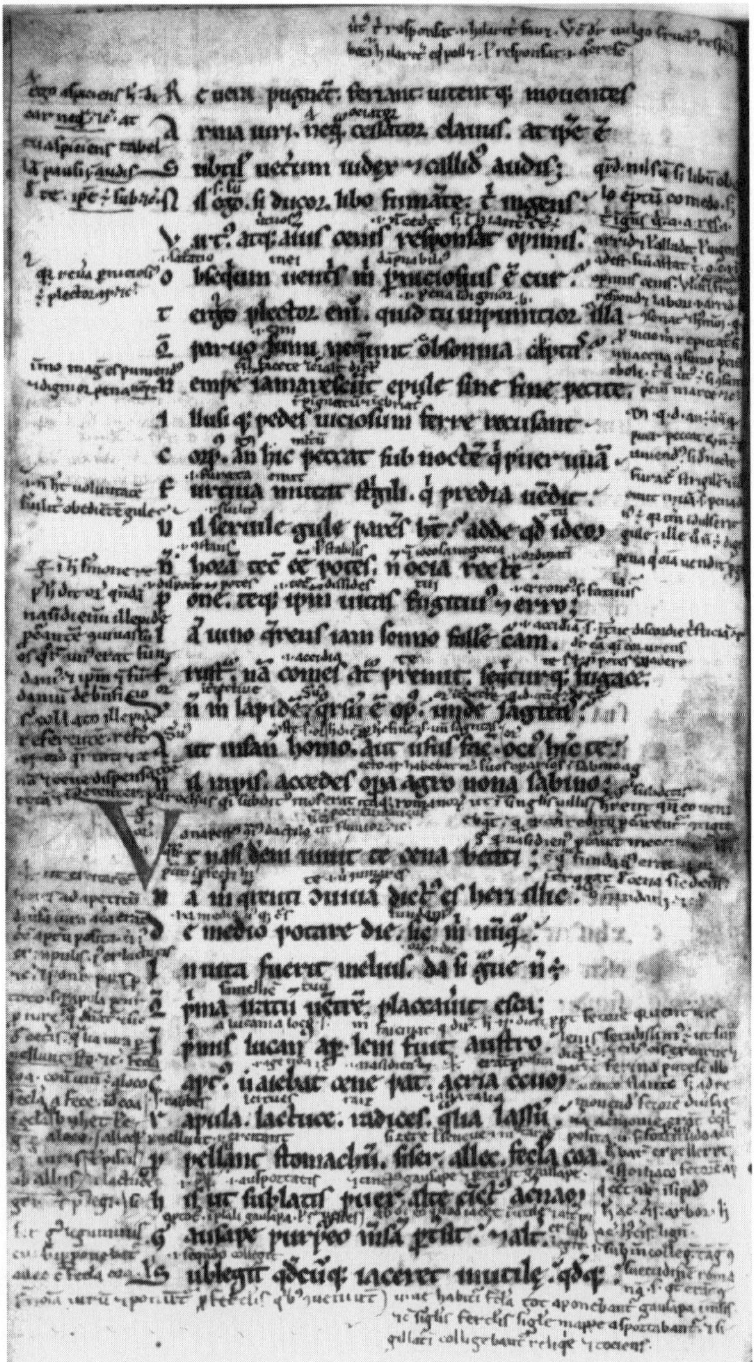
Re vera pugnent, feriant vitentque moventes
arma viri? nequam et cessator Davus; at ipse
subtilis veterum iudex et callidus audis.
Nil ego, si ducor libo fumante: tibi ingens
virtus atque animus cenis responsat opimis?
Obsequium ventris mihi perniciosius est cur?
Tergo plector enim. Qui tu impunitior illa
quae parvo sumi nequeunt obsonia captas?
Nempe amarescunt epulae sine fine petitae,
illusique pedes vitiosum ferre recusant
corpus. An hic peccat sub noctem qui puer uvam
furtiva mutat strigili? qui praedia vendit,
nil servile gulae parens habet? Adde quod idem
non horam tecum esse potes, non otia recte
ponere, teque ipsum vitas fugitivus et erro,
iam vino quaerens, iam somno fallere curam.
Frustra; nam comes atra premit sequiturque fugacem.
Unde mihi lapidem? quorsum est opus? unde sagittas?
Aut insanit homo aut versus facit. Ocius hinc te
ni rapis, accedes opera agro nona Sabino.
Ut Nasidieni iuvit te cena beati?
Nam mihi quaerenti convivam dictus here illic
de medio potare die. Sic ut mihi numquam
in vita fuerit melius. Da, si grave non est,
quae prima iratum ventrem placaverit esca.
In primis Lucanus aper; leni fuit Austro
captus, ut aiebat cenae pater; acria circum
rapula, lactucae, radices, qualia lassum
pervellunt stomachum, siser, allec, faecula Coa.
His ut sublatis puer alte cinctus acernam
gausape purpureo mensam pertersit, et alter
sublegit quodcumque iaceret inutile quodque

1 *facing*] Grammatical glossing of classical texts: Horace's *Satires*, ii, 8, 1–12, with glosses which suggest that this is a copy used in the schools. Biblioteca Apostolica Vaticana, MS Reg. Lat. 1780, f.90v: this particular set of glosses is discussed in depth in S. Reynolds, *Medieval Reading: Grammar, Rhetoric, and the Classical Text* (Cambridge, 1996, pp. 33–41).

---

authorities. The contest was usually overseen by the master, who issued the final determination to settle the dust.

As academic techniques and scholarly methods developed, there are signs of a significant mental shift taking place, placing greater emphasis on books as volumes, and on texts as repositories to be mined. This encouraged changes in book format, and the production of more compact and portable copies. It also stimulated attempts at mass production, aimed at a student market, through the so-called *pecia* system which arose at Paris in the thirteenth century. Rather than having texts copied out at length, volume by volume, an exemplar was split into sections, all of which were copied simultaneously (and in multiple copies), to be reunited on completion. Books also became more 'user-friendly': the text was separated into more manageable chapters. (This also happened to pre-existing works, most notably with the adoption of a system of chapter-division for the Bible, traditionally ascribed to Stephen Langton and accepted at Paris by 1203.) Concordances and indexes began to be produced. Page layout became more concerned with utility, glosses being set out to clarify their links with the text. Marginal signs sometimes indicated content. While memory remained essential to the learning process, the book as resource and substitute for memory became increasingly important.

While those who benefited from it naturally valued their education, education as such was not always praised. Indeed, even the educated complained about some of the practices. John of Salisbury's strictures against the so-called Cornificians for their misapplication of logic, about the under-appreciation of grammar, and charges that some were driven by a desire for profit more than for learning, convey a sense of real frustration. Specialisation in law and medicine, no matter how brief the spell of learning, could be the route to riches; a greed often decried. Others complained that those who spent their lives learning were wasting time, living in ivory towers, and concentrating on the wrong issues: anti-intellectualism has a long history. New religious orders in the period often began by shunning academic life: Bernard of Clairvaux (1090–1153), despite his own extensive learning, derided the new approaches of the secular schools, which he said blocked divine illumination and distracted from the truth. In the next century, Francis of Assisi was equally hostile to books: knowledge beyond Christ's gospel message was superfluous. Yet education was pervasive, and attractive. Within a generation of St Bernard's death the Cistercians were becoming integrated into the learned culture. Likewise with the Franciscans: their attractiveness was not confined to the unlearned. Within decades of the papal approbation of the Franciscan way of life in 1210, university students and masters were making dramatic conversions to the new Order, taking their books and learning with them. The Dominicans were less hostile to learning: their main function was to preach for conversion, giving them an educational imperative and a need for knowledge. They too invaded the nascent universities. By 1250 the friars' place at the universities was itself a bone of contention.

Within the religious orders the spread of the new learning brought its own tensions. Abelard's misfortunes at St Denis were partly due to his rather tactless demonstration that the house's founder was not actually Dionysius the Areopagite; his misfortunes at St Gildas perhaps owed something to his being over-educated for that abbey. Certainly discord could occur when learned and unlearned monks inhabited the same house. At Bury St Edmunds, the murmuring against Abbot Samson by unschooled monks towards the end of the twelfth century is reported by his contemporary chronicler, Jocelin of Brakelond; in some new religious orders tensions between *conversi* (the lay brethren who performed much of the manual work) and the choir monks perhaps owed something to different levels of education which encouraged a sense of elitism among the latter, and of inferiority among the former.

If education through the schools was treated as a route to preferment, it could not be the sole route. Those with jobs to offer had their own interests to consider. Their reasons for granting patronage might be many; a potential employee's education was one of several variables to be weighed. Yet the expectations of the educated remained. Some were, unavoidably, disappointed; either because they failed to gain anything, or because they felt that what they did obtain was less than they deserved. Resentment could and did result. Some anti-court satires of the time reflect the outrage of disappointed scholars, whose education had admitted them to the wrong elite, and who now complained about the elite in control. Sour grapes went with disappointment. Moreover, as the educated increased in number, the likelihood of gaining an 'appropriate' post declined: qualifications lost some of their value, patrons could pick and choose, and education gave immediate access only to the lower rungs of the ladder, perhaps leading to resentment when it did not produce the desired rewards.

† † †

The transformation in educational structures during the long twelfth century was profound, and permanent. Masters – identified by themselves and others by their new title – were gaining key posts. They had successfully persuaded prospective employers that they had some special qualities precisely because they were masters. The reality of the distinction may sometimes be questionable: the masters' success perhaps depended as much on the gullibility of the employer as on the qualifications themselves, by making the hiring of masters a fashionable decorative act of patronage (rather like some of the hiring of humanists in the later Renaissance). Sometimes the employment was purely utilitarian: particularly in the new legal systems, lawyers were needed to manipulate the structures. Even if education was not the sole justification for employing a particular individual (and in a world of networks and patronage, it was unlikely to be), it was a factor to be taken into consideration, and could be the most significant.

The rise of the schools also had broader social effects. By creating networks, by providing career openings, education increased mobility. Obviously, for many it did not improve matters much: the risks and costs of study at a distant centre precluded extensive mobility; and the number of students would always be a very small percentage of the total male (or even clerical) population. Despite its importance, the rise of the schools immediately affected only a very few people. This was no movement of mass education, yet those who went through these new schools had an importance far beyond their numbers, as they contributed to the changes in governmental, administrative, and intellectual traditions throughout Europe.

3

Past, present, and future: legacies, imports, memories

NOTIONS of 'renaissance' derived from the late medieval model usually include a sense of looking back, to a golden age of classical Greece and Rome. The emphasis on retrospection presumes that a renaissance somehow seeks to recreate and revivify that lost world, with a renewed interest in 'the classics' and a new concern for ancient languages, chiefly Greek and Latin. Such concern for the past, and specifically for the Greek and Roman pasts, does appear in the twelfth century. A sense of the gradual westward shift of civilisation overtly appealed to that 'classical heritage', in ideas of *translatio studii* (which made Paris the continuator of the Athenian academy) and of *translatio imperii* (according to which the Roman empire survived with the Franks and Germans); even, in the writings of Chrétien de Troyes, of the westward march of chivalry. The twelfth century also attests a renewed interest in Greek and Roman writers, and a flowering of Latin language and style, characteristics which in later centuries might be considered evidence of 'humanism'.[1] There are also signs of interest in the Greek and Hebrew languages, although most contacts with them were at second hand, and evidence of fluency among western intellectuals is rare. Attitudes to 'the classics' perhaps demand more attention than the use of languages; yet the quality of Latin at this time cannot be ignored, this being a period which produced some excellent Latin writing, but also many mundane texts. A conscious, even archaising, appeal to 'the classics' perhaps reflects 'renaissance' concerns more precisely. That appeal would unavoidably be confined to an elite, perhaps self-consciously élitist, whereas the expanding and developing use of Latin was less constrained, as part of a general process of cultural expansion and development. Here two distinct ways of looking at the renaissance

---

1 For twelfth-century 'humanism', see below, pp. 113–14, 139–41.

phenomenon, as conscious revival and as acceleration in cultural activity, appear together in a dynamic area of cultural evolution.

Examination of the attitudes to the past falls under two heads. One must consider the process of deliberate acquisition of old texts, facilitated by expanding cultural horizons and reflected in the translation movement which is a significant feature of the twelfth century. Wider cultural horizons also allowed the importation of recent works in addition to those of the past, a facet of the translation movement which must also be acknowledged. The second aspect is the concern with historical writing. In dealing with the past, twelfth-century authors were unavoidably affected by attitudes to the present, which must also be addressed.

Latinity

Basic to many of these twelfth-century concerns was an ability to use Latin effectively, both grammatically and rhetorically. The effect and impact of language were vitally important; hence the concern for correct pronunciation, and the development of rules for writing and recitation. Texts for reading needed an audible impact, to demonstrate their authors' refinement. Here floridity was common. Chains of adjectives, complex contrasts, made full play with the possibilities of the language. The style of the ancient texts was thus absorbed, to be reused in letters and other works in which awareness of these texts shrieks forth, even where they are not explicitly cited.

The continuity of Latin makes it inappropriate to argue for a major breach between the twelfth and earlier centuries: the florid rhetorical tradition had long antecedents. Yet twelfth-century Latin did differ from earlier forms, at least among the learned and cultured, attaining a higher and purer standard. The classical styles were followed, and developed. Although using the past, the writers were consciously going beyond their models, to derive new rules, and new methods of exploiting linguistic possibilities. In some ways they went beyond the Latin they had received by a stricter concern with linguistic rationality. The received ancient instructional texts – Donatus and Priscian – had merely recounted the rules of language, without validating them. New approaches to grammar sought to do just that. Peter Helias, writing in the 1140s, and Alexander of Villa Dei, at the end of the century, concocted new teaching texts which, by supplanting the received classical works, actually broke the continuity with the past. Particularly in letter-writing and poetry, the twelfth century reveals a 'new stylistic sureness [which] contrasts with the ineptitude, lack of complication, and indifference to rhetorical rules that characterize some earlier production'.[2] While restoring ancient stylistic practices, the new concern with language sometimes abandoned ancient conventions. In his *Ars versificatoria*, written before 1175, Matthew of Vendôme proclaimed the superiority of a modern style which adhered more closely to the linguistic rules. The faults of classical writers were to be excused, not imitated.

Much of this Latin (at least in its literary forms) also differed from ancient models in being produced according to the rules of *cursus*, a complex system of rhyme and accents which, while having old foundations, had to be to some extent recreated (and certainly extended geographically) during the course of the long twelfth century. The *cursus* of the papal court became the major form (and conformity to its rules a test for documentary authenticity), but a separate Orleans tradition existed from *c.* 1180 to *c.* 1250, closely associated with the distinct tradition of the *ars dictaminis* which had emerged there.

Some twelfth-century writers produced works with highly impress-ive classical appearances: a poem in praise of Rome by Hildebert of Lavardin was long considered a late antique work; opinion is still split on whether the so-called *Institutio Traiani* in John of Salisbury's *Policraticus* was composed in late antiquity (even if not actually by Plutarch for Trajan), or whether John of Salisbury simply wrote the whole thing himself.

Yet this highly polished Latin was not something everyone could write. Despite its strengths, Latin was not a first language: even if the Latin Bible and everyday Italian were still sufficiently similar to make a translated Bible unnecessary before 1200, that Italianised Latin was not the Latin of the schools or the clergy. Latin, however acquired, had to be acquired, as a second or foreign language. This could have advantages. It probably assisted uniformity of pronunciation and orthography across the continent. Regional residues of localised Latin may have been overwhelmed by the several conquests of the period, so that the Latin of northern France spread to England, Spain, the crusader states, and southern Italy. The common language gave a new unity to intellectual life: it facilitated discussion without the intermediary of translation, and so avoided the problem of discord through misunderstanding (although translation *into* Latin may have caused difficulties in interpretation). At the same time, the language was neither static nor dead. Changing demands ensured Latin its continued vitality: the need to deal with new issues – legal, economic, political, theological, and many more – in a

2 Janet Martin, 'Classicism and style in Latin literature', *Renaissance and Renewal in the Twelfth Century*, ed. Robert L. Benson and Giles Constable (with Carol D. Lanham) (Oxford, 1982; reprinted Toronto, Buffalo, and London, 1991), p. 550.

language whose original vocabulary had been created several centuries earlier forced Latin into life. It had to adapt, to adopt new terminologies to cover those new situations, to find new expressions, as it still does as the official language of the Roman Catholic Church.

Twelfth-century Latin was a language which worked at many levels, from deep intellectual abstraction to crude invective. The period's Latin heritage includes liturgical dramas, sermons and letters, songs and poetry (including the ribaldry and satires of those customarily called Goliards, despite some vagueness about exactly what types of work count as 'goliardic', and the identities of the poets themselves). Even Abelard may have joined in this 'low' Latin culture: the love songs which he wrote, and which Heloise mentions as well-known in the 1130s, were presumably in Latin. (None of them can now be identified, although some may survive, unattributed, in the *Carmina Burana*.) As an everyday language, Latin had to serve many functions. It clearly had a special role in the Church, but mastery of it was increasingly needed elsewhere, notably in law and administration, transcending the regionalism of dialects to ease communication and comprehension with a clarity and uniformity which might otherwise have been unattainable. Latin defined the internationality of the twelfth century, so that even ordinary letter-writing had its own rules for Latin composition in the *ars dictaminis*. This also facilitated the rise of a lay Latin culture, primarily in Italy, but also elsewhere in the phenomenon of the *miles litteratus*, the knight with a facility in Latinity. Such lay participation in a Latinate culture might well evolve beyond the confines and constraints of the intellectual, clerical, and ecclesiastical system. The call for a utilitarian Latinity meant that a highly classicised style would always be elitist, and sometimes counter-productive. While stylistic proficiency was to be lauded, practical Latin, for teaching, administration, and recording, was more mundane and businesslike: alongside praise for Latin skill, there was also insistence on communication, on using Latin at a level appropriate to the audience and the subject matter. This did not make the culture any less Latinate – it could make it more so – but it means that attention directed solely to the highly competent 'humanists' may be misplaced. Latin's role as an international language was perhaps its most important function overall.

The classical heritage and its implications

In tackling attitudes towards the classical heritage, the first issue to confront (but one rarely explicitly addressed) is, 'What are "the classics"?' Influenced by later 'humanists', modern attitudes view 'the classics' as mainly pre-Christian, but extending with paganism into the Roman empire. Even granting that extension, however, they remain non-Christian: the Greek and Roman classics are the works of pagan writers; of Cicero, Ovid, Horace, and their ilk.

Such preconceptions must be challenged immediately. Why constrict the 'classical' Greek and Roman by such criteria? They impose cultural and chronological categories which are purely arbitrary, and which in turn impose artificial distortions. They require twelfth-century thinkers to accept rules (or prejudices) not apparently established until the fifteenth century, and may reflect more the views of later commentators on 'the Renaissance' than those of fifteenth-century culture. Recent work has affirmed the importance of the Christian tradition in late medieval thought, suggesting that earlier emphasis on pagan writers in the search for 'humanism' was perhaps misplaced. The growing influence ascribed to 'Christian humanism' accordingly changes the tests to be applied to the twelfth century.

That shift allows reincorporation of the Christian Greek and Roman traditions into any search for 'classical' influences. This, obviously, has chronological implications. Christian 'classics' necessarily postdate Christ. How far into the Christian era a classical period should extend is debatable; but arguably all of the patristic age should be included, certainly up to Augustine (d. 430) and Boethius (d. 524/5). (The many citations of early Christian writers, including Augustine, in Gratian's *Decretum* perhaps merit mention with this in mind.) Much of this Christian writing was accessible only in Latin, not Greek. In part, this reflected the inherited tradition. The papal Church and its dependents existed within a western, Roman, tradition of commentary and exegesis. This western tradition was in Latin; linguistic contacts and training in other languages were not widely available. There was little opportunity, or need, to use Greek. This did not preclude access to works originally written in Greek; but it required that they first be translated into Latin. Any search for a Greek past might then stimulate a process of translation, which need not necessarily be limited to providing versions of classical Greek texts.

That said, non-Christian authors were important. With the exception of theology, the main intellectual traditions harked back (however imperfectly) to the pre-Christian past. However, the extent of their direct influence still remains uncertain. For 'the classics' to have had a role in the twelfth century, they had to be physically available. That a classical work had survived into the 1100s was no guarantee that it would feed a period of cultural development. To have a western impact, classics had to have survived in the west, or become newly available through importation and translation. They also had to exist where they would be used: survival in obscurity precluded influence. The fifteenth-century classicists were renowned for discovering ancient manuscripts in obscure German and Italian monasteries: the texts had survived, but had either not been considered significant enough to publicise, or the libraries were ill placed for their holdings to be appreciated and gain a wider readership through copying.

The question of how much knowledge there was of the classics can be addressed, but cannot be fully resolved. Library catalogues, and the surviving volumes themselves, allow the existence and distribution of classical works in the twelfth-century west to be noted and mapped. Citations and quotations from these works can be counted, twelfth-century writers who cite them can be listed, and the 'classical influences' can then be quantified. But what such information means is debatable. Library catalogues are, perhaps, reasonable guides to survival, but they cannot prove that the books were actually read. Twelfth-century volumes certainly reveal an interest in the classics, and that the texts were considered worth preserving and copying; but that again does not guarantee readership. Survival could actually reflect lack of interest: if these works had been popular, the volumes should have worn out, perhaps been discarded when better and more modern (which might mean more legible) copies were made later on. Quotations prove acquaintance, but leave open the scale of contact. Not every citation proves access to a complete text; quotations were often extracted from collections of snippets, *florilegia*, taken out of context but useful to lard another work (and, in the thirteenth century, also used extensively as sources for embellishing sermons, by providing illustrative stories or *exempla*). John of Salisbury, for one, used them. Such dictionaries of quotations would compensate for the lack of a full text; they could also result in incomplete understanding. (For Patristic and Christian Greek authors, equivalent collections of quotations were provided in collections of conciliar and ecclesiastical canons, or as fragments incorporated in historical works. Such, for instance, seem to have been the main vehicles for western awareness of the writings of St Cyril.)

Much, nevertheless, had survived, and affected many areas of intellectual life. Philosophical speculation was based on the 'Old Logic' – the corpus available up to about 1130 – which has to be separated from the 'New Logic' based on Aristotelianism and associated Arabic thought which was then brought into the tradition. Although the philosophical resources available around 1100 were decidedly limited, they included

Plato's *Timaeus*, works by Aristotle (usually as translated by Boethius, or accessible via his commentaries), and Cicero's *Topics*. The thought and analysis which this corpus generated had perhaps reached their limits by 1100; until new stimuli arrived to drive analyses in new directions, there was little scope for real advance.

Lacking from this concern with the classics was an editorial imperative, such as drove the later Renaissance humanists. There was seemingly little concern that texts might be incorrectly transmitted, or wrongly ascribed. Yet ascription gave authority, which could cause problems. Numerous works were wrongly labelled as being by Augustine; the users of texts often had to take them on trust. Where the real author and the writer to whom the work was erroneously ascribed were both either classical or patristic, this may have little importance for questions of attitude to the relevant heritage; but where the attribution misdated a text by centuries, generally to some time well before it was actually composed, this might well affect perceptions. Origen (d. *c.* 254) was sometimes named as the author of works actually by John Scot Eriugena (d. *c.* 877). Carolingian ideas (sometimes of questionable orthodoxy) transmitted in a third-century disguise presumably reflect a misconstruction of the classical heritage; yet it must be assumed that they were conveyed in ignorance of the misattribution. It is the acceptance of the misdating which is important, attesting a desire for contact with the early Church.

Questions of distribution and access thus underlie and precede any comment on the role of the classics in the twelfth-century west. Even if the term is, for the sake of argument, restricted to non-Christian writers (despite the artificiality and distortion this imposes), their treatment remains a real issue. Two points need to be addressed: how this material was dealt with as being from 'the past'; and how such non-Christian texts were integrated into an avowedly Christian culture.

The first issue is the easier to tackle. There is little evidence for the classics being hallowed as classics, as relics of a golden age. While they were obviously from 'the past', there is little sign of an awareness of cultural distance between 'then' and 'now'. In some contexts, they might be treated very prosaically: the use of ancient poets as a means to acquire good Latin might make the classical text 'no more or no less than a linguistic resource, a field of grammatical practice'.[3] Yet, as ancient texts,

---

3 Suzanne Reynolds, '"Let him read the *Satires* of Horace": Reading, literacy, and grammar in the twelfth century', in *The Practice and Representation of Reading in England*, ed. James Raven, Helen Small, and Naomi Tadmor (Cambridge, 1996), p. 39.

they were also treated as authorities, making them almost by definition valid for 'the present'. 'Authorities' in this sense, regardless of how they were used, were timeless, unconstrained by their own contexts of time and place. Their present utility caused them to be invoked, just as present utility likewise accepted the invocation of patristic authors. That present utility was, however, affected by an assumption that the world of the classical texts was, in essentials, little different from that of the twelfth century. Whereas appeals to the classics in the 'real' Renaissance were predicated on the assumption – or imposition – of a cultural void of the middle ages, twelfth-century citations of Greek and Roman writers assumed continuity: the Roman world still existed, and was peopled by Romans. That sense of continuity was important. It made the appeal to the classics less self-consciously a matter of artifice, although actual use showed no lack of artifice and artificiality. This also made the classics less remote.

One fundamental barrier separated the ancient writers and the twelfth century: paganism. How real this barrier was is hard to assess. Certainly paganism – sometimes overt paganism, sometimes just an absence of Christianity – was considered problematic by some twelfth-century writers. They feared that the paganism would rub off, and Christianity be undermined, especially in less mature minds. This concern focused especially on the impact of ancient philosophers in the schools; it extended to worries about the effect of the more prurient classical tales (notably those told by Ovid) on innocent young minds. Stephen of Tournai bluntly declared that 'Reading the books of the pagans does not enlighten, but darkens, the mind.'[4] However, the integration of the pagan past into a Christian world was no novelty, being legitimated by no less an authority than St Augustine in the topos of taking the gold of the Egyptians. This topos gave Christians the role of the Jews of Exodus, fleeing Egypt with the treasures of their former masters. It allowed them as successors to (or continuators of) the Jewish, Greek, and Roman traditions to adopt the most valuable aspects of those cultures. Likewise, exegesis of the verses of Deuteronomy 21.11–13 (describing the process for the marriage of an Israelite to a foreign woman seized as spoils of war) validated similar adaptation. Both traditions point to the chief weapon for neutralising any pagan threat: allegory.

Among the most important of late Roman or sub-Roman Latin authors was Martianus Capella (c. 410–39), whose De nuptiis Philologiae et Mercurii (Marriage of Philology and Mercury) had a twofold impact. It

---

4 Quoted in Stephen C. Ferruolo, The Origins of the University: the Schools of Paris and their Critics, 1100–1215 (Stanford, CA, 1985), p. 273.

provided the basic catalogue of the seven liberal arts, establishing a basis for commentary which would last for centuries. Mercury's search for Philology also provided a moral tale to be read through allegory, as the union of qualities required for human improvement, and as an epic narrative which could be further developed through moral exegesis. The continued attraction of some epic classical texts, and their interpretation through allegory to provide moral readings, often makes the interpretive process much less a recovery of the past than a continuation. Commentaries on Virgil, for instance, fit into a tradition which had continued virtually unbroken since the Carolingian period (and often drew on works produced then). However, this tradition was waning by the middle of the twelfth century. While it has later representatives, a critical change was the increasing Christianisation of the allegory: a merely moral or naturalising reading was no longer acceptable; an explicitly Christian layer had to be added.

For, whatever is made of twelfth-century culture, it was overtly Christian. Christianity was its proclaimed bedrock, especially among intellectuals. The Christian tradition had long experience of dealing with seemingly intractable texts, and to reinterpreting what seemed sterile or threatening, in order to aid the consolidation and confirmation of the faith. Nowhere were such challenges more robustly confronted than in dealing with the Bible. The interpretative tradition constructed around the fourfold reading of the Scriptures – in which looking below the surface of the words to an allegorical interpretation was common practice – constituted a transferable skill adaptable to deal with classical paganism.[5] The classical texts were accordingly reread, reinterpreted, as 'the purposeful deformation of literary material whose content for some reason or other does not meet with the [later] author's approval; or [in] … an attempt to derive information about some subject close to the allegorizer's heart, from a source which we should consider wholly unsuitable.'[6] No matter how overt the paganism, how blatant the lack of Christian influence, a Christian reading could usually be constructed. Pagan deities became representations of Christian qualities; rereading turned dubious texts into moral tales. Classical works acquired a new layer of significance, to reinforce Christian precepts, or to be used in other ways. The commentary on the *Aeneid* by Bernard Silvestris interprets the work so that the successive books reflect the progress of a human life (a long-established pattern for allegorising the work), while

5 For the fourfold interpretation, below, pp. 117–18.
6 R.R. Bolgar, *The Classical Heritage and its Beneficiaries* (Cambridge, 1954), p. 218.

also using it as a peg for a summary encyclopedia. Ovid moralised may read oddly to purists; but in the twelfth century (and later) it made perfect sense.

The reading of Ovid reveals another feature of the twelfth century: its literary awareness. In this era to be 'literate' was to be Latinate: skill in handling vernacular languages and texts was irrelevant to 'literacy'. This made the classics a key influence as repositories of good Latin and civilisation. An ability to refer to the great authors, to follow their styles or lard one's own writings with citations of their works, was proof of refinement. The texts themselves might be cited almost as padding: hence, perhaps, the to-and-fro citation of identical quotations in the letters of Abelard and Heloise. The addition and superaddition of authorities from the Latin classics, the catenae of quotations piling authority on authority, obviously served to emphasise the point being made. They also made a statement about their user and his awareness. Such dependence on authorities may now seem excessive, the citations superfluous almost to the point of being counter-productive. Among twelfth-century writers, however, there is no sign of any feeling that quotation might be overdone.

Appreciation of the significance of the use of the classics still needs further refinement. Counting citations indicates use, but little more. It may be necessary to differentiate between the instinctive citation of school texts, drummed in during the learning process so that they were cited almost by rote, and the deliberate reference to more obscure and elevated texts, which when recognised would provide signals to members of a smaller coterie. Possibly more important than actual citation and quotation is the stylistic imitation of ancient models. This can be a form of citation, if the model is recognised. Hildebert of Le Mans's poem lamenting his exile, modelled on Ovid's *Tristia* and *Ex Ponto*, would have gained added resonance from appreciation of the assumed parallel; yet the work could be appreciated independently. Similarly, speeches and descriptions inserted into historical works, although sometimes derived from ancient models and invoking classical parallels, did not require knowledge of those models and parallels to stimulate a response in their hearers or readers. On the other hand, a key point in using a quotation is that it be recognised and responded to by some at least; the quotation's message for those 'in the know' will differ from that received (if any) by those ignorant of the reference. Modern editors can often trace a citation (even if it is not exactly in the words of the original work from which it derives), but the extent of the recognition and the scale of the response – if any – are unrecorded. Some twelfth-century writers, while addressing a general audience, were also consciously writing for a smaller group, a sort of twelfth-century Bloomsbury.

Translations

One fundamental way in which the twelfth century's debt to the past could increase (with, in due course, its debt to other cultures) was by gaining access to further texts. This might be an accidental process; it might alternatively reflect a conscious urge to fill perceived gaps in the available corpus. The most important acquisitions proved to be ancient Greek scientific and philosophical works, supplemented by more recent Arabic thought and commentary: the newly available works of Aristotle had particular influence as they were integrated into western traditions over the twelfth and thirteenth centuries. The newly obtained texts had to be made available in Latin, a need which stimulated both translation and dissemination. These new texts completely changed western intellectual horizons, confronting thinkers with the major task of reconciling conflicting opinions, and challenging them to integrate the new material into their existing ideas on many subjects. The impact on philosophical thought (however considered) was fundamental; the knock-on effects in other fields – notably theology – were equally significant.

While the emphasis was on the recovery of ancient texts whose authority (being ancient) was unquestionable, other works also attracted attention. Arabic thinkers whose works were available in Spain had often commented on Aristotle; their works provided a medium for access to the original text. Unsurprisingly, therefore, their works were also translated. Beyond that, awareness – increasing awareness – of non-Christian cultures stimulated greater concern to use intellectual methods against Islam. The mid-twelfth century saw the first translation of the Qur'an into Latin, at the behest of Peter the Venerable of Cluny in 1142, to provide ammunition for Christians to argue their religious case with Islam. A final strand of this activity was stimulated by the growing interest in biblical studies after 1150. That included a concern to improve the accuracy of the received text, which for the Old Testament required access to the original Hebrew texts, through contact with Jews.

The translation movement thus had its broad context in the general intellectual ferment and hunger of the long twelfth century. Additionally, each individual act of translation had its own particular context, both geographical and intellectual. This increased activity owed much to the contemporary expansion of Latin Christendom, with the main points of access to these recovered and newly discovered texts being areas of recent conquest, primarily Spain and Sicily. Palestine was also a likely source, but there is little sign of translations being made there. The opening up of the Mediterranean after the First Crusade also eased access to Constantinople and the Greek lands. These, if defined by the spoken language, included southern Italy. (The Sicilian translators of Greek texts seem to have preferred to work from Greek, sometimes using inferior Greek texts rather than full Arabic versions.) The seizure of Constantinople in 1204, and the founding of the successor Frankish states, established a further link. Some of those who went east to these new states returned with Greek volumes, which duly fed into the western tradition when translated. Among such individuals was John of Basingstoke, who joined the group of translators of Greek texts which centred on Robert Grosseteste (c. 1168–1253) during his tenure of the bishopric of Lincoln. In the twelfth century translations of Greek works also came via Hungary, presumably reflecting either the land route to Constantinople followed by the First Crusade, or the cultural and commercial contacts between Hungary and Venice. The scale of this Hungarian activity and its western impact remains obscure. However, a partial translation by Cerebanus of Venice of *De fide orthodoxa* (*On the Orthodox Faith*) by John of Damascus, did travel westwards during the century. The short-lived Norman toeholds in North Africa may also have provided a route for importations.

The first major translator, active in southern Italy, was Constantine the African, who ended his life as a monk at Monte Cassino in Italy. He produced Latin versions of several medical works from Arabic, sometimes adaptations rather than real translations. Southern Italy remained a centre of translation through to the reign of Frederick II (d. 1250), although it is not certain that the Sicilian translations had much impact outside the kingdom. Most of the work involved translation from Greek, notably works by Euclid, and Ptolemy's *Almagest*. Henricus Aristippus also began the task of making additional works of Plato available, producing Latin versions of the *Meno* and *Phaedo*.

Spain was overwhelmingly the main source for the new translations. Why this was so is an intriguing issue. That it happened, and was important, is undeniable; but the mechanics need further thought. Particularly significant questions hang over the presence of so many foreign clerics in Spain at the time, who were available to translate, and to arrange for their labours to be transported northwards.

The combination of circumstances is certainly critical. Politically, the Reconquest meant a marked southward extension of Christian authority. Toledo fell in 1085; it was not lost. Although the Christian–

Muslim frontier wavered, the Christians were pushing south. That effort owed something to French aid for the native effort, under the aegis of crusading. More than that, Castile and Portugal were ruled by dynasties of French origin; while the rulers of Aragon-Barcelona had significant southern French contacts and interests.

This political advance was accompanied by other changes. The fluid border, and the reality of the Christian advance, encouraged Christian emigration from Muslim-ruled southern Spain. This brought new interests and information northwards, perhaps particularly works of thinkers like Averroes (Ibn Rushd, d. 1198), whose ideas were being rejected by the more rigid thinkers of Islam. Some of those involved in the translation process, as principals or assistants, seem to have been Mozarabs, like John of Seville (active 1133–42), or the Galib who assisted Gerard of Cremona later in the century. Major ecclesiastical changes also encouraged a foreign influx. The Reconquest carried with it a specifically Roman Christianity. The native Christian tradition, the Mozarabic Rite, suffered from that advance no less than Islam. The enforced suppression of the local rite meant that the advancing Church needed clerics who knew the new versions. Equally important, these clerics may have imported a particular type of Latinity, itself alien to Spanish traditions. This, too, had to be imposed by outsiders.

The upshot was a significant draft of northern and Italian clerics, united by their common tongue of northern Latin, into the Spanish realms, particularly Castile. The opportunities for new intellectual discoveries coincided with the temporary lack of a local clerical class to fill all the ecclesiastical posts, and a need for outside involvement. Non-Spaniards could accordingly exploit the particular cultural circumstances. The beginnings of *convivencia*, of a multicultural Spain inhabited by Christians, Jews, and Muslims, provided a unique opportunity for the Christians from beyond the Pyrenees to gain access to the intellectual heritage of the defeated Muslims states.

That said, the numbers involved in the enterprises, or the scale of their activities, must not be exaggerated. Indeed, the context remains largely conjectural; for one thing, there seem to have been few French translators. Although many texts are unascribed, the known non-Spanish translators were chiefly English (like Daniel of Morley, or Robert of Chester), or Italians (most importantly Gerard of Cremona). Again, the systematic work of translation is more characteristic of the second half of the century than of the first. Old ideas of a school of translators sponsored by Archbishop Raymond of Toledo (1125–52) were misguided; but Toledo was important in the second half of the century, activity there being dominated by Dominic Gundisalvus and Gerard of Cremona. A striking and problematic aspect of the Spanish endeavours is the proliferation of translations of Arabic scientific and mathematical texts and astronomical and astrological tables, material which would not find a ready home in the northern schools. On the other hand, the schools would in due course play ready hosts to the translations of Aristotle which were being made in the first decades of the twelfth century, their effect being attested at Paris from the 1130s. The obscure James of Venice probably worked at Constantinople, producing direct translations from the Greek of the so-called 'New Logic'; others in Italy and Spain also contributed to this first stage of the Aristotelian influx. Translations of Aristotle's more naturalistic works appeared later on. The progress of this work, and its assimilation into the northern intellectual tradition, still have some uncertainties: David of Dinant, in Paris at the turn of the twelfth and thirteenth centuries, seemingly had access to Aristotelian works before they are otherwise known to have been translated, but where he obtained them is unknown (he may have translated them himself, as a result of his own studies in Greece).

Just as important, the Spanish translators provided versions of the works of the Arab philosophers who had commented on Aristotle's works, notably of Avicenna (Ibn Sina, d. 1037) and Averroes. The integration of their ideas into the northern intellectual tradition would exacerbate the tensions generated by the attempt to reconcile Aristotle's own works with inherited ideas.

Important as they were individually, and as evidence of intellectual curiosity, the overall impact of the translations was variable. Knowledge of their existence was often limited; their manuscript tradition is often weak; evidence of their use is patchy. Northward transmission was haphazard, often perhaps dependent on the translators themselves returning home with their texts, as seemingly happened with Daniel of Morley. There was duplication and confusion: Cerebanus translated part of *On the Orthodox Faith*, but the first full translation was by Burgundio of Pisa in the 1150s. That translation correctly identified John of Damascus (d. *c.* 754) as the author; Cerebanus had ascribed the work to the earlier, and perhaps more authoritative, St Basil (d. 379). Peter the Venerable's translation of the Qur'an remained unknown; the work was repeated by Mark of Toledo at the start of the thirteenth century.

The motivations behind the production of particular translations are often obscure. The much-travelled Adelard of Bath (*c.* 1070–early 1140s) may have produced his translations of Arabic astrological works in England on his return, possibly in association with (or dependent on) work by the converted Spanish Jew Peter Alfonsi, sometime physician to King Henry I. While many translations occurred almost fortuitously, some texts were acquired intentionally. This was, after all, why Peter the Venerable commissioned the translation of the Qur'an. Theological disputes were behind some of the forays to acquire Greek material directly from Constantinople. Hugh Etherian (a Pisan then resident in Constantinople) compiled his *Liber de differentia naturae et personae* (*Book of the Difference of Nature and Person*) in the 1170s in response to a western appeal for partisan material to validate the Trinitarian views of Gilbert of Poitiers, which had been condemned in 1148. Alongside Greek theologians long accepted in the west, such as St Basil, he included texts from several extremely obscure writers.

The translation movement was one of the most important cultural trends in the long twelfth century. It certainly stimulated enquiry; once the scale of the material available was appreciated, the work gained a momentum of its own. The task continued into the thirteenth century: William of Moerbeke eventually completed the Aristotelian corpus in mid-century. Moreover, it continued outside Spain. Michael the Scot produced translations in Frederick II's Sicily; in England Robert Grosseteste worked on translations of Aristotle (including revision of earlier defective versions). Without these labours the intellectual transitions of the long twelfth century could not have been achieved.

Historical awareness, historical writing

The difficulty over the awareness of the classical heritage and its impact becomes perhaps most concrete when considering a broader attitude to the past in the twelfth century, which might be summed up as the period's sense of historical awareness. The importance of history in the long twelfth century is undeniable: chroniclers abounded across the continent, often producing works of style and scholarship. This was an outstanding period for historical writing in western Europe, particularly in England and Normandy. The work of numerous historians in England in the generations immediately after the Conquest of 1066 was among the country's main contributions to the contemporary cultural movement. A twelfth century without Orderic Vitalis (1075–c. 1142), William of Malmesbury (c. 1090–1143), or Henry of Huntingdon (1109–55) (to name only three of the most prominent writers) would be considerably diminished.

Yet an assessment of historical attitudes in this time faces many obstacles. One basic problem is that 'history' was not an academic discipline; any appeal to modern ideas of what history 'should be' to assess the writers of the time is quite anachronistic. This makes comment even harder. Should the focus be on 'perceptions of the past', or be directed to immediate contemporary awareness of change and the need to address its implications? Should it consider historical writing in terms of its sources and place in a classicising or humanistic movement? Each can validly be considered; each provokes different treatment and appreciation.

For twelfth-century (and earlier, and later) writers, 'history', *historia*, 'a story', did not have to be 'historical' in modern terms. The contrast lay not between true and false 'histories', but between *historia* and *fabula*, tales which did or did not merit belief. Those most deserving credence were contained in the Bible, which was certainly history. This distinction counters any charge that the twelfth century was uncritical about the past. Attitudes to evidence indicate a strong awareness of the need to balance authorities, and cite evidence. Chroniclers appreciated the difference in evidential value between oral tradition, eyewitness accounts, and documents. Authors' interjections affirming the veracity of their statements were relatively common, although this convention was easily exploited to seek credibility for falsehood. The traditions of the academic *questio* were easily transferred to assessments of the reliability of historical accounts: the introduction to Abelard's *Sic et non* would not be out of place in a modern lecture course on historical source criticism. That the nature of physical historical evidence changed over time was also appreciated, appearing in occasional vignettes like the discussion of sealing practices in a dispute over some Battle abbey charters, or investigations into the validity of papal bulls. Sometimes the investigators were taken in; but the process of testing, and the processes applied, are more important. With William of Malmesbury, writing in England in the early twelfth century, there are even indications of conscious antiquarianism and an ability to balance evidence to establish a new historical record.

Historical writers were certainly aware of the past, and of a continuity with that past. Henry of Huntingdon, in the preface to his *Historia anglorum* (*History of the English People*), set himself in a tradition derived on the one hand from Homer and other classical writers, on the other from biblical history. In the following century (but in the same tradition) Matthew Paris set himself in a line from Moses through the Evangelists, Eusebius, Bede, and Sigebert of Gembloux. The long twelfth century saw a massive expansion in the production of 'historical' material, in chronicles, annals, biographies (which include saints' lives, despite the problems they create as documents), and records of recent events. Attitudes to the past (which are also attitudes to the present, and to the future) are also shown in other ways, especially the growing emphasis on documents in the move 'from memory to written record', and the emergence of various types of historical fictions (including 'forgery') to create an acceptable past.

Yet in many ways 'history' was not about the past, but used the past for the present and the future. Even though there are signs of an awareness of change over time, historians did not feel obliged to appreciate the past on its own terms, did not strive for 'empathy'. Rather, history offered moral and ethical guidelines which were applicable to the present. The prefaces to historical works often stressed this aspect of history. Henry of Huntingdon noted that

> in the recorded deeds of all peoples and nations, which are the very judgements of God, clemency, generosity, honesty, caution and the like, and their opposites, not only provoke men of the spirit to do what is good and deter them from evil, but even encourage worldly men to good deeds and reduce their wickedness. History therefore brings the past into view as though it were present, and allows judgement of the future by representing the past.[7]

Jocelin of Brakelond said that his *Chronicle* was written as an inspiration and a warning: to record the good as a model, and the bad as a warning. The same sentiments appear in the *Historia pontificalis* of John of Salisbury. The author notes that he was writing 'to profit my contemporaries and future generations'. Historians, he comments,

> relate noteworthy matters, so that the invisible things of God may be clearly seen by the things that are done, and men may by example of reward or punishment be made more zealous in the face of God and pursuit of justice ... and nothing, after knowledge of the grace of God, teaches the living more surely and soundly than knowledge of the deeds of the departed.

However, history also had a more mundane purpose, for John also points out that 'the records of the chronicles are valuable for establishing or abolishing customs, for strengthening or destroying privileges'.[8] History had a purely utilitarian side; although sometimes the recording, as in the charters in Hemming's cartulary from Worcester cathedral, was a nostalgic echo of lost causes rather than the proclamation of a determination to retain and regain.

---

7 *Henry, Archdeacon of Huntingdon, Historia Anglorum: the History of the English People*, ed. and trans. D. Greenway (Oxford, 1996), p. 5.
8 *John of Salisbury's Memoirs of the Papal Court*, ed. M. Chibnall (London, 1956), p. 3.

The very variety of twelfth-century historical production defies any attempt to impose coherence. Alongside novelty, there was also continuity with previous traditions, and no anticipation of change: the annalist at Melk, in 1123, left space in his volume for additions through to 1300 (at two lines per year). The quantity of production can also mislead: very little was meant for 'public' consumption. Most compilations were relevant only to a restricted audience, perhaps only a single town or monastery. Even 'national' histories, like Henry of Huntingdon's *History of the English People*, had limited readership in foreign parts. The rise of academic history in the past 150 years, and the extensive publication of historical sources, can give these texts a prominence and readership hitherto unknown. The survival of works like John of Salisbury's *Historia pontificalis* (if it is by him: he is not actually named as its author), Jocelin of Brakelond's *Chronicle*, or Galbert of Bruges's *Murder of Charles the Good*, all hang on the thread of a single manuscript; for others the position is similar. This weakness in transmission most affected writing about recent events: those wishing to go back before their own memories could acquire that past from a previous writer, whose work could provide a prologue (in full or abbreviated form) to the new additions.

The role of the past in the long twelfth century, and the way it was treated, varied considerably. All historical writers addressed the present in some way. Here, perhaps, is where a line can be drawn, between 'literary' history and the more mundane process of recording simple facts in annals or similar compilations. However, this cannot be a precise demarcation, because of the nature of some of the compilations (Jocelin of Brakelond's *Chronicle* comes to mind here, with its mixture of personal comment, record, and lists).

When not concerned purely with a record, historical writing was intentionally moralistic, a branch of ethics. For those who were authors rather than mere recorders, it offered opportunities for rhetorical display. In such circumstances, the classical heritage acquired a new role. History as morality, ethics, rhetoric, gained a stylistic pattern, visible in the set speeches and elaborate descriptions which adorn the great texts of the period. But history as a means of maintaining a specifically classical view of the past is less visible. For one thing, very few classical historical texts survived into the twelfth century. Most awareness of Roman history derived from late antique Christian writers like Eusebius and Orosius. Texts by Suetonius, Livy, and others were known, but attempts to show their influence sometimes rest on shaky foundations. Yet non-historical classical allusions abound in the twelfth-century histories, used for rhetorical effect rather than to convey information. The writers might cloak the lives of their subjects in Roman rhetoric; while that might give them Roman characteristics, it could not transform them into real Romans.

In its moralistic exploitation, the recent past was no different from the distant past: it was all part of that continuum going back to Genesis. This gave twelfth-century historians a peculiar status. Because he could and did provide moral lessons from history, someone like William of Malmesbury was little different from Peter Comestor. The latter's *Historia scholastica*, completed in 1169–73, offers 'a constructive historical, geographical, and chronological basis for reading Scripture'.[9] While focused on the simplest and clearest level of biblical comprehension, hovering over it are the more advanced allegorical and moral levels of interpretation. A literal historical meaning, no matter what the period covered, always implied the possibility of a moral reading, of a chronological transference from Old to New, and from Then to Now. The Bible was not the only history to carry multiple meanings.

Access to the past might depend primarily on written texts, but need not be so confined. Visual stimuli were another way to communicate the past to the present. The importance of the artistic and visual heritage is considered further elsewhere;[10] but an important feature of the period is the use of visual stimuli for recollection. These might be inscriptions, like those placed on the walls of Pisa cathedral to recall past maritime victories; or they might be paintings or images. More than mere reminders of a past event, they served to conjure up a mental and emotional re-enactment of the scene, despite anachronisms in depiction. Frescoes depicting imperial surrender in the Lateran, statues of saints, crucifixes, were all intended to provoke a reaction. Stirring the viewer's memory to encourage involvement, they made that viewer a participant in a kind of interactive history, a synchronicity of past and present. Clearly, visual stimuli alone were insufficient: a narrative link (however provided) was usually needed as well. In many ways this emotional approach to the past was ahistorical, atemporal; it is much like the attitude which made every celebration of the mass a re-enactment of the Passion. Accordingly, it was most effective and evident in devotional recollection, producing a reaction which, for the thirteenth century, has been labelled a 'mysticism of the

9 David Luscombe, 'Peter Comestor', in *The Bible in the Medieval World: Essays in Memory of Beryl Smalley*, ed. Katherine Walsh and Diana Wood, Studies in church history, subsidia 4 (Oxford, 1985), p. 120.

10 Below, pp. 158–72.

historical event'.[11] It also appears in ideas of the imitation of Christ, and in the recreation of the apostolic life, which are such features of twelfth-century spirituality.[12] The desire to recreate the apostolic life, which in its appeal to an imagined early Church was also a search for a relevant past, sought also to make that interpreted past real, and to use it as a programme or blueprint for the future.

This link with devotion and spirituality affected other attitudes to the historic past. The use of the past to provide models, and instruction, made it highly manipulable. This is most obvious in the writing of saints' lives, which remained an important genre. Although often derided for their lack of historical veracity, especially when dealing with a saint long-dead, such lives do reflect a view of history, and of its function. They were often more concerned to depict someone relevant to the present than with historic reality, being rewritten to meet current needs and ideas of what a saint should be, avoiding the constraints of verifiable facts. Although often fantastic, that did not make them 'unhistoric'.

Perhaps most importantly, the past which the historians wrote about was part of a continuum going back to Genesis, but also going forward, towards the Last Judgement. Historians were accordingly writing within a confined time, filling a gap (even if one of unknown length) between a known past and a known future. Otto of Freising's first historical work was *The Two Cities* (*Chronica sive historia de duabus civitatibus*), an explicit cross-reference to Augustine's *City of God* (*De Civitate Dei*), and heaven as the 'other' city which contrasts with the present world is implicit in his text. Hugh of St Victor's view of time is reflected in the divisions of his *De sacramentis*, whose second book runs 'from the Incarnation of the Word until the end and consumation of all things'. This sense of being between two fixed points makes the future a part of history, something which can be built into the structure of time and might itself be penetrated and explained. The structuring of history was important. The Incarnation was a major break between ages, so that although world chronicles might begin with Genesis, the birth of Christ was an equally valid starting point. Allegorical interpretations could be applied: the Seven Days of Creation were equivalent to the Seven Ages of Man, and to a scheme of world history based on Seven Ages. Similarly, the seven seals of the Book of Revelation could represent the Seven Ages of the world (with ideas varying about which particular age the twelfth century was in). The

11 Ewert Cousins, 'The humanity and the passion of Christ', in *Christian Spirituality: High Middle Ages and Reformation*, ed. Jill Raitt (London, 1987), pp. 383–4.
12 See also, pp. 10, 143.

concept of the Ages could be used to create an idea of progress – as can be found in the writings of Hugh of St Victor and Anselm of Havelberg – but this was not automatic. Progress might have occurred in the past, before the Incarnation, but in the Sixth (and current) Age the world was growing old and cold, declining in preparation for (and anticipation of) the Seventh, Final, Age. Even the proud claims for the *translatio imperii* and *translatio studii* could cloak an inherent pessimism, as the move from east to west traced a path from sunrise to sunset, and thereafter – perhaps – a new dawn. The sense of expectation and decrepitude which runs throughout the remainder of the middle ages appears repeatedly in attitudes to past, present, and future during the long twelfth century.

This use of historical allegory created a dilemma, because it also made prophecy – futurology – a legitimate part of history. This need not mean apocalypticism, and the anticipation of the end of time. Such fears were clearly far from the mind of the Melk annalist, who had foreseen history lasting until at least 1300. They were, presumably, also far from the mind of whoever copied a set of Easter tables for Thorney abbey at the end of the eleventh century, which extended beyond AD 2600. However, the importance of prophecy seemingly increased during the twelfth century, with appeals to the sibyls and Merlin, and with the visionary writings of Hildegard of Bingen. In the late 1100s, Joachim of Fiore reinterpreted the structure of the past to propose a new model of world history, dividing the past into two separate blocks (as ages of the Father and the Son), in preparation for an incipient Age of the Spirit, initially calculated to begin in the middle of the thirteenth century. Although little known at first, Joachim's new interpretation of history gained massive influence during the thirteenth century, establishing a prophetic streak which lasted throughout the middle ages. A more mundane boost to prophetic endeavours came with the importation of Arabic astronomical works, and the consequent improvement in astrology. On one level this was a purely scientific enterprise, working out by appropriate calculation the impact of astral influences on the future. On another, it created major theological concern, by challenging the idea of human autonomy and free will. The struggle to legitimate or control astrology would develop further in later centuries.

A notable feature of some of the historical writing of the twelfth century is that it reaches back into the distant past, especially to Greece, with a revival of interest in Alexander the Great and the Trojan Wars. Alexander provided material for northern French vernacular histories in the late twelfth century; Troy was written up in Latin in the *Ylias* of Simon

Chevre d'Or (written at the request of Count Henry the Liberal of Champagne), and in the *De bello Troiano* of Joseph of Exeter. Little distinguishes such works from epic romance and Virgil transformed, but they appear of a piece with contemporary concerns to trace national roots. This search, which often found those origins in the flight from Troy, was part of a pattern stretching back to Gregory of Tours in the sixth century; although the fact that most western nations (except for the Spaniards, who had other concerns) made the discovery during the long twelfth century does point towards a newly wakened interest. The French myth of Trojan origins was the oldest, but seemingly gained strength at this time: Robert of Clari, chronicling the capture of Constantinople in 1204, has a French participant transform that event into a Trojan Reconquest. In the early eleventh century, Dudo of St Quentin had put forward claims for Trojan origins for the Normans (through the Danes). Godfrey of Viterbo created a history for the Hohenstaufen which likewise established a Trojan descent. In England the creation of the Trojan myth achieved its zenith in the 1130s in the work of Geoffrey of Monmouth, uniting Trojan origins with the tale of Arthur. No matter whether Geoffrey wrote seriously or as parody, and despite immediate condemnation by contemporaries like William of Newburgh, his *Historia regum Britanniae* (*History of the Kings of Britain*) was soon embedded into the English past and present, to influence British history for centuries. Stage-managed as it was, the 'discovery' of the graves of Arthur and Guinevere at Glastonbury in 1189–91 (chroniclers vary on the date) confirmed Geoffrey's veracity. (The exhumations may also have tamed his history by proving that Arthur was really dead: if Geoffrey was constructing a Welsh national myth against the Anglo-Normans, the Glastonbury graves trumped his claims, and allowed England's rulers to make Arthur one of them.)

The search for ancient pasts was not confined to kings and nations. Individual towns and cities also sought origins with the Romans (or, at Trier in the Rhineland, even earlier). Strikingly, this seems to be a feature mainly of German cities, at least initially: the Italians, who might be expected to lead the field, delayed such inventions until the thirteenth century. This is not to deny the importance of the past in Italy (certainly at Rome, for obvious reasons); but Roman continuity appears as less of an issue. Rome did play a prominent part in twelfth-century Pisa's view of its past but, significantly, Pisa saw itself as a replacement Rome, *altera Roma*: classical allusions created parallels for self-adulation, but not a specific past.

Most historical works did not look back to Rome and Troy. They were more localised, and chronologically limited, on family, city, realm, estates, generating immediate histories for present use: dynastic histories of French magnatial families; regnal histories in Castile. Often the real starting point for histories was in the ninth or tenth century, in the world of Charlemagne and his heirs. This is also the world adopted and adapted in the *chansons de geste*, the world of Roland and Oliver; a world whose existence could not then be disproved, despite all the blatant anachronisms which shriek at the modern reader. The historicity of such epics was confirmed *c*. 1140, in the *Chronicle* of pseudo-Turpin, which treated the tale of Roland in Latin prose, and with numerous additions. This was among the first texts to be translated into Old French, with six different versions being commissioned between 1200 and 1230, plus one in Anglo-Norman. The world of the *chansons de geste* was a world to look back to, and to recreate, by defeating Saracens, by restoring the Carolingian dynasty. The first was the task of the crusades and the Reconquest; the second found voice in the myth of *redditus regni* in France of the late twelfth and early thirteenth centuries, which interpreted the accession of Louis VIII as a Carolingian restoration (his mother being descended from that dynasty).

Other histories were more local. This might reflect the weakness of central authority, as in Germany (where the focus tended to be on bishops and dioceses), or Italy (where the centre of attention was the city). But this was not a necessity: English monasteries produced their own annals, for instance; and Orderic Vitalis's *Historia ecclesiastica* (*Ecclesiastical History*) germinated in a commission to produce a history of the monastery of St Evroul. Estate history generated a different response, in administrative records (notably the collection of charters into cartularies), and forgery. Estate archives were here the main concern, to record rights and inheritances, privileges and powers, which were to be maintained for the future. Here the contemporary changes in attitudes to legal evidence were important: the past began to matter in a very practical way.

What happened, though, when documents were lacking? The period from 1050 to 1200 is a great age of European forgery, the deliberate production of pseudo-historical material to satisfy a need for documentary proof. The motivating spirit requires more comment, however, as the aim was rarely to defraud. The 'forgeries' were often created to validate the present by filling in the gaps in the record, rather than trying to deprive others of their rightful possessions. Monasteries were particularly apt to engage in such practices, to secure their possessions; but the

need to do so varied across Europe. The worst offender seems to have
been Peter the Deacon in twelfth-century Benevento; but houses in
England and France also indulged in the practice, to varying extents. Few
at the time knew that these documents were concoctions, and their
originators usually kept quiet. There was, though, an awareness of the
practice, and the papal chancery certainly acted to curtail it. Generally,
increasing awareness of the value of documents, and of their historical
development, made the testing increasingly rigorous, and put the forgers
out of business. However, once the forgeries were accepted into the
documentary and historical record, there was no reason to challenge
their status. In any case, later papal and princely confirmations arguably
gave them whatever validity they otherwise lacked.

Of course, some forgeries did aim to defraud, perhaps by slipping an
additional place name into a request for confirmation of property rights.
Others sought to avoid the costs and risks of securing genuine documents: Rome was a good source of fraudulent papal bulls; Innocent III
was to be praised for his attempts to prevent their production. Such
forgery, like the counterfeiting of coins, is in a different category from
mere gap-filling exercises; but where the documents were not produced
'in-house', the judgements become more complex. Guerno of St Médard
at Soissons confessed in 1119/31 to having forged papal privileges for his
own house, and for other houses which made gifts to his abbey in return:
the motivation and justification for his work would have varied from
document to document.

Most of this historical production was private, but there are hints of
the developing use of history as an official memory, even as a propaganda
tool. Ideas that the early Hohenstaufen encouraged a 'court
historiography' are no longer upheld, but the historical tradition at the
abbey of St Denis did emerge during this period, as a kind of official
record of the Capetian dynasty, setting a tradition which lasted throughout the middle ages. An official historical tradition also emerged in the
Italian communes, in a different format. The annals compiled by the
Genoese Caffaro were adopted as official memory by the communal
authorities in the 1160s, and thereafter continued by a communal official.
Similar practices emerged in other cities in the later twelfth and thirteenth
centuries. Most history remained, however, privately produced,
sometimes for patrons. Perhaps just as important, history shifted into the
vernacular, notably in north-west France and Flanders. (In England it had
already shifted out of Anglo-Saxon into Latin; but Anglo-Norman writers
began to create a new vernacular tradition by 1200.) Here the links with,
and transition beyond, the histories of the *chansons de geste* and similar

tales are important. Local dynasties were effectively commissioning their own histories, to validate their own status, in response to the aggressive activities of the French monarchy under Philip II. Some of this vernacular history was also biographical: the first decades of the thirteenth century saw the appearance of verse biographies, of Rodrigo Diaz in the *Poem of the Cid*, and of William Marshal in the *Histoire de Guillaume le Mareschal*.

These very varied and very different types of historical activity cannot be welded into one tradition. Nevertheless, the evident, and evidently increasing, concern with the past in this period was one of its main bequests to later centuries. Although some argue that the historiographical peak had passed by 1200 – with the main Anglo-Norman contribution perhaps completed by 1130 – the legacy was considerable. The early thirteenth century was also important: then Matthew Paris was at work in England, Vincent of Beauvais produced his massive historical compilation in the *Speculum historiale*, and the chronicle tradition was firmly established at St Denis. While much historical writing after 1200 was derivative, the continuation and broadening of the tradition is notable. The practice of local history – especially in the towns of Italy, Germany, and elsewhere – also expanded in the thirteenth and later centuries. While some historiographical genres would decline after 1200, others came to the fore, especially the vernacular histories. The first real signs of these new forms had appeared during the long twelfth century; some would achieve enduring importance.

 † † †

Disparate though the aspects treated here have been, they are linked by an awareness of influences and inheritances which could be used to reflect on the present, and to mould the future. Their impacts naturally varied. The new translations perhaps had the most immediate and dynamic significance, with their effect on contemporary thought. The concern with the classics and the revival of Latin proved less enduring, giving way to a more mundane and practical approach and leaving an evident gap before the classical revival of the later Renaissance. Nevertheless, the concern with the Roman inheritance in particular did preserve texts which later humanists would rediscover. The reinforcement of Latin's status as the standard language of international contacts, academe, and administration, also had lasting importance. The most novel development was the emergence of awareness of the past as history (however it was used for practical purposes), and the consolidation of memory in writing. Most important of all was the awareness that the past was relevant, and that humans did change over time. Arguably the main legacy of twelfth-century historical writing was the emergence of 'that comprehensive but limited view of human progress which dominated European historical thought from the twelfth century to the eighteenth',[13] displaced only with the rise of academic history in the nineteenth century.

---

13 R.W. Southern, 'Aspects of the European tradition of historical writing: 3. History as prophecy', *Transactions of the Royal Historical Society*, 5th ser., 22 (1972), p. 159.

4

Law, politics, and government

MODERN ideas of 'politics' are very remote from the notions regarding power and its exercise which circulated in twelfth-century Europe. Developments during that century were highly important in the evolution of Europe's political society. They can be considered under three different heads, all closely related. The main issue, where the debate about rebirth or renewal is directly relevant, is the evolution of law and legal structures, particularly of Roman and canon law. Closely allied, because of the links with ideas of Romanness, are the signs of emerging political thought. Finally, there is the intensely practical issue of the growth of government – or governance – and the increasing sophistication of administration. These trends are different and distinct, but they do overlap, combining to make the twelfth century a critically formative period.

All the changes in some ways reflect the greater awareness of social complexity which appears during the period. The inherited view of society, such as it was, divided the population into Three Orders: those who prayed (the clergy), those who fought (knights), and those who worked (the rest, usually equated with peasants as agricultural producers). Some in the twelfth century considered it flawed, but it remained the standard treatment of social division throughout the late middle ages.

Nevertheless, greater social differentiation in the twelfth century made the Three Orders model increasingly obsolescent. Where, for instance, did townspeople fit in? What of the many kinds of cleric – monk, canon, priest, and so on – and their different orders? Writers produced new hierarchies to reflect such developments, although none gained wide acceptance; and the exponents of the *ars dictaminis* in the Italian cities formulated ever more precise rules, a kind of etiquette, to deal with the changing situation.

The recognition and advocacy of difference was most profound when dealing with the fundamental division in western Christian society, that between laity and clergy. Although Christendom was perceived as the supreme social unity, the most radical outcome of the 'Gregorian reform movement' was the imposition of a basic cleavage between clergy and laity, in status and identities. The battles to impose celibacy, eliminate simony, and secure clerical exemption from secular jurisdiction, lasting throughout the twelfth century (and, indeed, well beyond), created a distinct caste whose position within the broader society would henceforth always be somewhat anomalous, and conflictive.

'Christendom' – western Europe – was also being divided in other ways, as the hollowness of the imperial tradition became increasingly obvious, and new territorial authorities emerged. Within those territories, new balances had to be constructed between different social groups, regarding their power and claims to status. A society of privileges emerged, often with a decentralised distribution of power, jurisdiction, and immunities. New social categories were identified, notably acknowledgement of the towns, and an increasingly formal and rigid division between the free and unfree.

Little of this social change was addressed specifically in a political context. Yet a political dimension was acknowledged, being formulated in terms of the body politic. The idea that the constituent parts of the social and political structures paralleled the different parts of the human body, under the ultimate direction of the soul (identified with the priests) was most succinctly and effectively asserted by John of Salisbury in his *Policraticus* (completed in 1159), although he was not its originator. He may indeed have introduced a significant modification to the existing tradition, by arguing for a co-operative view of the way the organs were to function, rather than a hierarchical approach seeing the separate organs as subordinate to a ruling head. John's view (which he ascribes to, and claims to derive from, Plutarch) declared both the indispensability of any particular part of the body, and the need to maintain the proper balance between the parts for their mutual benefit and survival:

> those who direct the practice of religion ought to be esteemed and venerated like the soul in the body ... just as the soul has rulership of the whole body so those who are called prefects of religion direct the whole body ... The position of the head in the republic[1] is occupied ... by a

1 This is not a 'republic' as now understood, but refers to the political unit as a commonwealth, which would normally be expected to have a monarchical head.

prince subject only to God and to those who act in His place on earth, inasmuch as in the human body the head is stimulated and ruled by the soul. The place of the heart is occupied by the senate ... The duties of the ears, eyes and mouth are claimed by the judges and governors of provinces. The hands coincide with officials and soldiers. Those who always assist the prince are comparable to the flanks. Treasurers and record keepers (I speak ... of the counts of the Exchequer) resemble ... the stomach and intestines; these, if they accumulate with great avidity and tenaciously preserve their accumulation, engender innumerable and incurable diseases so that their infection threatens to ruin the whole body. Furthermore, the feet coincide with peasants perpetually bound to the soil, for whom it is all the more necessary that the head take precautions, in that they more often meet with accidents while they walk on the earth in bodily subservience; and those who erect, sustain and move forward the mass of the whole body are justly owed shelter and support. Remove from the fittest body the aid of the feet; it does not proceed under its own power, but either crawls shamefully, uselessly and offensively on its hands or else is moved with the assistance of brute animals.[2]

The concept of the smoothly integrated body politic, with its inherent idealism of the common good, was an ultimate goal. The difficulty was to attain it. To some extent that search is represented in the developments considered here, but it must be firmly stated at the outset that no one at the time justified or commented on the particular evolutions precisely in such terms.

Law

The evolution of legal ideas, which were then transposed into the 'political' arena, was a major feature of the period 1050–1250. Relationships between people and institutions were increasingly defined in abstract terms of jurisdiction, making legal judgements opportunities for the application of theory within a framework of rules. (Of course, the exercise of power was also a key factor, but the framework imposed important limitations.) Concurrently, those claiming authority sought to resolve quarrels between parties by using their own legal structures – a process which might include pronouncements on and of law – making the provision of legal remedies an aspect of the economics of power. By

---

2 John of Salisbury, *Policraticus: Of the Frivolities of Courtiers and the Footprints of Philosophers*, ed. and trans. Cary J. Nederman (Cambridge, 1990), p. 67.

offering opportunities for dispute settlement which attracted suitors to their courts, those in authority enhanced their own claims to power and jurisdiction. One outcome of this trend was a developing sense of unity, which might be considered political unity, at various levels. Whether this was essentially an imposed or an evolved unity is open to debate, for such centralisation was not universally welcomed; but its creation was critical.

This growth of legalism had two key manifestations, which are particularly important to traditional ideas of a 'twelfth-century renaissance'. The first is the revival of the study of Roman law, and its consequent influence on other legal systems. The other is the growing importance of canon law, the law of the Church, especially after the appearance of Gratian's *Concordance of Discordant Canons* (otherwise known as the *Decretum*) in the 1140s. This became the standard text of canon law, in turn encouraging standardisation of canonistic studies, and allowing the structures in which that law was used to develop as well.

Beyond these two key features, several other developments reflect the growing interest in law and legal systems. Most are regionalised: the emergence of the English common law; the definition of 'feudal law' (notably in Italy); and the gradual cohesion of custom in parts of France and in Germany. That process of cohesion led to the appearance of provincial German codes in the thirteenth century, the first being Eike von Repgow's *Sachsenspiegel*, dating from 1220 to 1235.

Although the revival of Roman law is a central aspect of the twelfth century's legal history, its tale has been subtly rewritten in recent years, so that the re-emergence of the Roman system now seems less radical a change of direction than once thought. The re-emergence was undeniably important, although it perhaps owed much to a specific political context: had the emperor Frederick I (1152–90) not seen himself as the new Justinian, the revival of Roman law might have remained little more than an intellectual exercise. As it was, his explicit claim to the status and rights of the old Roman emperors (as at the Diet of Roncaglia in 1158),[3] and his affirmation of continuity by making his own additions to the body of Roman legislation (notably the *authentica Habita*, issued in 1155/8, which enshrined the legally privileged status of students), made Roman law a present rather than merely antiquarian concern.

The 'revival of Roman law' was not a process of sudden rediscovery and adoption, in which the new law shone forth as a total novelty in the world. The post-Roman world of Languedoc and the Italian cities

3   See below, p. 87.

(especially perhaps those places which were not merely post-Roman, but post-Byzantine) had not entirely lost its Roman heritage. The legal system, however, had evolved into a more customary form than the precise textuality normally associated with 'Roman law'. Much of northern Italy had developed an amalgam of Lombard and Roman law, which was to some extent customary. Pavia and Milan had a more learned tradition of Lombard law, the text known as the *Lombarda* setting out the material on lines much like those of Roman law. There were some enclaves where Lombard law had not been applied, and where the Roman inheritance was presumably more vital. However, this inherited Roman law was textually incomplete: the *Digest*, a key component of the Roman corpus, had effectively disappeared from circulation since the sixth century. Nevertheless, other components were available, and elements of the law may have been widely known. Moreover, direct access to the legal texts was not absolutely necessary: extracts were available, for instance, in Isidore of Seville's *Etymologies* (a massive compilation of material, even in the incomplete state in which it was left at Isidore's death in 636), which could be plundered as needed.

Although 'Roman law' had remained alive in northern Italy for practical purposes, as an academic subject its origins date from the late eleventh century. Some of the polemical writings of the Investiture Contest suggest a revival of interest even in the incomplete law, for example in the *Defensio Heinrici IV regis*, written in 1080 or 1084. However, it was the rediscovery of the *Digest c.* 1070 which provided the major stimulus to a revival of Roman law studies, most markedly at Bologna. Two copies of the text were actually found, but only one of these survives, being located at Pisa in the twelfth century. Historically it is the lost copy which was the more important, being the source text for the Bolognese revival.

There Roman law was first taught by Irnerius (d. 1130), originally a grammarian. His grammatical concerns may well say something about his academic approach to the text. The new legal discipline was soon firmly entrenched, attracting students from across Europe, although its emergence as a fully independent discipline took some time. Initially, indeed, the academic study may have been considered subsidiary to canon law; while the connection to the liberal arts (and specifically to grammar) was only definitively broken later in the twelfth century by the *Summa institutionum* of Placentinus (d. 1192). The recovery of the law (completed with the acquisition of the final segments of the Roman corpus in mid-twelfth century) permitted a highly literate society to proclaim a return to a pristine legality, even if one seen through spectacles tinged by centuries of change. Bologna became the acknowledged centre for such legal studies, although practical reasons for the city's attraction are hard to find. The tradition begun by Irnerius did not falter. The legal texts were treated according to the new academic procedures: glosses, disputations, commentaries, built up around them. The *questio* technique of positing opposing authorities for reconciliation also appeared, resulting in texts called 'brocards'. Eventually the commentary process culminated in an 'ordinary gloss', produced by Accursius at Bologna between 1220 and 1240.

The ripple-effect of the revival spread widely. 'Civil law' (as it was generally known) became a regular discipline at the leading educational centres, although continuity in studies and teaching are sometimes hard to establish. Montpellier soon gained a reputation as a major school, although on rather slim grounds. Traditions like that which had Vacarius lecturing on Roman law at Oxford in the 1140s, and so contributing to the emergence of the university, are now discounted. Nevertheless, Vacarius was in England, and there compiled his textbook, the *Liber pauperum*, summarising the main elements of Roman law. He also taught in England, although exactly where remains uncertain; and he was not alone. An English lecture course on the *Institutes*, one of the simpler Roman texts, survives from around 1200. Roman law was also taught at Paris, although there papal opposition to the implications of such study led to a ban on further teaching in 1219. Geographically, the centre of interest lay in the south of France and in northern Italy, with significant schools at Mantua and Modena. Roman law was apparently being taught at Avignon in the 1120s; while in the 1140s an epitome of the law, *Lo codi*, appeared in Provençal, to be translated into Latin, probably at Pisa, later in the century (exactly when is debated).

Despite its antiquarian attraction, Roman law's immediate utility was limited. Europe did not suffer a major crisis of identity, and replace unsatisfactory customary and local law with the rediscovered norms. Instead, Roman law was often treated as a supplementary law, to augment local custom. *Lo codi* shows this, occasionally commenting that Roman practices no longer applied. However, there are hints of adoption of Roman notions. Genoa ceased to stress its Lombard legal heritage after the mid-twelfth century; and Roman provisions were regularly referred to in Pisan court cases from the 1160s. The study of Roman law was important in the late medieval universities, but it was only in the fifteenth and sixteenth centuries that, with all its magistery, Roman law was formally adopted as a legal norm over a wide area. Frederick Barbarossa's attempt to re-establish imperial authority by claiming and asserting imperial continuity proved a failure.[4] Outside northern Italy and southern France, the academic tradition of Roman law (at least in the twelfth century) was seemingly based on the simpler texts – notably the *Institutes* – rather than the *Digest*. Yet, once available, Roman law had unavoidable influence. Indeed, the frequent complaints that lawyers were mercenary money-makers probably apply to those who were exploiting Roman law. In the 1180s, such complaints were voiced in England against the *pauperistae*, those whose knowledge of Roman law derived from Vacarius's *Liber pauperum*. Their legal knowledge was based on insufficient foundations, yet was still lucrative.

Perhaps the new law's main effect was its conscious and sub-conscious influence on other legal systems. Its stress on princely authority seems, for instance, to have been significant in the recension of the *Usatges* of Barcelona compiled in 1149–51; while *Lo codi* has been identified as an important source in the evolution of the law of the Kingdom of Jerusalem. The English *pauperistae* were attacked for demanding that local law conform to Roman ideals of justice. Certainly, the incorporation of Roman tags into non-Roman legal texts subtly affected attitudes on the force and authority of law; and commentators aware of the Roman structures and their implications transposed those readings into other arenas. Carlo Tocco's apparatus to the *Lombarda*, produced in southern Italy in the early thirteenth century, was strongly influenced by his knowledge of Roman law. In the Italian cities, the realities of government and the different needs of the times made formal application of Roman law impractical; but it remained an ideal, and communal laws were gradually assimilated to Roman models as lawyers were asked for opinions on specific cases. Possibly the Romanists' ideas had greater impact in procedural matters, an aspect of Roman law where the details given in the texts were scattered and often uninformative. The procedural norms newly established (in co-operation with the canon lawyers) could then be adopted more widely.

The merging of the mental world of the original Roman law with contemporary political experiences also meant that the revived law influenced political ideas. This might be the revived 'Roman republic' of the mid-twelfth century (and, beyond Italy, possibly also the communes of Languedoc and elsewhere). It might be the revived imperialism of Frederick I (and, later, Frederick II), who occasionally suggested that politics was primarily a secular concern.[5] Such secularisation (although

4   See below, pp. 69, 87–8.
5   *Ibid.*

the word, and the mentality normally associated with it, are anachron-istic for the twelfth century) created a polarity in political attitudes between 'empire' and 'papacy' which bedevilled Italian politics through-out the thirteenth century.

The secular universal legal system of Roman law was one of two universal legal structures created during the long twelfth century, and was arguably the less significant of the two. While Frederick I battled to become a Roman emperor, the papacy was slowly establishing and consolidating its own claims to universal authority, based on a code of law specific to the Church: canon law.

The Church had always claimed to be ruled by law. A series of conciliar assemblies had proclaimed rules and regulations in many spheres, ranging from the degrees of consanguinity within which marriage was prohibited, to rules for dealing with heresy. This canonical tradition was well established and widely acknowledged; but it lacked clarity and cohesion. Although it was agreed that canons governed the Church, precisely what was canonical or authoritative was uncertain, and the lack of any code cleared the way for creative legalism. Individuals compiled collections which might gain popularity, but were essentially ad hoc and unofficial. In Germany, Burchard, bishop of Worms, produced his *Decretum* around 1020. This was one of the century's most important collections, and its balancing of contradictory canons antici-pated the format adopted by Gratian in the 1140s. Burchard's collection reflected its author's episcopal rank and interests: its approach was essentially decentralising, asserting the rights of bishops as local prelates, and denying an authoritarian papal monarchy. South of the Alps that stance was increasingly unacceptable as the eleventh century wore on. Canonical collections made there during the Gregorian reform – for instance, the *Collection in Seventy-Four Titles* – were more authoritarian and centralising in outlook. Another important collection was made in France by Ivo of Chartres, in two versions: the undigestible *Decretum*, and the considerably shorter (and accordingly more popular) *Panormia*. In the 1070s Archbishop Lanfranc in England tried to create a settled local tradition of canon law by compiling his own collection, which provided a common code there for roughly a century.

The mishmash of patristic statements, conciliar decrees, and papal statements which passed for canon law around 1100 was clearly open to exploitation. Its ambiguities fuelled the Investiture Contest polemics of 1073 to 1122: it was Gregory VII's rediscovery of a neglected conciliar canon which sparked his condemnation of lay investiture, in an approach which was essentially backward-looking. Yet Gregory's reign (1073–85), and the subsequent crisis over papal authority, showed the potential of canon law: whatever the intended purpose of the *Dictatus papae* of *c.* 1075, it seems to work best as a statement of canonical principles; although that it constituted a programme is less certain. Over the next quarter century, papal statements disseminated at synods and other gatherings spread the papalist understanding of canon law across Europe. It was after attending Urban II's synod at Bari in 1098 that Archbishop Anselm of Canterbury returned to England with the decrees against clerical homage to lay lords, to rekindle England's version of the Investiture Contest.

Although canon law existed, lack of codification and organisation made it an unwieldy weapon. Yet it was used. The Church gradually defined its jurisdictional claims during this period, operating its law through its own courts and its claims to penitential authority. William I of England, for instance, acknowledged the Church's juridical independence when he issued his writ separating lay and ecclesiastical courts in the 1080s (although the practical separation of their structures and jurisdictions took some time). Throughout Europe, a groundswell of canonistic activity, enforced through Church courts, was firmly running by the mid-1100s, although lack of sources makes evidence for their operation relatively scarce.

Canonistic studies evolved alongside other legal studies. It can be no accident that it was from Bologna that, around 1140, there emerged – unheralded, and initially perhaps unheeded – a compilation which would transform the study and utility of canon law. Traditionally ascribed to a Camaldolese monk named Gratian, the *Concordance of Discordant Canons*, or *Decretum*, offered a highly utilitarian compilation, which rapidly established itself as the essential textbook of canon law. Facing head-on the complexities and contradictions of the existing traditions, Gratian's text adopted customary academic techniques of compilation and argument, and applied them to the canonical heritage. The various approaches to a problem were posited by citing opposing authorities, which were then reconciled. The whole, though, was informed by a papalist stance: Gratian effectively transferred Roman law ideas of sovereignty to the Church and papacy, acknowledging that the latter possessed a formal legislative power. This was a vital weapon, which would be used to the full.

Yet Gratian's work was not adopted as an official code of canon law. Its widespread acceptance as the basic compilation, a status secured within half a century, was primarily a testimony to its utility; it remained an unofficial text. The first formal papal collections were not issued until the early thirteenth century, beginning with the so-called *Compilatio tertia*, sent by Pope Innocent III to the masters of Bologna for use in their schools in 1210. The most significant milestone after the appearance of the *Decretum* came in 1234, when Pope Gregory IX promulgated the *Decretals* as a definitive supplementary volume.

Uncertainties about how the *Decretum* was compiled, and its obscure early history as an academic text, cannot diminish its significance as a reasonably coherent corpus which could be cited directly when appropriate, and whose utility could expand as lawyers argued their cases. But to produce one volume was not enough. In some ways, the *Decretum* reflects the encyclopedic tendencies of its time; like other encyclopedias, its claims to completeness were soon outdated. The *Decretum* could not settle all problems: further clarification was often needed, and new problems required new solutions.

Here the legislative authority which Gratian had conceded to the papacy proved critical. After 1150, as they laboriously constructed the 'papal monarchy', the popes used law to tie the provinces more firmly to the centre. The construction of an exceedingly complex web of courts (centred on the papal curia as final court of appeal), and the popes' power to grant privileges and resolve issues, combined to enhance papal authority and thereby increase the importance of canon law. Not a static system, this law could evolve in response to demand, and did. Bishops sought advice on procedures and interpretations; new problems arose and had to be resolved; old solutions seemed inappropriate and had to be reconsidered. All such difficulties met a ready response: the pope would issue a decretal to settle the matter. Such letters were issued in abundance, often in response to specific queries from local prelates. (Many went to England, where interest in canon law in the late twelfth century was such that it has been suggested that these years 'may be called the "English period" in the history of canon law'.)[6]

The proliferation of these papal decretals – ipso facto binding on the whole Church (whether aware of their issue or no) – was a major addition to the canon law, but remained unregulated and uncoordinated. The need to keep track of the new decisions forced canon lawyers (the decretalists) to make their own private collections; the system was again

6 C. Duggan, 'The reception of canon law in England in the later-twelfth century', in *Proceedings of the Second International Congress of Medieval Canon Law*, ed. S. Kuttner and J.J. Ryan, Monumenta iuris canonici, ser. C: subsidia 1 (Vatican City, 1965), p. 377 [reprinted, same pagination, in C. Duggan, *Canon Law in Medieval England* (London, 1982), ch. XI].

threatened with the incoherence and contradictions which existed before the *Decretum*. The way commentaries on canon law were distributed only added to these problems. They, like other academic works, were disseminated somewhat haphazardly, in a process not so much of publication as seepage, in varying recensions rather than distinct editions. This is clearly shown with the monumental *Summa decretorum* of Huguccio of Pisa (usually identified as a teacher of the future Pope Innocent III), of which the fullest version represents the last in a series of five distinct stages, each of which is represented in the manuscript tradition (often with additions written by others to fill the gaps). Moreover, the canonists were interpreting the laws (including decretals), extending their application beyond the original intention and context. Lawyers like Huguccio or Alanus Anglicanus pushed the law to its limits, and in so doing also pushed the popes. Some of the more extreme papalist political concepts emerged initially from the discussions and analyses of canonists, only later being adopted by popes.

This living law, adaptable and flexible, used to augment a papal jurisdiction which constantly expanded its claims until it demanded universal authority, represented a major transformation, with major implications. On the one hand, it perhaps provoked others to issue their own legal statements (as Henry II's Constitutions of Clarendon sought to block the challenge which canon law posed to princely authority). On the other, it generated extensive academic discussion and real litigation, becoming a major formative force in contemporary society. By the middle of the thirteenth century an extensive range of issues was being claimed as subject to canon law and ecclesiastical jurisdiction, although the claims were not always conceded unopposed. Backed up by the Church's (and especially the pope's) supreme moral obligation to intervene in earthly matters *ratione peccati* – on account of sin – the extension of ecclesiastical jurisdiction gave the Church oversight of heresy, marriage, slander, perjury (which, covering breaches of oaths, included breach of contract and debt cases), and wills. The stress on sin marked a critical difference in approach between the secular and ecclesiastical laws, emphasising the moral dimension in the canons. As Huguccio noted, something could be perfectly legal under secular law (which for him was primarily Roman law), but still be a sin. The attempts to enforce the Church's jurisdictional claims (and therewith its morality) were especially contentious when they justified intervention in matters affecting secular inheritances, to apply views which might well clash with lay traditions. One such conflict occurred in England in 1236 over differing common and canon law concepts of bastardy, with the Statute of Merton upholding the local view that children born out of wedlock remained illegitimate even if their parents subsequently married.

Regardless of such local clashes, canon law was a practical and learned law, which functioned internationally. Although its court structure did not cohere fully until the thirteenth century, a court system did exist, reaching up to the final court of appeal and the pope himself. This law had to be learned and taught, and soon had its own academic structures, with glosses, questions, disputations, as well as instruction through practical experience. The interlinking of theoretical and practical learning may explain why some universities developed where they did, for instance alongside the courts of the bishopric of Ely at Cambridge. The demands of study, and the speed of the changes in both Roman and canon law, may also account for a marked regionalism in the history of legal scholarship in the twelfth century, being noticeably concentrated in Italy. Legal studies in France had a very different history. The flourishing of academic Roman law in the Midi was but a passing phase, Montpellier losing its importance by the end of the century. In the northern schools, including Paris, the study of Roman and canon law was at first only shallowly rooted. Even at Paris the disciplines developed late, with extant texts mainly from the 1190s and later. Evidence of canonistic and Roman activity elsewhere in France is sparse, although there was some. This had died out by 1220 at the latest, and was dormant for some fifty years. A convincing explanation for this pattern is elusive; a suggestion that the legal commentaries were developing so fast in Italy that the French schools simply could not keep up and the students all decamped to Bologna has some appeal,[7] but then must confront the counter-argument that study of both laws was buoyant in England at precisely this time.

Roman and canon law were not the sole legal systems in this period. Across Europe, statements of law – sometimes legislation – attest a developing interest in such matters, allied to the growth of government. In Italy, for instance, Lombard law continued as a scholarly tradition in southern Italy. It remained the common law in Norman Italy, alongside other imports and traditions. In northern Italy, the early twelfth century saw an upsurge in interest in the law of fiefs, evidence for which survives in the collection of *Libri feudorum*. Much of this discussion seems to be

---

7 A. Gouron, 'Une école ou des écoles? Sur les canonistes français (vers 1150–vers 1210)', in *Proceedings of the Sixth International Congress of Medieval Canon Law: Berkeley, California, 28 July–2 August 1980*, ed. S. Kuttner and K. Pennington, Monumenta iuris canonici, ser. C: subsidia 7 (Vatican City, 1985), p. 239.

academic, perhaps deriving from Pavia or Milan, and treated as an aspect of Lombard law. The collection was brought together in mid-century, the tracts being supplemented by letters of the Milanese judge Obertus de Orto which show the principles being put into practice. By the end of the twelfth century, this formal feudal law was being treated as a branch of Roman law, included in the corpus as the *decima collatio*. Other evidence of legal proceedings in Italy also shows ideas taking shape in practice, as communal courts extended their areas of competence.

The formulation of 'feudal law' outside Italy also seems more coherent during the twelfth century, although it often occurs ad hoc, and without much theorising (and with the ever-present danger that historians may be identifying trends with the anachronistically tinted spectacles of hindsight). The intervention by Louis VI of France in Flanders in 1127–8, claiming as overlord to determine the succession after the death of Charles the Good, is open to a legalistic justification and interpretation after the event, but was essentially a matter of him trying his luck. Likewise, Philip II's appeal to law against John of England in 1203 was manipulation rather than precise legalism. In Germany, Frederick I's actions to break the power of Henry the Lion in 1180 were formulated in legal terms to justify action against a contumacious vassal, but appealed additionally to the greed of those invested with Henry's lands in anticipation of his deprivation. Two aspects of this affair are important. Firstly, a sense of legal constraint clearly affected this case: Henry lost only those lands considered fiefs; his allodial lands – the dynastic inheritance not held from the crown – remained to his heirs even after the other lands had been taken. Secondly, perhaps more importantly, the very law which Frederick invoked limited his room for action. He might use the law as a weapon in power politics, but he could not crush Henry completely.

Elsewhere, the extent of legalism remains questionable. Some instances of 'law-making', or 'legislation' now appear less firm than they once did. What was once thought to be a code issued by Roger II of Sicily in 1140, the so-called Assizes of Ariano, are now treated more as a collection compiled later from regulations issued by successive kings. Developments in Spain were episodic, and varied in the separate kingdoms. There a mediatised tradition of Roman law had lingered, inherited via the Visigothic *Fuero juzgo*. To some extent that provided an inherited code, and had remained valid in the Basque country during the period of Muslim rule further south. As Islamic power collapsed, the advancing Christians revived that legal tradition, although with uncertain effect. On the one hand, there was considerable fragmentation in legal norms with the granting of *fueros* to reconquered or newly founded settlements, or to particular social groups. They acquired privileged status in relation to the *Fuero juzgo*, often by codifying local customs and giving them the force of law. On the other hand, social change undermined the legal tradition. Following massive social transformation in eleventh-century Catalonia, the old norms collapsed. Catalan appeals to law in the early 1100s were no more than 'a romantic invocation of the ancient force of Visigothic law, not a legal system founded ... on the scrupulous observance of its rules'.[8] In 1149–51 the final codification of the *Usatges* of Barcelona (a codification influenced by both Roman and canon laws) provided the foundation for the reconstruction of a public system of law in the county. Significant change elsewhere in the Iberian peninsula was delayed until the thirteenth century, with Ferdinand III of Castile imposing the *Fuero juzgo* on the areas he reconquered, and his son, Alfonso X, compiling the *Siete Partidas*.

The one place which clearly experienced major advances in the twelfth century was England, although even here there are uncertainties. Perhaps because the emergence of English common law has been studied in considerable detail, the appearance of a new body of legal ideas and practice seems to mark a major contribution to the developments in law, government, and politics. The kingdom certainly had a strong tradition of law-making, dating back to before the Norman Conquest. This in itself may have been peculiar. The constant appeals to the Laws of Edward the Confessor, the composition of the *Leges Henrici primi* by 1118, and the translation of Anglo-Saxon law codes in the *Quadripartitus*, reveal a striking continuity in appreciation of the value of law, even if its implementation remains obscure. This was mainly royal law, although other authorities had law-making functions, down to the customs decreed in manor courts across the country.

However, legislative activity does not appear as the English kings' main legal concern. Justice, much more lucrative, attracted more attention. While the twelfth-century rulers issued legal statements, like the Constitutions of Clarendon of 1166, these were also statements of policy. The Clarendon decrees, for instance, were concerned with the relationship between English practice and the international law of the Church, and as such were defensive, if not retaliatory. Even more significant was the evolution of a royal (and, because royal, national) system of legal procedures, and legal practice. The first steps occurred

8 S.P. Bensch, *Barcelona and its Rulers, 1096–1291*, Cambridge studies in medieval life and thought, 4th ser., 26 (Cambridge, 1995), p. 74.

under Henry II (1154–89), who made his courts the final courts of appeal against seigneurial justice (which slowly atrophied), and also offered procedures by writ to settle inter-party disputes in his courts, especially disputes about land and inheritance. Growing procedural complexity and formality, which made knowledge of the system essential for its successful exploitation, encouraged the emergence of legal specialists, as judges, and as lawyers employable for their knowledge. Greater emphasis on record keeping, on precedent and rules, also aided that transition. Nevertheless, the numbers directly involved were small, and the emergence of properly professional lawyers, and of the arrangements for training them, were delayed until well into the thirteenth century.

The overall impact of the legal changes was considerable, but remains relatively hard to assess. Part of the problem here lies in the overlap between the different strands, produced as much by the personnel as by the ideas themselves. Connection and overlaps between the laws were unavoidable: in due course the scholarship of the Roman and canon laws had much in common, and by the later middle ages it was almost normal for university-trained lawyers to be doctors in both. However, the first generations after 1140 showed some uncertainty about the relationship between Roman and canon laws. Gratian himself cited little explicitly from the Roman laws, yet asserted that they could be applied to supplement and fill gaps in the canonical system, and to provide supporting arguments in decision-making. Initial wariness centred on whether this relationship gave the emperor a legislative authority over the Church; and on whether imperial privileges and amendments to the law automatically applied to the Church, thereby undercutting its own legislative and jurisdictional autonomy. The demarcation of the respective legislative powers of pope and emperor settled that issue, decreeing that imperial legislation could not apply to the Church without tacit or explicit adoption by the ecclesiastical authorities. On the other hand, the Church could still use Roman law and procedures to supplement its own, as Gratian had suggested. Canonical scholarship often drew on Roman law ideas, and papal decretals likewise showed the cross-fertilisation, as in Innocent III's *Vergentis* of 1199, which adopted Roman ideas of treason to criminalise heresy. The effects of this simultaneous and joint evolution were also apparent in legal procedures, as a combined 'Romano-canonical' system emerged, based very much on written materials and judicial determination.

The learned ethos surrounding Roman and canon law, adopted by the lawyers of both, also affected other traditions, although the impact is not easily assessed. Tags and ideas from Roman law certainly floated around, to be used (and sometimes misconstrued) elsewhere. The creation of a 'learned attitude' to law, derived from the academic study of the texts, may be more significant than actual citations and direct influence; the *Tractatus de legibus et consuetudinibus regni Anglie* (*Tract on the Laws and Customs of the Kingdom of England*), written 1187–9 and ascribed to an otherwise unknown 'Glanvill', reveals minimal direct influence from Roman law, but the fact that it was written shows a new approach in England to law and its practice.

Also significant were changing approaches to proof. A change in attitude appears in the abandonment of methods of proof which tested God, the so-called 'unilateral ordeals', mainly by water and hot iron. This broke the tie between the supernatural and justice, and brought the latter firmly down to earth. Clerical dissatisfaction with such ordeals had been growing for some decades before the Fourth Lateran Council of 1215 banned clerical participation (thereby ending the ritual which committed the test to God) and administered the death-blow. Trial by battle lingered, but proved increasingly anachronistic except in a chivalric context.

Procedural changes, and new attitudes to proof, suggest a tilt in the balance of legal proceedings, from making a defendant secure exoneration, to requiring a rival or accuser to establish responsibility or guilt. However, there was no sudden and whole-hearted switch to 'rational' methods of proof, even if greater use of juries (as teams of fact-sifters, often effectively witnesses) and reliance on documentary proof changed the bases of assessment. One common way to 'prove' innocence remained compurgation, whereby people acting effectively as character witnesses swore oaths that they believed the defendant's own oath of innocence. This reliance on community support also gradually withered, but only over centuries (the pace varied regionally). Compurgation, despite its obvious flaws, remained a normal method of proof in Church courts throughout the pre-Reformation period.

In combination, these novel legal changes set social evolution on new paths. Yet a sense of balance is needed, a caveat against making the impact too radical, and against stressing innovation whilst ignoring continuity. Traditions of compromise and arbitration were well established, highly important, and would long make recourse to law something of a last resort. It has rightly been pointed out that 'If ... habits of collective deliberation, decision-making, and responsibility were entrenched in traditional law from at least the tenth century, then the legal changes of the twelfth century, impressive as they were from other points of view, look much less important.'[9] Nevertheless, even here the greater formality of decisions imposed by writing, and the recording which made decisions into precedents, would have altered attitudes to traditional practices.

Politics

By 1200, although politics was still primarily about lordship, ideological and theoretical interpretations and approaches were becoming increasingly influential. Recent legal developments had also affected political systems: the twelfth-century changes have been summed up as 'the juridification of political life'.[10] Certainly law and justice were fundamental to any political structure, although views on their nature varied. The assumption that structures were needed to reduce conflict, which would require an authority to enforce the peace, was widely shared. In the fifth century, St Augustine had opined that a kingdom without justice was merely organised brigandage, and although some twelfth-century subjects probably felt themselves the victims of such brigandage, the idea of justice, and of a ruler's responsibility to guarantee it, was gaining ground. Indeed, the ruler's duty as guarantor of justice became a major element in political thinking of the high middle ages. Justice was not, however, solely the concern of the head: for John of Salisbury the search for and maintenance of justice (seen as a form of the common good) was a collaborative effort, in which all components of the body politic had a share and a responsibility.

The changes in political ideas and action which derived from this new sense of morality and collaboration should not be exaggerated: the relationships between monarchs, Italian cities, rulers, and subjects, remained everywhere conflictive, everywhere requiring the enforcement of authority through the exertion of power and use of violence. Even as new ideas legitimated power relationships, only a very small minority among those affected adhered to them as theories rather than rationalisations, excuses, or justifications of brute force. Theories often underpinned propaganda rather than practice. Nevertheless, the physical conflicts were now being paralleled by explicitly verbal battles, in which victory was gained by convincing both opponents and third parties.

9 Susan Reynolds, *Kingdoms and Communities in Western Europe, 900–1300* (Oxford, 1984), pp. 65–6.
10 Timothy Reuter, 'Debate: the "Feudal Revolution", III', *Past and Present*, no. 155 (May 1997), p. 185.

Although the arguments are now known only from their written remains, at the time equally important (if not more so) were the oral rhetoric of embassies and meetings, exploiting skills with words acquired at the schools. These, unfortunately, cannot usually be recalled. Explicit theorising for its own sake occurred less often, and it has been claimed that 'by the twelfth century we have passed beyond a period in which political thought had developed remarkably'.[11] Indeed, most analyses of twelfth-century political thought, usually confined within narrow chronological limits, mention little beyond John of Salisbury's *Policraticus*, finished in 1159. That work certainly had an enduring influence, being regularly cited in later centuries; but whether it counts as a work of true 'political thought' is debatable. 'In so far as [it] ... was a work of political thought, it had obvious faults of organisation: it can appear as a strange farrago of political and moral observations interspersed with more sustained passages containing something like a systematic treatment of issues.'[12] Yet, regardless of the seeming hiatus, 'it is nevertheless true that the twelfth century was a time when horizons were extended and some new ideas emerged that were eventually to provide a backcloth to political thought in the thirteenth century, and even play a part in it directly'.[13]

The prominence given to the *Policraticus* may reflect a failing of the historians of political thought as much as an absence of material. Contemporary biblical commentaries should prove a fruitful source for further investigation, especially when discussing critical texts like Romans 13.1–6, which deals with 'the powers that be'. Abelard's commentary on this text leads him into discussion of tyranny. Defining a tyrant as someone who had usurped authority and therefore lacked divine authorisation for his rule, he argued that subjects had a legitimate right to resist.

The importance of tractarian writings, and of the debate they reflected, appears in the works produced during the Investiture Contest, between 1073 and 1122. The papacy then sought to expand its influence across Europe by, among other things, undermining secular monarchs' claims to supervise their local churches, notably by trying to smash the alliance

---

11 D.E. Luscombe and G.R. Evans, 'The twelfth-century renaissance', in *The Cambridge History of Medieval Political Thought, c. 350–c. 1450*, ed. J.H. Burns (Cambridge, 1988), p. 307.

12 Joseph Canning, *A History of Medieval Political Thought, 300–1450* (London and New York, 1996), p. 114.

13 *Ibid.*

of kings and prelates epitomised in Germany in the practice whereby monarchs invested prelates with regalian rights and fiefs. As this conflict developed in Germany and Italy, it became a major polemical battle, with writers on both sides putting their case, theorising their stances, and challenging their opponents. Because of the struggle's many ramifications, the arguments ranged widely, dealing with relations between kings and subjects, popes and bishops, and secular and ecclesiastical authorities. Whether they reflected precisely political thought is debatable: there is a developing tendency to locate such discussions in the realms of political *theology* instead, with political *thought* emerging only in the thirteenth century, perhaps only after Aristotle's *Politics* became available in translation in the 1260s. Although it would be hard to ascribe particular outcomes specifically to the theorising of the Investiture Contest (the Concordat of Worms of 1122, which traditionally marks its termination, was more an armistice than a peace), the ideas advanced did reflect contemporary opinions, and the possibility of real changes in the balances of power, legitimated through argument.

Historians' discussions of the Investiture Contest usually focus on a perceived conflict between papal and royal power (often confused with imperial power, although Henry IV only gained the imperial crown at the hands of the antipope in 1084). In practical politics rather than theoretical debates, the key issue was the balance of powers and responsibilities between king and princes in Germany. This became particularly significant when, in 1077, the princes claimed to depose Henry IV (with papal backing) and elect an alternative king. The legacy of this novelty was the uncertain status of kingship in twelfth-century Germany, until Frederick I tried to reinvigorate the monarchy by creating a new relationship between himself and his magnates founded on more legalistic interpretations of vassalage.

Different developments occurred in the local version of the Investiture Contest fought out in England. This lacked the vehement extremism of the continental conflict (but there was one fervent participant, the 'Anglo-Norman Anonymous', whose views on the relationship between crown and Church are among the most extreme statements of a royalist case). The English solution was arrived at by gradually defining the spheres of influence for secular and ecclesiastical authorities. In 1088 the trial of William of St Calais, bishop of Durham, distinguished church holdings tied to spiritual duties from those held as temporal fiefs of the crown; a distinction based on the precedent set in actions against Odo, bishop of Bayeux, in his capacity as earl of Kent in 1082. Archbishop Anselm of Canterbury clashed fiercely with William II and Henry I over investiture and clerical homage, but if he was aiming to establish the principle that Church lands were beyond the normal property relationships of the kingdom and exempt from secular authority (albeit, presumably, under ultimate archiepiscopal control in a form of patriarchate), his claims were forcefully rebuffed.

In 1107, a practical formal division of obligations was set out for newly appointed prelates, with 'spiritualities' being received from the ecclesiastical hierarchs, and 'temporalities' from feudal superiors (often the crown), thus ending that aspect of the quarrel. It did not, however, end the jockeying for superiority between lay and ecclesiastical authorities, which recurred intermittently over the century, and beyond.

In the varied political evolutions of the long twelfth century, three main themes stand out. The first is the impact of the Roman inheritance: the history, institutions, and laws of Rome. This directs attention to imperialism, to republicanism, and to the influence elsewhere of tags derived from Roman law.[14] The second focus is on kingship, as something different from imperialism but realistically more important. Here a different spotlight is needed, on concerns with justice, on biblical models, and on the evolution of 'feudalism'. The third strand appears when these models are applied to the changing relationship between centre and locality in the Church, as an aspect of the creation of the so-called 'papal monarchy', in which the Church was to acquire many characteristics of a 'state'. These changes had not been completed by 1250; but what has to be highlighted here are the first steps towards a new order, a change in direction rather than the end of the line.

The appeal to Roman traditions and ideas is the most obviously 'renaissance' aspect of twelfth-century politics. Several strands coalesced, sometimes in contradiction. Particularly important was the role of Roman law, in changing the definition of emperorship. Increasingly, what was stressed was the emperor's status, and the exercise of his powers. Earlier ideas of 'empire' had been vague. Although it was recognised that, following the Roman tradition, the unique emperor was secular lord of the world, the formal bases of 'empire' had been uncertain. Because imperial authority was seen as cosmological, not territorial, the stress had hitherto been on the process of acquiring authority in those terms: imperial status was gained by being crowned by God, even if the crowning was mediated through the papacy.

14 Above, pp. 69, 72.

The twelfth-century appeal to Roman models and law changed the bases of the debate. Whereas earlier discussion had simply been about 'empire' (and later debates would likewise centre on abstract and ethereal concepts), the twelfth century's new insistence on Romanness carried connotations of a territorial and secularised sovereignty. The emperor, with Rome as a real capital, might yet reactivate that imperial power which had been in abeyance in the west since the fifth century. This presented a latent challenge both to other secular rulers, and to the papacy. Through the appeal to law, and insistence on the continuity of the imperial tradition from the times of the Caesars, the emperor's cosmological status (and with it the bases of the dispute with the papacy on the meaning of 'empire') were radically changed. A tradition of empire predated Christianity; there were emperors before there were popes. This stimulated a redefinition of the sources and contexts of imperial power, making the new imperialism more secular. God was not a prerequisite, although it was inconceivable that God would actually be excluded. Even with God left in, the revived Romanism raised the spectre of an empire which did not need priestly (that is, papal) mediation to transmit the divine favour, as was suggested in 1149 when the Romans invited Conrad III of Germany to receive the imperial crown at their hands, ignoring the pope. Any necessary theocratic element could be inserted directly into the relationship between God and emperor. Although the legal tradition did not explain the processes of imperial continuity, appeal to the *Lex regia* (whereby the Romans had transferred their inherent sovereignty to the emperor) could eliminate the papacy's role in the appointment of an emperor: what mattered was the irrevocable transfer of power from 'the people' to the ruler. Precisely such ideas were advanced by the canonist Huguccio, who argued that the emperor acquired his powers at election, not by papal confirmation. They were publicly voiced in the Declaration of Speyer, issued in May 1199, by those who had elected Philip of Swabia to succeed Henry VI as emperor. (Innocent III reacted, in his *deliberatio* of 1201, to reclaim and reassert papal authority to determine suitability for the imperial crown as a quasi-ecclesiastical office, altering the coronation ceremony for Otto IV to remove any hint of territorial power in Rome, or any likelihood of papal ideas being misconstrued.) Twelfth-century legists produced increasingly refined analyses of the relationship between the prince and the law, as the source of law but existing also to defend the rights and traditions of his subjects. This formal, to some extent static, system, was eminently exploitable. Its Roman origins gave it the authority of antiquity and memory: a revived imperial power could be portrayed as a restoration of rights, a challenge to the illegitimate structures which had replaced the old empire, rather than as startling innovation (although implementation would be innovative in practice).

This new Romanism was openly expressed in the reign of Frederick I (1152–90): his activities made the imperialist threat abundantly clear both to his subjects and to the papacy, provoking reactions from both. Frederick saw himself very much as a *Roman* emperor; in his reign the empire was for the first time referred to as the *sacrum imperium*, the holy empire. The stage on which Frederick I acted was too big to allow his actions to be completely co-ordinated; his policies in Germany necessarily differed in conception and application from those adopted in Italy. Yet he may have had an ultimate goal. In seeking it, the Roman inheritance was important, nowhere more so than in Italy.

Frederick I's Italian activities openly appealed to Roman traditions. The Italian cities' acknowledgement that their status was affected by Roman law was crucial, amounting to an admission that they were not independent sovereign entities, but parts of a larger body (at least the Kingdom of Italy, perhaps the Roman empire). They were not sovereign republics, but provincial *civitates*, parts of the greater entity.

In 1158 Frederick I sought to make the legists' construct of empire real. At the Diet of Roncaglia he requested a statement of his rights in Italy under Roman law. A panel of lawyers duly confirmed his regalian powers and privileges, over both cities and countryside. Frederick then sought to act on the statement. It was not this in itself which produced conflict with the Italian cities: Frederick was seemingly prepared to integrate their communal realities into the imperial scheme provided that they recognised his supremacy and that they exercised their powers by delegation. The communal governments would still exist, but under the emperor's overriding sovereignty and authority, recognising that their powers derived not from popular grant but imperial concession. Initially, the cities seem to have accepted that compromise: perhaps the fact that Frederick had law on his side (not to mention force), and was promising to restore peace within Italy, boosted his chances of success.

The development of northern Italy during the preceding century meant that the restoration of imperial authority would not be achieved. The details are unimportant here; nor did the dream die completely: the secular appeal to empire marked Hohenstaufen attempts to assert authority in Italy well into the thirteenth century. However, that Frederick I did not gain everything does not mean that he gained nothing. At the Peace of Constance in 1183, the civic authorities still accepted that they were imperial subjects. Even if Frederick had renounced the power to interfere, the cities were autonomous by concession, not right. Latent imperialism still overshadowed their existence and evolution, a shadow which might yet become concrete if circumstances permitted. Moreover, although the cities' powers in their hinterlands were also recognised, the formal statement of imperial rights and powers made at Roncaglia was not abrogated: again, control was delegated. Later imperial action in Italy (by Frederick II in the thirteenth century, and Henry VII and Louis IV in the fourteenth) would reopen the debates about imperial rights, and revive the conflicts.

While Frederick I invoked Rome's monarchical imperialist tradition, another strand of political Romanism also had an appeal. The historic Rome was not solely imperial: the city's republican tradition was recorded in literary texts, and in parts of the law. The *Lex regia*, the very law which validated the monarchy, presupposed a transfer of power by voluntary grant from the people to the prince. It therefore presupposed a republican system, with the possibility (duly debated by lawyers in the twelfth century and later) that the grant might be revoked. Classical tradition suggested that the Roman people might reclaim for themselves their headship of the world, and the empire which went with it. Far-fetched and unlikely as that was, they might also, more positively and practically, reclaim their self-governance, against either emperor or pope.

That did happen in the 1140s, although in somewhat confused fashion. In 1143 a revolt led to the re-establishment of a senate (which was misunderstood as being a popular institution), and to attempts to curtail papal power in the city. Arnold of Brescia, a reformist preacher once associated with Peter Abelard, had a role in the proceedings, emerging as leader. The rest of the world was invited to acknowledge the newly revived Rome, but seems not to have responded; just as Conrad III failed to take up the offer to receive the imperial crown from the Roman people. The republican experiment, although lasting for a decade, was crushed by concerted papal and imperial opposition. Arnold of Brescia was executed by imperial forces in 1155; the whole affair ending up as just another of the power struggles known in contemporary Italian cities. The Roman inheritance nevertheless remained, with the senate retaining a role in Rome's civic government. However, its real power was minimal, and eventually gave way to rule by a single senator, effectively acting as a papal governor.

The immediate impact of the revived republic was limited, but the experiment, in conjunction with lingering Aristotelian ideas of civic self-rule, may have aided the birth of an Italian civic ideology, encouraging the Italian communes' self-perception as real political bodies, and

justifying their legislative and administrative actions. Yet the practicality
and practicability of those claims were limited, as the conflicts with the
Hohenstaufen showed. The continuing shadowy existence of an Italian
kingdom compromised and undermined the 'city states' throughout the
later middle ages. The twelfth-century Italian cities certainly were not
'states': although practically self-governing, they lacked solid theoretical
support for their autonomy, or to justify claims to sovereignty. Their use
of old terminology evoked memories – although 'consuls' may have
more connotations to later historians than they did to twelfth-century
governors – but reality was very different. Only after 1300 did a
theoretical shift occur to justify the cities' claims to sovereign self-
governance, on the basis that the city was *sibi princeps*, a prince unto itself.
Even this did not eliminate the problem of continuing imperial claims to
sovereignty in Italy, or (by this stage) those of the pope.

The theorising about the political implications of the Roman past was
both impressive and fundamental, but there was one major weakness: it
concerned a lost world. Originating in a unitary political system which
claimed authority over all of western Europe, the Romanising ideas
sought to recreate that system in a context where that was simply
impossible. While twelfth-century Europe had an emperor, whether
there actually was a Roman empire is debatable, involving questions of
identity and authority. A sense of continuity perhaps encouraged those
living nominally under the sway of the emperor to think of themselves as
Romans, or to be ascribed a Roman identity by outsiders (as the non-
Slavs – Germans and others – enticed eastwards by the Polish rulers to
expand agriculture in their territories were generally labelled *Romanos*).
But in terms of practical governance, any real Roman empire would have
to be a new creation. Here the implications of territoriality and sovereignty in Frederick I's imperialism were innovations. His de facto
authority derived from his status as King of Germany, King of Italy, and
King of Burgundy, kingdoms whose territorial bounds set the limits of his
actual power, regardless of any universalist connotations of 'empire'. For
practical purposes, twelfth-century western Europe was a complex of
kingdoms, and the Roman system said little about kings. They (or their
advisers) would in time appropriate Rome's law-based imperialist
monarchical ideology for their own ends; but this was a slow process.
Kings existed in reality, rather than theory; empire – and papacy – had to
accommodate themselves to their existence. Concurrently, partly in
response to aspirations of empire and papacy, partly in response to the
challenges posed by their subjects (lay and ecclesiastical), and partly in

order to fix their own authority, these kings needed a theoretical basis for their status and authority, to ensure the continuity, security, and reality of their power.

The problem of finding and securing a theoretical foundation for kingship in twelfth-century Europe had to be resolved within the individual realms, generating specific conflicts and resolutions from kingdom to kingdom. Other developments occasionally raised slightly different issues, but these often worked within a broad structure which was essentially the same. Papal claims to establish kingdoms (as with the creation of the Kingdom of Sicily, or the attempt to elevate Ireland into a kingdom in 1185), or to have kings as vassals (most obviously with the submission of King John of England in 1215), essentially matched the claims made by kings over their own vassals. When the Emperor Henry VI forced Richard I of England to hold his realm as an imperial fief, he was operating on the same principles. Here questions of 'Roman empire' seemingly did not arise; and if the relationship was not immediately considered invalid because involuntary, it was perhaps treated as a purely personal obligation, which did not outlive the parties.

The emphasis on practicality, and on relationships, appears in one of the most significant comments on the status of kings made in the period, by Pope Innocent III in his decretal *Per venerabilem* in 1202. In declining an appeal from the Count of Montpellier to legitimate his children, the pope threw out the chance remark that 'the King himself recognizes no superior in temporal matters'.[15] These were words to cherish: Peter could be used against Caesar. If the King of France – and, by extension, any king – had no terrestrial secular (as opposed to spiritual) superior, this clearly abrogated any imperial claims to authority over him. Universalist imperialism's challenge to kingship was immediately, directly, and radically undermined, at least from a royalist perspective. Similarly challenging to universalist imperialism were ideas circulating among canonists at the papal curia, which congealed in the formula that 'the king is emperor in his own kingdom'. Building on such foundations, the thirteenth century saw the consolidation of royal authority by the adoption of the Roman ideology, a territorialised royal imperialism, with all that that implied. Moreover, such independent sovereignty justified a process of territorial and jurisdictional consolidation, the creation of a 'state'.

The Romanisation of territorial monarchy occurred primarily in the thirteenth century. Before 1200, theorists of kingship worked with

---

15 Brian Pullan, *Sources for the History of Medieval Europe, from the Mid-Eighth to the Mid-Thirteenth Century* (Oxford, 1966), p. 70.

different materials. If Roman tradition dealt mainly with empire, and its ideas did not really apply to kings, there was another – greater – source of legitimation available to be mined: the Bible. Its picture of kingship could be exploited to establish the relations between monarch and subjects.

The Old Testament offered a good picture of divine sanction for kingly government. It also decreed the nature of the king's joint relationship with his subjects and, more importantly, with God. In the New Testament, Paul's epistle to the Romans (13.1) bluntly enjoined obedience: 'the powers that be are ordained of God', which generally meant kings. Still, kings had obligations. They were ministers of God, with obligations to those under them, primarily to maintain justice. Unlike 'empire', kingship was necessarily Christian, inevitably therefore it had a religious dimension, which added further complications. Coronations, with their anointing and oaths (where such ceremonies were used), were constitutive acts, interpreted as conveying divine approval for the new monarch. It was only in the twelfth century that clerical writers concluded that coronation should be denied sacramental force, denied the power to grant an indelible character equivalent to baptism or priestly ordination. In the English rite, the symbolic possibilities of the retention of the practice of anointing with chrism (the ointment used in priestly ordination), and the covering of the newly anointed ruler's head with a quasi-baptismal coif, were matters of concern to canonists and popes by 1200. The quasi-sacral status of the king could also be demonstrated in other ways. In some kingdoms (England among them) repeated ceremonial crown-wearings restated and reinforced the monarch's elevated status, especially when accompanied by the *laudes regiae*, ritual acclamations which proclaimed and invoked divine assistance for the king.

Despite the biblical background, ideas of kingship lacked intellectual rigour in the early part of the period. Any theorising dwelt primarily on a king's authority over the church, as in the works of the 'Anglo-Norman Anonymous', or the tracts produced during the Investiture Contest. More 'political' considerations appeared only gradually. The main focus was on practicalities, on 'feudal' relationships which were essentially founded on power and, although strengthened by appeal to law, on ideas of property: that vassals really held only the usufruct (even if hereditarily) of lands and property which rightly belonged to the monarch, and might in due course revert to him. In the property-based relationship of 'feudalism', the vassalic and legal ties centred on kingship were almost identical: the pyramid allowed the king to claim the supreme position as guardian and guarantor of justice. Precisely how this should be done varied. A concern for law and the proclamation of laws had been part of the job description of monarchs for centuries; what really mattered, however, was the effectiveness of their implementation, and how the kings used that legal system to their own advantage. In Germany, for instance, it has been argued that the twelfth-century monarchs failed to advance beyond a declamatory role; that their apparently legal pronouncements remained essentially dead letters, being no more than vague generalisations which proclaimed a desire for peace but were incapable of imposing it. Yet Frederick I clearly exploited a legal system against Henry the Lion in 1180.

In contrast to Germany, royal use of law in England and France provided an effective boost to royal power and authority, in differing ways. In Angevin England, Henry II exploited his position at the head of a legal system to undermine his rivals for power, and thereby enhanced the status of the monarchy. His judicial reforms, including the innovative property assizes which allowed disputes over land to be determined without recourse to violence, challenged the competence of his vassals' courts, and eventually forced most of them out of business. The effectiveness of the changes owed much to market forces: the crown offered solutions, encouraged suitors, and rival courts proved unequal to the competition. Indeed, the erstwhile competitors appreciated the value of the royal courts for their own ends: Henry's reforms were at first resented, but had been accepted by John's reign. Magna Carta called not for their elimination, but for assurances that they would work more effectively. Of course, the kings were not driven by altruistic abstract concepts of justice: control of the legal processes was a means of exerting influence, demonstrating power, controlling and limiting opposition, subjecting subjects. It also brought in large sums of money. But once England was ruled by a system of justice which was conceptually *crown* justice, this was a considerable advance in the process of state building, and towards an ideology of monarchy. The process remained incomplete for some time; but the twelfth century set it in motion.

In France, meanwhile, a less overtly aggressive approach was adopted, but still one with considerable potential. French kings claimed not to supplant, but to supplement, local judicial authorities. They transformed the ideal pyramid of vassalage into a practical pyramid of legal relationships, with the vassals themselves and with their subjects. The appeal to a property law of fiefs allowed the kings to increase their territorial authority: initially within the crown domain under Louis VI, and then expanding aspirations to intervene in the great magnatial fiefs. The latter strand appears in Louis VI's attempts to control the Flemish succession in 1127–8 (although there he was, ultimately, thwarted), and in the recreation of homage relationships with the Angevins which applied a brake to Henry II's ambitions (most obviously when he abandoned an attack on Toulouse in 1157) and was used to exploit Angevin intra-familial rivalries in the 1170s and 1180s. The most dramatic and significant exploitation of the relationship occurred in the dispute between Philip II and John; first in Philip's claim that his intervention in the succession dispute between John and Arthur of Brittany was legally justified; and more importantly in the declaration of forfeiture issued against John when he ignored a summons to Philip's court in 1203. No matter that the judgement was legally excessive, it was a legal judgement, which was enough. In some ways the attack on John matches Frederick I's assault on Henry the Lion in Germany, differing, however, in that Philip II did gain the prizes.

The second component of the French crown's exploitation of justice was the creation of direct links with subjects of the great vassals. As guarantors and supreme exponents of justice, the French rulers sought to undermine magnatial power not by direct confrontation and rivalry (which was basically what the Angevins did in England), but more subtly by making the royal court the final court of appeal. As royalist ideology developed, local and private rights of justice were reinterpreted as powers delegated from the crown. While the crown would not normally interfere with or challenge their use, the parcellisation of justice could be reversed by the imposition of a royal appellate jurisdiction. In some ways matching the development of papal claims to universal jurisdiction, within their kingdom the French kings offered a ready ear to complaints of injustice, or of failure to provide justice. Subjects thereby gained a channel for redress against their lords. It was a short step from offering an ear to encouraging complaints: the channel for redress of grievance became a means whereby the crown could undermine and subdue the magnates. This was only incipient in the twelfth century; but the possibilities were again demonstrated by Philip II's action against King John. That was, after all, initiated by Hugh de Lusignan's appeal to Philip against the alleged bad lordship of his Angevin master. The commodification of rights of justice, which allowed kings to purchase judicial powers outside their own territories, either outright or by the sharing arrangement of *paréage*, offered yet another way to increase their power.

Although they faced rebuffs, kings could bide their time, nurse their wounds, and then return to the fray. They could base their claims on ideological foundations derived from old traditions of theocratic kingship. At heart the Investiture Contest was really about kingship, and about the real meaning of royal claims to be Vicar of Christ. That title – not yet a papal title – asserted terrestrial supremacy within the realm, what James I of England later called the 'strange divinity [that] doth hedge a king' (although the eleventh century had nothing like the specific formulation or ideology which became the Divine Right of Kings). Royal claims to power could be buttressed by appeals to the peculiar status confirmed in coronation, and by conscious creation of a monarchist ideology, stressing God's sanction for their position. Royal powers and duties thus acquired a spiritual edge, one hard to controvert. Although notions of theocratic monarchy were buffeted by the Investiture Contest, they were not annihilated. The major revisions and developments here occurred during the thirteenth century, but premonitions appear in the twelfth, particularly in France.

There – or, to be precise, in northern France, where the Capetians were based – the growth of a political religion owed much to the alliance between Abbot Suger of St Denis and King Louis VI. This laid the foundations for a royalism whose religious tone became increasingly intense in later centuries. The relationship originated as a basis for mutual support, with Suger aiming to harness the power of the crown to defend his abbey, while the king sought ecclesiastical support to expand and consolidate royal authority. Its outcome was an insistence on divine approval for monarchy in general, and particularly for the Capetian dynasty. The strong alliance with St Denis (the person, rather than the place), and that saint's promotion to quasi-patronal status of both realm and dynasty, reflected back on the monarchy as supported by its heavenly protector. Coronation was emphasised, setting the king at the pinnacle of the political order, and defending the dynasty against possible challenges. Despite clerical assertions that coronation was non-sacramental, the French ceremony retained strongly sacramental features. The anointing itself, with the oil of the *sainte ampoulle* (the miraculously inexhaustible flask of oil supposedly brought from heaven to St Rémi by an angel, to crown Clovis as first Christian ruler of France), proclaimed God's approval of the new king, making resistance an act of sacrilege. (This was perhaps particularly important in the twelfth century, when prophecies declared the Capetians a caretaker dynasty, awaiting the return of the Carolingians: a prophecy supposedly fulfilled with Louis VIII's accession in 1223.) The healing royal touch, the quasi-priestly status allowed to the king at his coronation (although a layman, he took communion in both kinds), increased the sacrality of kingship. Although only the French kings developed this kind of royal religion at this time, others soon followed, notably the Plantagenets in thirteenth-century England. The only close twelfth-century parallel was the ritual of the Norman court in Sicily; but that derived mainly from Byzantine and Arabic sources, and although it clearly promoted the crown, it was more effective as court ritual than as royalist propaganda.

The development of kingship was neither smooth nor unperturbed. There were practical difficulties in exercising authority, and issues of accountability. Rebellion (broadly defined as all violent actions which challenged monarchs' emerging self-perceptions of their role and powers) was virtually endemic, but could it be justified? Could rebellion be validated as self-defence, or as a public-spirited attempt to return the ruler to a role which he himself had threatened? Such formulations smack of hints of constitutionalism, which are anachronistic for this period. Yet a sense of balance was there, in the oaths sworn at coronation, reciprocated by homage to the new ruler. The language of politics here becomes significant. The seventh-century writer Isidore of Seville was the source for the potent tag that a king (*rex*) was so called because he ruled *rightly* (*recte*). Right rule, in opposition to unright, distinguished a true ruler from a tyrant who, by definition, was illegitimate. Here was an implicit (rarely explicit) sense of mutuality: that a ruler who threatened to go off the rails might be called to account. Whether that accountability was to subjects, or to God, was debatable; but the subjects' role was certainly being considered. A tyrant ruler, one who ruled wilfully, abandoning paternalism for self-interest, threatened the whole political system. By definition, a 'tyrant' was not (or no longer) a 'king'. Manegold of Lautenbach argued in 1085 that the transition to tyranny automatically dissolved the ties between monarch and subjects (identified as the leaders of the kingdom, not the people in general), moving the right of rebellion from the blunt appeal to self-interest in the feudal *diffidatio* (where the link of vassalage or homage was dissolved to legitimate conflict between the former partners) to a more principled stance of defence of the 'community' against an errant monarch. In reality, of course, the appeal might still be to self-interest; the views of the overall community were not canvassed.

Formal accusations of tyranny are rare in the twelfth century, partly because the necessary political language was still evolving. There are hints of such charges in the English civil war in Stephen's reign; and in anti-Angevin agitation later in the century. Elsewhere, Roger II of Sicily was sometimes called a tyrant, perhaps less for the nature of his government than because he occupied territories claimed by the emperor, because classical tradition made Sicily a land of tyrants, and because he

was determined to dominate the south Italian Church. Almost unavoidably, since clerics controlled the language, charges of tyranny tend to
erupt from an ecclesiastical milieu: a king's failure to act in Church interests
was usually what made him a 'tyrant'; although some laypeople may
have been appropriating the language by the end of the twelfth century.

The main statement of ideas on tyranny appears in John of
Salisbury's *Policraticus*. He makes much of the distinction between
kingship and tyranny, and on one reading accuses Henry II of England of
tyranny. But John's proposed response to tyranny is unclear. The
traditional reading has him advocate tyrannicide: that the tyrant, by
abandoning his kingly role, dissolves his links with God and his subjects,
and may justifiably be removed – even killed – to restore good governance. Other readings differ: the matter was to be left in the hands of God.
Subjects had no right of anything other than passive resistance, in the
hope either that God would act, or that the tyrant would respond to pleas
and advice and revert to true regality. The issue here, as elsewhere,
centred on the balance of forces: was the king primarily accountable to
God or to his subjects (which really meant the magnates and other
landowners)? Translated into the practical issues of the time, that battle
could be regularly fought and refought, and would continue to be
debated long after the twelfth century had drawn to a close.

Meanwhile, another type of political accountability evolved from the
realities of urban experience. The Italian communes offer the key
instance here, but many other towns – in southern and northern France,
in the Rhineland, and in England – were seeking and achieving greater
autonomy. The process was most marked, most obviously 'political', in
northern Italy, which lacked any overarching effective rulership (a
situation matched in southern France, where political fragmentation
likewise encouraged urban self-rulership, notably in Toulouse). Northern France and England saw some attempts to reject local lordship, like
the communal rising at Laon in 1108, which led to a period of disturbance
ended by royal confirmation of the commune in 1128. Reactions to such
movements varied, with ecclesiastical lords appearing particularly hostile
to such attempts to assert autonomy. Yet many lords recognised the
profits to be gained from compromise, which reduced the need for
conflict. Where (as in England) towns were not forced back on their own
political resources, the fact that they were welded into a kingdom, and
did not need to exert physical control over the surrounding countryside,
eliminated that opportunity or impulse to dominate their hinterlands
which drove the Italian communes to establish *contadi*.

The experience of urban self-government created a sense of mutuality, of shared participation; but this experience was not widely shared. Most Italian communes began as self-interested pressure groups which had managed to seize and share power; they were not representative of the whole populace. The transfer of powers occurred in a context of privileges (granted and confirmed by a recognised superior authority), and against a background of practical ad hocery (powers being seized or negotiated in response to immediate issues and opportunites, to be justified and validated after the event). Even though some communal statutes, like those of Pisa in 1154, validated consular actions by declaring their ratification at popular assemblies, there was no communal ideology in the twelfth century, and certainly not a 'democratic' ideology. 'Even in the most independent, rich, and splendid cities of Italy very few revolutionary ideas about society and politics seem to have been produced before the fourteenth century.'[16] Instead, the early communes were exclusive: full membership was a restricted privilege, even if the self-perpetuating communal rulers claimed to speak for the whole urban body. As self-appointing and self-appointed representatives, the communes negotiated with, and sometimes constrained, those who in turn claimed authority over them; yet there was no necessary incompatibility between the continuance of Italian communal structures, and effective imperial overlordship. A *modus vivendi* between the communes and Frederick I was initially a real possibility, although ultimately not achieved.

Outside Italy, urban elites similarly secured power for themselves as 'citizens', excluding all others. Sometimes these elites appealed to the communal model, but could not develop in the same way. Nevertheless, the model could be transported in other ways. If (as has been claimed) King John's opponents in England appealed to communal ideas to redefine the relationship between crown and subjects in Magna Carta and later disputes, they were likewise self-appointed spokesmen for the kingdom, even if they appealed to different forms of accountability by recalling the pact between king and subjects established by the coronation oaths.

So far, the stress has been on the secular application of politics, a world of emperors, cities, and kings. But 'politics' functioned elsewhere. The historical tradition that the twelfth century saw the rise of a 'papal monarchy' shifts attention from the secular to the ecclesiastical arena. Certainly, there are many parallels between secular and ecclesiastical

---

16 Reynolds, *Kingdoms and Communities*, p. 156.

developments. The papacy's own dependence on Roman traditions, or what were seen as such (like the Donation of Constantine), was fundamental. Indeed, 'tradition' was critical for the Church because the very essence of its self-identity derived from the past: Christianity, and ecclesiastical order, was a *traditio*, a 'handing-over' from generation to generation, a continuity. For the popes that was manifest in their proclaimed status as successors to St Peter, and as inheritors of the commission which he had received directly from Christ to rule the Church, as recorded in Matthew 16.18–19. With this insistence on tradition and continuity (even if necessarily amended in response to circumstances), it is hardly surprising that the revived Romanism of the twelfth century, especially in law, made a mark. The popes' increasing adoption of Roman imperialist ideology caused them to see their powers in equivalent terms: Pope Honorius III (1216–27) would draw the precise analogy between pope and emperor, with the cardinals in the role of senators. In this (re)construction, the role of bishops declined: they became mere provincial governors, increasingly answerable to Rome for the governance of their sees, exercising power on behalf of the papacy through that channelling of authority which has been defined as a 'descending theory of government'.[17] Reusing formulae originally advanced by St Bernard, Pope Innocent III stated the relationship bluntly: the pope alone had the *plenitudo potestatis*, the totality of power; lesser ecclesiasts – cardinals and bishops – had only a *pars solicitudinis*, a share in the duty of care.

The subtle links between Roman and canon law also affected developments: the pope was much more self-consciously a law-maker than any contemporary king, much more involved in legal matters through the rise of the papal courts as places of resort for answers to legal issues from across western Europe. St Bernard indeed complained that Pope Eugenius III (1145–53) was too much a Justinian, too little a Peter. Papal monarchism, using the weapons of law and justice, effectively crushed notions of co-operative episcopalism, but the embers of that conflict were to be a long time a-dying.

Government

While theory affected the developments in law and the balance of authority, practice was of more immediate significance than writings.

---

17 Walter Ullmann, *Principles of Government and Politics in the Middle Ages* (London, 1961), pp. 19–26.

This is hardly surprising. The essential change here was the growing sophistication of government. The twelfth century has rightly been identified as central to the shift 'from memory to written record', as governmental systems evolved to deal not merely with revenues, but with administration, law, and other aspects of rule. The Italian cities, the Norman kingdom of southern Italy, and the Anglo-Norman realm appear most precocious in these matters, followed (not led) by the papacy. Administrations (including ecclesiastical administrations) evolved increasingly sophisticated – sometimes increasingly cumbersome – methods of record keeping. There was a general burgeoning of organisation and archives, which penetrated way below the top layers of the lay and ecclesiastical hierarchies, continued to develop into the thirteenth century, and expanded even more thereafter. In England, for instance, one response to royal initiatives in legal matters included attempts by those with local rights of justice to make their courts conform more to the new royal models, especially when dealing with free tenants. This may have stimulated increasing documentation of manorial administration in late twelfth- and early thirteenth-century England, notably court rolls (a type of document almost completely unknown in continental Europe), although the processes require further elucidation.

Yet there is a difficulty here. How far administrative activity is recognisably and properly 'government' is questionable. There is little sense of policy, of conscious decisions being made (except possibly about war). The scope for action by twelfth-century governments was extremely limited, and although balls might be set rolling (notably in legal changes), there was no telling how soon (or if) they might come to a halt. For kings and princes, what passes for government was mainly patrimonial administration, based on lordship and the realm as the king's land, his demesne. Administration accordingly dealt mainly with that demesne and its revenues, and with the fruits of attendant rights derived from the creation of 'feudal' structures and profits of justice. But the only real difference between royal administration and that of another lord was in scale. As owner of a large estate, the king needed a large and complex administration, especially when the switch to a cash economy was liberating the value of payments in kind by allowing them to be converted into coin.

That transition to cash also permitted centralisation of accounting, perhaps made formal accounting a necessity because embezzlement and misappropriation of coin was a serious threat to authority. Hence, perhaps, the stabilisation of the exchequers of the Anglo-Norman realm; hence also the emergence of written accounts in Catalonia and Flanders, and the first signs of their existence for the French royal domain. The commodification of justice also contributed. Fines and such like had to be accounted for, fees collected. The official memory recorded in writing could be exploited both fiscally, and for private purposes.

This administrative development was significant, but it was largely ad hoc. There is no sense of planning, of deliberate decisions. The machinery established was often unwieldy: records give the impression of being made for immediate purposes, with little thought for their overall and later utility. Searching through them to discover a past event would have been a laborious task.

As most fiscal regimes initially dealt mainly with domain finance, the critical point in the emergence of 'government' came when those landed revenues proved insufficient, and extraordinary revenue – taxation, which had to be both assessed and imposed – was needed. The emergence of taxation 'marks most clearly the capacity of rulers to separate themselves structurally from the ruled, and create a separate economic foundation for the state'.[18] Few places had made the change by 1250, other than England (where the inherited Anglo-Saxon geld had withered in the twelfth century, making the emergence of wealth-taxation under Richard I and his successors a new start) and the Italian cities (whose need to pay for armies had required means to tap wealth). There had been experiments elsewhere, some amounting to little more than a regularisation of tributary exactions, like Frederick I's attempted annual imposition of the *fodrum* in north Italy in the 1160s. If few governments could tax, even fewer could impose taxes effectively: assessment and collection systems were rudimentary, even if the taxation process generated a considerable array of documents and encouraged further administrative development as the arrangements were recorded and consigned to memory. The practical needs of assessment and collection encouraged a search for consent and collaboration, and might evoke opposition at intervention in local rule. Concerns about taxation were occasionally voiced in terms which appear 'constitutionalist' (as in Magna Carta, or the negotiations over consent under Henry III in England), and taxes were resisted and rejected; but once the principle of taxation was established, it would not be abolished.

The new bureaucracies (if that is an acceptable word for them) employed clerks – clerics – to run the system and keep the records. Notaries in north Italian cities, exchequer clerks in Winchester, attest a

18 Chris Wickham, 'Lineages of western European taxation, 1000–1200', in *Actes: Col·loqui corona, municipis i fiscalitat a la baixa edat mitjana*, ed. M. Sánchez and A. Furió (Lleida, 1997), p. 27.

growing concern to record, to have evidence, which accompanied the evolution in government, to support the ruling authorities. While accounting practices had their local forms, in general documentary history there is a clear basic contrast between the notarial tradition of the Mediterranean, whose prime legacy is the runs of notarial registers whose first examples survive in Italian cities from the late twelfth century and, north of the Alps, greater reliance on charters with witnesses and seals (although notaries were seemingly important in Flanders). Almost inevitably, the administrators gave their own rationales for the system they served, as their offices became self-perpetuating, and self-justifying. The formation of administrative systems stimulated the formation of administrative minds. Many administrators were products of the schools. Trained to quibble, they quibbled for others by challenging charters, arguing cases, pushing the claims of authority (including their own) for the benefit of their employers. That is, when they were not confined to mere pen-pushing and copying, in those mundane tasks which in a manuscript culture made administration a tedious and time-consuming business. However, while the usual focus when discussing the 'twelfth-century renaissance' is on the clerical role in these new administrations, which set in train a Parkinsonian proliferation of parchment, this neglects the often important role of lay administrators. They were especially significant in Italian cities, and in the notarial culture of the Mediterranean. They appear also in Catalonia, where Guillem Durfort oversaw comital finances at the end of the century as 'the very type of an urban entrepreneur and moneylender'.[19]

This expansion and multiplication of administrations allowed the hierarchies of rule to become more formal. Centres created machinery for communicating with and asserting authority over the localities, based on writing rather than speech (or, for that matter, force). Nevertheless, the shift to written records was neither abrupt, nor absolute. The speed of adoption of what was a form of new technology varied considerably, as the staggered inception of episcopal registers in the dioceses of England shows. Administration also retained a strong oral tradition – in communicating, ordering, explaining, sometimes translating – during the thirteenth century and beyond.

Yet, because of records, jurisdictional claims were formalised, and relationships defined, to tie units together more effectively. The accumulation of parchment – sending orders, confirming their receipt, recording

---

19 Thomas N. Bisson, *The Fiscal Accounts of Catalonia under the Early Count-Kings (1151–1213)*, 2 vols (Berkeley, Los Angeles, and London, 1984), 1, p. 148.

subsequent action, filing records – made it increasingly difficult to evade oversight (but still by no means impossible). Debts, inaction, could now be pursued; pressure could be exerted, precedents cited. In combination, such development opened up the possibility of welding a disparate collection of authorities into a single unit, of creating greater political cohesion. They could also be counter-productive: the reaction against King John was partly because his government was proving too efficient, too interventionist.

† † †

The disputed relationships between components of the political structures of western Europe repeatedly caused conflicts in the twelfth century, conflicts centred on practicalities as well as theories, and in which attempts to impose a theory challenged and threatened the preceding balances. Law was proclaimed and used, power was theorised; yet a 'rule of law' which operated in the context of a genuine politics was still missing. The growth of monarchism meant that, in theory, royal and imperial powers were extensive, almost unlimited. In practice the underdevelopment of administrations and the dependence on the willing self-subjection of at least the highest layers of politically active society meant that monarchical authority was severely limited by a lack of real control in the localities. For subjects this meant that the contacts with local rulers – whether landed magnates or urban authorities – were often more meaningful than contacts with the nominally supreme ruler. Nevertheless, the king (or emperor, or pope) had a notional power to intervene at the lower levels of the structure, was theoretically responsible for and to all below him, might yet act of his own volition if it seemed necessary. The struggle between centre and localities played out between papacy and bishops can be matched by struggles between kings and local rulers in each of the kingdoms, and would last throughout the middle ages. If the debates and transformations of the long twelfth century had been linked to attempts to construct an ideally balanced society, they were a sorry failure. There is, however, no sign of such a conscious concern. The main bequest to the future was the first steps in the construction of frameworks which would influence later political evolutions and struggles. That may not appear a particularly weighty outcome to the dramatic struggles of the period as a whole; yet insofar as the evolutions of the long twelfth century allowed the battle lines to be drawn, they also let the battle commence, to continue in succeeding centuries.

5

Intellectual transitions: philosophy and theology, humanism and individualism

O NE accompaniment of the educational changes of the long twelfth century was a massive transformation in western intellectual life. The acquisition of new resources – mainly the gradual rediscovery of the Aristotelian corpus, enhanced by translations of the works of Arab commentators and internal incremental growth – stimulated major advances in ways of thinking and, perhaps more importantly, ways of arguing. A growing need was felt to resolve doubts, to settle contradictions between authorities, and to reconcile thought systems which had originated under paganism with the requirements of Christian faith, a faith itself considerably refined in this period. Taken in conjunction with the contemporary educational changes, the outcome was a legacy which overshadows the rest of the middle ages: the rise of 'scholasticism' as an effective and finely honed argumentative method. Although the vituperations of Renaissance and Reformation polemicists have given scholasticism a bad name, it is ill deserved: the fifteenth- and sixteenth-century revulsion against scholasticism was in reality a reactionary movement which actually curtailed intellectual progress in some areas.

Significant developments occurred in philosophy, where a new emphasis on argument and reliance on reason imparted new vitality and rigour. Alongside, and on a different plane, theology acquired the character of an academic discipline, becoming increasingly speculative and doctrinal, and leaking out of the academic milieu into the wider world through a heightened concern for pastoral care which acquired greater momentum as time passed. A third strand of intellectual development – if it occurred – is more contentious. The long twelfth century has been linked with 'the discovery of the individual' and the appearance of something labelled 'humanism'; although both terminology and content are debated. Much of the philosophical and theological work occurred in the increasingly organised academic environment of the schools, especially the French schools, and particularly those of Paris. So intense is this French emphasis that it is hard to identify equivalent developments in England, Germany, or Italy; but there are signs that they occurred, leaving appropriate textual evidence. This Franco-centric emphasis raises further issues for appreciation of the whole cultural and intellectual movement, and about whether a 'renaissance' in the twelfth century can be a single all-encompassing movement or is best viewed as a series of concurrent but disconnected developments.[1] Each intellectual issue – the philosophical changes, the rise of academic theology, and the problem of humanism/individualism – could justify a chapter to itself. To bring them together here does not diminish their separate significance, but addresses them as components of a single broad strand of intellectual change whose overall significance was perhaps greater than the sum of its parts.

Philosophy

An immediate issue arises with regard to twelfth-century philosophy: the vexing question of definition and content. Philosophy is now an independent academic discipline, with its own sense of identity and language; but modern conceptions cannot be automatically transposed into the twelfth century. The term 'philosophy' was then applied in many different contexts, with very different implications.

A broad usage occurs in Hugh of St Victor's *Didascalicon*, written in the late 1120s, covering a wide range of knowledge arranged in several subsidiary 'arts'. The 'theoretical arts' comprised theology, physics, and mathematics (itself subdivided into the four arts of the *quadrivium*). The next main strand consisted of the 'practical arts' of ethics, economics, and politics. Then come the seven 'mechanical arts', ranging with a striking display of comprehensiveness from clothmaking and hunting to drama and medicine, with commerce, agriculture, and armaments thrown in. Last come the 'logical arts', those of words, initially separated into grammar and argument, with the latter being subdivided in further stages which include dialectic and rhetoric. This dauntingly compendious definition of philosophy offers a striking contrast to current precision, yet is justified by Hugh's concern to inculcate a love of learning in the broadest sense. Such breadth would not be maintained in reality, not even at St Victor itself.

1 See below, pp. 208, 210–11.

Other notions of 'philosophy' also circulated. Responding to the appeal of the schools, defenders of monasticism claimed that their life was the only true 'philosophy'. Other disciplines, like civil law, also claimed to have or be a 'philosophy'. The term's implications also varied: some linked it with disdain for wordly cares (especially money); monastic philosophy sought fulfilment with God; others limited the divinity's role, treating philosophy as a way of rationalising to which God was not absolutely necessary. That stance is dramatically and poignantly rejected in Peter Abelard's anguished declaration that he did not wish to be a philosopher if it cut him off from Christ. However, while twelfth-century writers might talk of (and portray) abstract philosophers who could do without God, they did not actually exist at the time. The writers who talked of such people had 'the disadvantage of never having met an individual who would call himself a philosopher as opposed to a Christian'. In the twelfth-century, as in other medieval centuries, 'we are ... dealing with Christian thinkers who have read a little ancient philosophy ... not [people] ... whose lives are guided by a philosophical system'.[2]

Two main types of philosophy coexisted in the twelfth century, something which makes discussion problematic. At times, indeed, the same writers appear as exponents of both types, dissection of their thought falling under different headings. Historians' imprecision often leaves it unclear which type of 'philosophy' is actually being discussed. Both, however, need attention.

The first approach treated philosophy as a specific science of thinking, the acquisition and refinement of a transferable skill with potential vocational application. It was probably in that practical sense that most thinkers (and their students) considered themselves 'philosophers': students in particular would be 'doing' philosophy (or, more precisely, its component disciplines) rather than 'being' philosophers. The second definition is more demanding, less precise, and contained within it the greater threat to the pre-existing intellectual culture. This saw philosophy not as a skill, but as an intellectual act, a way of thinking about, and thinking through, significant problems of existence. It became the science of analysing 'life, the universe, and everything', working out humanity's place in creation. Perhaps more significantly (and more threateningly), it sometimes sought to do that without insisting that God fit into the equation. Based on its pagan Greek origins, philosophy sought

2   G.R. Evans, *Philosophy and Theology in the Middle Ages* (London and New York, 1993), p. 7.

to answer the questions by assuming a creation, but not necessarily a Creator-God. By leaving God out (except by implication, and sometimes not even then), such interpretations offered new approaches to major issues, which might then produce equally major and far-reaching clashes, and stimulate further developments in reaction. While a 'skill-based' approach could evolve simply through greater sophistication and aware-ness of the insufficiency of accepted rules (and, therefore, to some extent through trial and error), cosmology had to respond to, and seek to reconcile itself with, the implications of the developing influx of new material which challenged preconceptions and existing solutions.

Here a second major point about the evolution of twelfth-century philosophy becomes pertinent: the low base from which the growth occurred. Few key texts were available in 1100: mainly the so-called 'old logic' of Aristotle (384–322 BC), based on his *Categories* and *On Inter-pretation*; the *Isagoge* of Porphyry (d. *c.* AD 304); and translations and commentaries on Aristotle by Boethius (d. 524/5), whose own *Consolation of Philosophy* also dealt with significant problems about the nature of being and of good and evil. Although the Aristotelian material was important, a significant strand of thought derived from Plato (428–347 BC), even though the only work of his widely known in the west was the *Timaeus*, which dealt with the process of the world's creation. At a very simplistic level, Platonism (or, rather, the Neoplatonism which had evolved in the late antique period), offered possibilities for abstract and idealised thought within a structure which might be considered 'holistic', and open to a spiritual – even Christian – interpretation. Aristotle's thought, by contrast, was more firmly based on practical experience, more naturalistic, and left less room for the supernatural. Despite the quantitative dominance of the direct Aristotelian heritage, Aristotle's impact in 1100 was limited by being seen through the strongly Neo-platonist outlook inherited from the Church Fathers, notably Augustine. He was appreciated mainly as a linguistic philosopher, a logician; the avowedly secular Aristotle, whose arguments posed massive problems for later Christian thinkers, was yet to be discovered. (That said, how-ever, recent research has demonstrated that there was considerable indirect access to Aristotelian ideas before direct translations became available. This '"underground tradition" of Aristotelian thought'[3] meant

---

3 C.J. Nederman, 'Aristotelian ethics and John of Salisbury's letters', *Viator*, 18 (1987), p. 173; reprinted, same pagination, in his *Medieval Aristotelianism and its Limits* (Aldershot, 1997). The volume contains several other articles examining this underground Aristotle.

that when direct contact did occur, the intellectual effects were perhaps not as traumatic as is sometimes alleged.)

Awareness of the differences between Plato and Aristotle made their reconciliation a major aspiration, precisely because their status as 'authorities' meant that they were both 'right' in their different ways. In the early twelfth century, Bernard of Chartres struggled to achieve such a reconciliation, to no avail. Even had he done so, the whole kaleidoscope would have shifted when further Aristotelian material became available, making the achievement redundant. Nevertheless, the goal of reconciliation remained, but it was not until the appreciation of the results of the monumental labours of Thomas Aquinas (c. 1226–74) that the reconciliation would be considered to have been attained. (Even that proved to be wishful thinking: the reconciliation almost immediately began to fall apart, as rival camps exploited Aquinas for their own interpretations.) Other classical traditions were influential alongside Plato and Aristotle, like the Stoic tradition mediated primarily in analyses of the Virgilian myths.

Over the long twelfth century, a flow of translated texts made more Aristotelian works available in Latin, the corpus being virtually completed by c. 1260. The Platonic corpus was also expanded, but here progress was rather slower, and less directly influential.

The influx of the new Aristotelian logic had generally positive and beneficial effects. The texts helped to refine linguistic logic, exploring and defining meanings which terms might have in different contexts, explaining the different meanings which they might be assumed to convey, and aiding the clarification of philosophical ideas. Only later did the threat of the more scientific Aristotelianism become apparent, with the introduction of translations of the *libri naturales*. These were more subversive in the long run, especially when their ideas were introduced into theological debate. The backlash against this more scientific Aristotelianism is evident in the Parisian ban on reading the *libri naturales* in 1215. However, that move may have been premature: among Parisian scholars at that date the *libri naturales* 'were admired more than read, frequently referred to, sometimes quoted textually but rarely understood', perhaps playing second fiddle to some of the Arab commentators.[4] Even making allowance for the influence of its earlier underground current, it was only after 1240 that Aristotelianism really took off, and even then with the interpretation much influenced by Arab ideas. In 1270 (at Oxford) and

4 John Marenbon, *Later Medieval Philosophy (1150–1350): an Introduction* (London and New York, 1987), p. 55.

1277 (at Oxford and Paris) the response was forthright: extensive condemnations of assorted Aristotelian ideas considered incompatible with accepted theology. Needless to say, the bans could not last.

Despite the acquisitions, the scope for 'philosophical' enquiry was limited by purely physical considerations. Basic matters like the distribution of texts were important: this is where hindsight, and the search for intellectual genealogies, creates and obscures problems. The problems of texts and manuscripts, and of the purity of the available tradition, apply as much to the legacy of the philosophers in the early twelfth century as to the newly acquired works of later decades. If manuscripts were hidden in obscure places, they could not be used. Such problems continued throughout the period: the distribution of new texts was a vital matter. The works produced by the twelfth-century thinkers were themselves affected: writing preserved outdated ideas; if re-encountered they might again stimulate further thought. On the other hand, the mechanics of production meant that even if new ideas were available as texts, their wide dissemination could not be guaranteed.

Critical in the development of philosophy was the educational focus on the three arts of the *trivium*, the sciences of language: grammar, logic (or dialectic), and rhetoric. As the basic requirements for more sophisticated thought, they also provided 'transferable' and (particularly in the case of rhetoric) 'vocational' skills.[5] For most thinkers the basic concern was with the relationships between words, and language and the science of language were central to many contemporary arguments. Words and their meanings – and implications – were basic to any attempt to comprehend the world. The linguistic dissection which resulted sometimes went to extremes which even contemporaries considered ludicrous: John of Salisbury castigated the trivial pursuits of those who debated whether purchase of a cape presupposed purchase of the attached hood, or whether a pig being led to market was precisely 'led' by the string, or by the person holding the string.

An understanding of grammar was a fundamental requirement for all linguistic knowledge, particularly important in an inflected language like Latin, in which word-forms were affected by cases, declensions, and conjugations. 'Grammar' in the twelfth century specifically means *Latin* grammar. Although vernacular languages existed, and by 1200 had their own literatures, there is no sign of concern, or even awareness, that they might be subjected to grammatical analysis. However, Latin, the

5   See also above, pp. 29–30.

universal authoritative language, the common tongue of the educated classes across western Europe, was so analysed. That Latin was always a second language (with its degree of divergence from the first variable, depending on whether that was basically Romance or Germanic) may have stimulated a greater concern with grammar: it was necessary to know and understand the connections between words in a sentence before they could be understood and used in argument.

Grammar was taught in 'the schools', but was very much the first step in knowledge, almost an access course, enabling pupils to understand and use the language through which they would receive their subsequent education, and introducing them to the sophistication of an inherited textual culture. Here again, the necessity and utility of Latin is important: even if an artifical language (being no longer natively spoken, and possibly an erudite reconstruction with little real connection with Latin as originally spoken), it provided a common tongue to transcend the many vernacular languages represented in the schools. (Many of these would now be considered 'dialects', but that understates their mutual incomprehensibility.)

For John of Salisbury, citing Isidore of Seville from the seventh century, grammar was 'the science of speaking and writing correctly – the starting point of all liberal studies'. Furthermore, it was 'the cradle of all philosophy, and in a manner of speaking, the first nurse of the whole study of letters. It ... guides our every forward step in philosophy.'[6] Moreover, the methods adopted to make grammar comprehensible were themselves transferable to other sciences. Glossing, for instance, was used to explicate the works of the classical authors, by providing synonyms and explanations for difficult words, explaining figures of speech, and exculpating 'ungrammatical' poetic licence. The gloss as an explanatory tool was easily transferred to theology for discussions of the Bible, to Roman or canon law, or elsewhere.

Having sufficiently mastered grammar, the student could progress to the more advanced linguistic sciences of logic (or dialectic) and rhetoric. The latter needs no consideration here, being used mainly for public speaking, letter-writing, and occasions where words had to be manipulated to play on the emotions.[7] Logic/dialectic had a more rational function, in the science of asking and solving questions. As such,

---

6 *The Metalogicon of John of Salisbury: a Twelfth-Century Defense of the Verbal and Logical Arts of the Trivium*, trans. Daniel D. MacGarry (Gloucester, MA, 1971), p. 37.
7 See p. 30.

it developed understanding and the ability to argue by analysing the relationship between statements. From around 1140, newly acquired Aristotelian texts – the 'new logic' of the *Prior Analytics, Topics, De sophisticis elenchis,* and *Posterior Analytics* – stimulated new analyses. Hence the centrality of the syllogism to twelfth-century modes of argument, and the formulation of rules to test validity and prove falsehood. The syllogism was the basic analytical tool, establishing and formulating argumentational relationships in an almost algebraic manner.

In its simplest form, a syllogism tests the argumentative veracity of a statement (which is not the same as its actual truth). If A equals B, and B equals C, then A equals C. However, if A equals B, but B does not equal C, then A does not equal C. Complications set in when words are used rather than signs, and when they provide identifications and definitions. Thus, if (A) is 'Socrates is a man', and (B) is 'X is Socrates', it follows (C) that 'X is a man'. However, if (A) 'Socrates is a man', and (B) 'X is a man', then (C) 'X is Socrates' may be true, but does not necessarily follow. The syllogistic mode of argument can also create strings of statements which are seemingly valid, but plainly wrong: 'What you have not lost you retain'; 'You have not lost horns'; 'Therefore you have horns'. In their various valid, invalid, and infuriating forms, the understanding of syllogisms was a major contribution to the evolution of logic and the rules of argument.

Those rules of argument became increasingly complex. Many, after several centuries, now seem almost banal: it is perhaps a testimony to the effectiveness and importance of the foundations laid down in the twelfth century that stages in argumentative processes which then had to be carefully thought through and elucidated are now taken for granted, with stages in the process being skipped as not needing individual proof. Moreover, textbooks are not written for the 'great minds', but for those being taught: many of the logical rule books had a status little higher than that of the grammar texts, operating on a level very different from the arguments of someone like Abelard. The somewhat tedious listing in the *Abbreviatio Montana,* produced at Mont Ste Geneviève, shows this well, laboriously guiding from basic statement to basic statement, but providing an effective and accessible guide to logic and the science of argument.

It was on these rules that twelfth-century thinkers like Abelard raised their logical and argumentative edifices, with ramifications way beyond the basics of logic. (It was, perhaps, on the basis of teaching such fundamentals that some of them also earned their livings.) The fluidity of the times and the constant flow of novelties meant that everything was always in flux: all resolutions became provisional, because the questions were constantly changing, and the resources available from which to construct a solution changed as well. This constant and continuing challenge to thought was important: it forced development, made old ideas constantly outdated. Abelard, although the most dynamic thinker of his time, was rapidly overtaken and outmoded. The progress of twelfth-century thought in some ways matches the current succession of computer generations. Individuals had immediate impact, but it was often transient, as new ideas came along to supplant them. Once supplanted, they were rarely recalled.

Rules became particularly important as they began to influence ideas, mingling with the intellectual inheritance of the past to affect current interpretations of the world and modes of human perception. This was most explicit in the fiery debates over 'universals', the manner of labelling and comprehending labels through conceptualisation. When people talk of a 'table' (or 'man', or 'dog', or any other general term), whence does the generic recognition of the concept – the 'universal' – derive? Does it come from an inherent and distinct 'tableness', a generalisation which has some kind of independent existence? Or is it the result simply of having seen numerous tables, and therefore knowing what one looks like, even if any specific table does not in all respects match the imagined generalisation? The issue's crux was the intellectual distinction between 'substance' and 'accidents'. 'Substance' contained the distinctive essence of an object in a universal sense: the ideal 'humanness' of humanity, the 'tableness' of a table. 'Accidents' were the distinguishing characteristics of the individual, or which tangibly differentiated it generically from other things: the features which made Richard the Lionheart of England visibly and characteristically not Philip Augustus of France; the ability to bark which means a dog is not a cat.

Put so baldly, the question of universals seems to be one of those silly debates which give philosophy a bad name. Yet the issue generated a major fault line in twelfth-century thought, and had important side-effects in theology, which will be considered elsewhere.[8] On one side were those originally known as 'vocalists', and later as 'nominalists', for whom the individual object was the only reality; the universal had no independent objective existence and was only a word or a name. Opposing them were the 'realists', for whom the universal had real existence, although precisely how was not universally agreed. Realism

8 Below, p. 127.

was at first the more common view, with vocalism only beginning to find
a voice in the late eleventh century. The first real exponent of the stance
to become nominalism was none other than Peter Abelard, whose
followers at the schools were to be identified as *Nominales* in the later
twelfth century. Between the two extremes, before opinion polarised, lay
a range of opinions tending one way or the other. The clashes on the
issue could be intense. Peter Abelard's tale of his battles with William of
Champeaux on this matter shows the heat which could be generated.
The split between nominalists and realists would become a radical
cleavage in the western medieval philosophical tradition, re-emerging
repeatedly in theological debates.

As concern with the sciences of words became the primary feature of
twelfth-century philosophy, it sidelined the second strand of the
discipline, the concern for the natural and cosmological. This had been
particularly important up to around 1150, being associated with Bernard
Silvestris, William of Conches, and others who were once grouped with
the 'School of Chartres'. Scattered comments made by several writers of
the time have been seized upon to suggest that the period almost
developed a truly scientific approach, but these early signs were soon
snuffed out. There clearly was an appreciation of the potential for
investigating nature and comprehending its internal rationality, and an
awareness of the utility of the *quadrivium* as 'four types of reasons which
lead men to an understanding of the Creator' (to quote Thierry of
Chartres).[9]

However, the selective abstraction of small quotations does not
convey the whole picture. The cosmological approach revealed in the
works of Bernard Silvestris and William of Conches meshes in with other
aspects of their writings, based in other traditions. While William's
comments on the *Timaeus* suggest the scientific approach, he also interpreted Virgil in a naturalistic allegorical manner, as one of the group of
early twelfth-century 'mythographers', interpreters of the classical
myths, who very much followed and developed an older tradition. They
read the tales of the Roman gods as allegories (or, to use their word,
integumenta, coverings) for natural processes which explain the cosmos.
That tradition was both backward-looking, and a continuity, of which
they are the last real representatives. Later unveilings of the deeper

---

9 Nikolaus M. Häring, S.A.C., *Commentaries on Boethius by Thierry of Chartres and his School*, Pontifical Institute of Mediaeval Studies: Studies and texts, 20 (Toronto, 1971), p. 568.

meaning of the classical myths would lack their profundity, as theology and a more scientific and naturalistic approach to nature marginalised the tradition. The idea that nature's truths lay concealed in classical texts, awaiting discovery, could also apply to the Bible, especially the creation story in Genesis. The process of unveiling sometimes generated ideas which seem very modern, but perhaps for the wrong reasons. In his *Hexameron*, Thierry of Chartres interpreted the Genesis story in a way which seems to posit something like evolution. God initiated the creation process, but it continued independently, without specific divine action or intervention, along a trajectory established by the qualities imbued in the individual elements at that initial moment of creation. In some ways, Thierry postulates God as the Big Bang. Moreover, the Six Days were treated not as periods of twenty-four hours, but as Ages, in a way which again appears almost evolutionist. William of Conches likewise exploited ancient interpretations of creation to develop a kind of atomic theory, analysing the world in its smallest particles. However, neither Thierry nor William was a scientist as that term would now be understood: they were trying to comprehend and rationalise a received intellectual tradition, not reconstruct the creative process itself.

The cosmologists had a real concern to understand humanity's place in creation, motivated by a Platonic sense of a cosmic balance which had been disordered and needed to be restored. This restoration could amount to a regeneration and almost a new creation. The stance is especially noticeable in the *Cosmographia* of Bernard Silvestris; it later appears in a more moralistic and spiritual sense in the *De planctu naturae* and *Anticlaudianus* of Alan of Lille, the latter particularly concerned with the creation and ensoulment of a 'new man'. These writers often centre their attention on an abstract 'Nature', producing a world picture in which God – or at least the Christian God – had only a minor, if any, role. But these writers were not atheists, nor did they deny a role to God; rather, God has little active role, responsibility for change being assigned either to Nature or a generalised humanity. This was especially the case with the generation ending with Bernard Silvestris: by 1200 God was allowed back in, as a 'supernatural' entity without whom the creation – especially the giving of a soul to man – is incomplete. That, at least, is the divine function in the *Anticlaudianus*. Also notable is the emphasis on the human role in this world: humans are largely responsible for their own salvation, must accept the moral responsibilities of distinguishing between good and evil, and defeat the latter. To some extent (but without the twentieth-century overtones) humans were seen as environmentalists: as overseers of creation, they would have to account for their stewardship to the divinity. This human-centredness is a key feature of many writers, perhaps making them 'humanists' in one definition of the term.[10] It is the absence of God and the stress on humanity which makes these people philosophers in one twelfth-century usage of the word: working without God to understand the world solely on its own terms. However, while the twelfth-century thinkers sought to penetrate Nature's secrets, the evidence for an explicitly empiricist attitude is scanty: Plato, their guiding light, had distrusted experience and experiment, and they followed suit. While practical experience was sometimes cited (but the citations may have actually come from other texts), the general approach can be summarised by quoting from Abelard's *Glossulae super Porphyrium*: 'The man of understanding is he who has the ability to grasp and ponder the hidden causes of things. By hidden causes we mean those from which things originate, and these are to be investigated more by reason than by sensory experiences.'[11]

Plato's intellectual influence on the 'naturalist' writers is clearly shown in their abstraction of Nature, and the references to the 'world-soul', or *Nous*, which derive explicitly from Platonic sources. Sometimes their writing is fairly florid, and in verse. This gives it affinities with the eleventh-century texts, derived from the highly developed rhetorical writing of the cathedral schools. Replete with classical allusions and demonstrations of knowledge almost for its own sake, this can become tedious. Yet it is important, in showing that people were really addressing the links between humans and creation, were 'philosophising'.

Such texts also show a remarkable self-confidence, which seems to evaporate in mid-century. That disappearance may help to validate claims that early twelfth-century authors were trying to maintain a decaying tradition; it seems more likely that they were simply supplanted by new developments. The self-confidence is clear in the encyclopedic concerns of some of the writers. These were people who knew that humanity had the capacity to triumph, to know everything, perhaps to become God-like. They thought, moreover, that they already possessed all the requisite knowledge, that there was little more to learn. Everything could be, and was, digested. This feeling stimulated the production of massive works like Thierry of Chartres's *Heptateuchon*, which is the largest of the twelfth-century encyclopedias, intending to provide full

10 Below, pp. 139–41.
11 B. Geyer, ed., *Peter Abaelards philosophische Schriften*, 4 vols, Beiträge zur Geschichte der Philosophie und Theologie des Mittelalters, 21 (Münster-in-Westfalen, 1919–33), 4, p. 506; translation from A.C. Crombie, *Robert Grosseteste and the Origins of Experimental Science, 1100–1700* (Oxford, 1953), p. 30.

coverage of all seven liberal arts in a single compilation. The ambition of such compilations is striking: Thierry's work was so massive (some 1,400 folios) that it would have been almost literally impossible to reproduce; so ambitious that it was never actually completed.

Yet the desired total picture would not be constructed. Fate cheated these ambitious and confident writers. Just when they thought everything could be summarised, new waves of information and ideas destabilised their intellectual world. The encyclopedias became outdated, to survive only in the occasional manuscript. While the encyclopedic tradition continued elsewhere – in Gratian's *Decretum*, Peter Lombard on theology, and (in the thirteenth century) Vincent of Beauvais on almost everything – there was now just too much knowledge for one text, or one mind, to contain it all. The future lay in specialisation and fragmentation, not amalgamation and comprehensiveness. The self-confidence also disappeared: as the futility of seeking to know everything became obvious, as outbreaks of argument and discord increased, as awareness of change grew, so writers seem to lose the robustness of the early 1100s. Perhaps this owed something to the development and formalisation of 'academic' conventions; perhaps it was one result of awareness of the built-in obsolescence of most scholarship. By 1200, the aspiration to be all-encompassing was past its peak.

The speculative linguistic analysis, the philosophy, was central to the intellectual advances of the long twelfth century. It provided the momentum for major developments, bringing to the fore individuals like Abelard, and stimulating great debates. The development of the argumentative techniques and the appreciation of the complexity of language were in themselves significant developments; but if they had remained mere verbiage their importance would have been considerably diminished. The application of the linguistic rules and syllogistic reasoning in other fields, most particularly theology, meant that the philosophical debates and analyses did not occur in a vacuum: they contributed to understanding of the real world in a very real way.

Theology

Arguably the most important area to which the advanced skills and techniques developed by the changes in philosophy and philosophical methods could be applied was the new science of theology. Theology's emergence as an academic discipline may count as the key transition of the whole period. It seems to be the strand which unifies the disparate evolutions into a whole, feeding on and evolving in the context of intellectual and institutional changes, and making its own contribution to them.[12] By 1250 theology was regarded as the highest of the higher faculties in the emergent universities. It was also the rarest of faculties: until the mid-fourteenth century there were only three, at Oxford, Cambridge, and Paris. Theological education was also offered in the *studia* of the new mendicant orders, and the parish clergy were meant to receive cathedral-based theological instruction after 1215, but that was nothing like as effective or widespread as intended.

The significance of theology's rise in the twelfth century has long been recognised, but is not always given its due prominence. Until recently a stress on philosophy and the schools, and on the more immediately arresting translations and legal changes, perhaps allied to a reluctance to take theology seriously, have conspired to push it into the background. Possibly, too, theology has been overshadowed by the scale of the institutional changes within the Church during the period: the growth of papal monarchy, birth of new religious orders, and eruption of heresy, which together constitute 'the medieval Reformation', and which individually appear more amenable to historical analysis and understanding than discussions of the nature of God.

Like 'philosophy', 'theology' as a coherent identifiable discipline did not exist in 1100, although it had gained an identity by the thirteenth century, even if the word was rarely used of it. There were theolog*ii* – 'theologians' – in the twelfth century, but perhaps in a generic sense of 'people who talk about god(s)' rather than as analysts of the specifically Judaeo-Christian God. Peter Abelard was the first to use the word 'theology' in the title of a work; moreover, in defiantly calling a revised version of the work condemned at the Council of Soissons in 1121 *Theologia christiana*, advocating a specifically Christian theology, the adjective is as important as the noun.

By 1250 theology had come of age as a discipline. In the scale of production, and the range and intensity of analysis, the long twelfth century bears valid comparison with the age of the Fathers, and with the Reformation, laying down lines of development for the rest of the middle ages. Setting firm chronological boundaries for discussion here is particularly problematic. A valid starting point is the debate over the ideas of Berengar of Tours on what happened at the moment of consecration in the mass, begun in the late 1050s.[13] The basic controversy went back centuries, but the Berengarian debate is generally taken to

12 See below, pp. 208, 210.
13 Above, pp. 20–1.

initiate the discussions which brought 'transubstantiation' into the theological vocabulary, to be used at the Fourth Lateran Council of 1215 to describe what happened to the bread and wine at consecration. (However, although the word existed, its meaning remained imprecise: transubstantiation as now understood – with the substances of the bread and wine being replaced by the substances of the Body and Blood of Christ at the moment of consecration – may only have become the dominant interpretation in the late thirteenth century, if then.) A closing point is less easily established. An obvious choice is the supposed attainment of the long-desired reconciliation of Plato and Aristotle in the monumental *Summa theologica* of Thomas Aquinas, left unfinished at his death in 1274. This takes the concluding point beyond even the longest of long twelfth centuries; but a credible alternative is elusive. An alternative is the Fourth Lateran Council itself, whose credal statement sought to settle recent theological controversies and terminate debates on them; but that perhaps cuts things too short.

However confined chronologically, the period saw fundamental changes in approaches to the science of God. Ideas expanded in response to the introduction of new material and new techniques of analysis. There was a significant shift of emphasis: away from the specific study of the *sacra pagina*, the holy page, characteristic of the meditative monastic biblical tradition, to a concern with examining the nature of God and other features of the evolving faith, towards the analysis of what might be called unwritten verities. Of course, meditation and biblical exegesis were not abandoned, but the approach changed. Comprehension of the Bible still structured the outline of study, with a literal/historical analysis providing a skeleton for Peter Lombard's *Sentences*; but it was surrounded – perhaps overshadowed – by a concern for greater doctrinal analysis and understanding. The Bible's continued centrality is attested by the importance of its *glossa ordinaria* (although that declines in the early thirteenth century), and by the appearance at Paris in the early 1200s of a new standardised Bible, arranged into a set order of books with chapters, which was seemingly created primarily as a school text.

The analysis of the Bible was enhanced by using a fourfold method of interpretation, which allowed the text to be read on several different levels: literal/historical, moral/tropological, allegorical, and mystical/anagogical. The first (literal or historical) provided a basic grammatical interpretation and took the narrative at face value as a factual statement. The tropological sense provided moral edification, reading the narrative as a guide to behaviour and the divine response. The allegorical sense reinterpreted the narrative to reveal parallels with the life of Christ and the work of the Church (particularly important when reading the Old Testament to prefigure the New). Finally the anagogical sense gave access to the text's mystical or spiritual meaning, to aid understanding of God. The balance of interpretation necessarily varied depending on which bit of the Bible was being analysed, but the literal/historical reading was usually considered preliminary to all the others. (This application of different levels of interpretation was not confined to the Bible: it was also applied to classical texts, allowing them to be read allegorically and morally.)

Expanding beyond its biblical core, 'theology' now directly addressed a whole range of issues covering morality and ethics; the status of humankind and its reason for existence, future potential, and the search for salvation; God and His relationship with the creation, especially humanity; and doctrine. This expansion of content raises questions about the precise border between theology and philosophy, and also brings in the spectre of 'humanism'. The clearest sign of the shift is Abelard's self-proclamation as a theologian, in reaction (he said) against the dull exegetical teaching of Anselm of Laon. Although lacking specialised theological training, Abelard thought his skill at dialectical linguistic analysis sufficient qualification to allow him to interpret the Bible, which he proceeded to do, to the horror and consternation of Laon's masters of the sacred page. Among theologians Abelard – 'one of those academics constitutionally incapable of finishing anything he started'[14] – left a complex legacy, often causing problems rather than solving them precisely because of his application of dialectic methods to matters theological: a good deal of writing after 1130 was produced to counter his ideas.

The new academic theologians – and, through them, the western Church – addressed the technicalities of their proclaimed beliefs. The faith itself also changed, to meet new situations and challenges: changing social structures which demanded different approaches to pastoral issues; contacts with Jews and Muslims which produced debate and clarification of Christianity; the emergence of heresies which demanded definitions of orthodoxy in response. Although many of the issues were old, the twelfth-century theologians sought new precision in their understanding of the sacraments, of sin, of the Incarnation, and of the balance between predestination and free will. They sought to understand the Trinity, worried over Christology, and tried to make sense of angels (but without cramming them onto pinheads). In a circular process, greater precision

14   Marcia L. Colish, *Peter Lombard*, Brill's studies in intellectual history, 41, 2 vols (Leiden, New York, and Köln, 1994), 1, p. 48.

generated greater conflict, between groups and between individuals, as academic solutions and propositions stimulated debate and discord. This was perhaps particularly evident in the emerging tensions between monastic and scholastic traditions, between intellectualism and an approach which was almost anti-intellectual, tensions which proved highly important in the development of the schools.[15]

In a context where new knowledge had to be incorporated into or change pre-existing ideas, and new social issues had to be confronted, using new intellectual skills to specify and resolve the questions, the basic issue boiled down to one of faith versus reason, the polarisation between an understanding inspired by God or achieved by human intellectual effort. In a sense, this debate still continues, between 'religion' and 'science', but the twelfth century lacked the secularism of the present confrontations. A world which undeniably existed, and so must have come into existence, self-evidently had been created, and must have a creator. For an intellectual to deny God's existence in the twelfth century was the height of irrationality; even more irrational than choosing the wrong God. The encroachments of Aristotelianism would challenge aspects of this view, but many of those debates were for the thirteenth century rather than the twelfth. Twelfth-century Christianity needed no defenders against atheism; but there was a growing and insistent need to uphold the definitions of this increasingly precise Catholic orthodoxy against Jews, Muslims, and heretics, and even against academic rivals. Yet no matter how precise and rational the analyses, a residue would always be incapable of clarification and 'rational' explanation. At some point, as Alan of Lille showed in his *Anticlaudianus*, reason became insufficient. Theology as a science, as a mode of interpretation, had its limits. Ultimately, ineffability was unavoidable, the search for comprehension had to be abandoned, and faith took over as guide: incomprehensibility was part of the definition. In *c.* 1148 the anonymous author of the *Sententiae divinitatis* could thus deal with the issue of God's divinity 'by an act of reason but not by the form of speaking, by reason of faith, not by reason of human philosophy'.[16] Faith had to lead argument, because argument alone could not fill all the gaps.

Theology's scientific development was a change of form as well as matter. As already noted,[17] the earlier monastic system had aimed

15 Above, pp. 19, 37–8.
16 Colish, *Peter Lombard*, 1, p. 141.
17 Above, p. 13.

essentially at replication: the main issues had already been settled by the Fathers, whose investigations and ruminations had by the end of the sixth century established the norms and defeated heresy. Monastic theology aimed not to ignite mental fireworks, but to resolve doubts as they arose, and to ensure continuity: the underlying aim was traditional – really traditional – by handing on the received wisdom to succeeding generations. Doubts and disputes did arise, but the monastic context and tradition limited their occurrence. There may have been more doubt than the sources reveal; but doubts could be resolved by the self-abnegating submission to authority demanded by monastic obedience. There are few signs of such intra-monastic uncertainty, at least until the writings of Anselm. Some of his works were written to resolve his own uncertainties; others dealt with questions posed by pupils; yet the doubts did not produce major turmoil, nothing like heresy. Indeed, insofar as there was awareness of heresy, it was largely retrospective: the Fathers and the Councils had already identified the key areas where heresy was possible, and had already decreed the orthodox reaction. There was accordingly little appreciation that heresy might actually be new. A common assumption in the twelfth century, and later, was that any outbreak had merely revived an old error, that the genealogy of all heresies could be traced back to ideas already condemned.

Just as Anselm hints at uncertainties, even cracks, in traditional monastic thought, he also gives the best example of that system in operation. Few of his works are truly argumentative, in the manner of scholastic theology. Although operating with words, and with logic, his stance was in essence illuminist: by meditating, and opening himself to inspiration, he would allow the self-revealing God to resolve his doubts and provide enlightenment. The technique is best exemplified in his *Monologion* and *Proslogion* (completed respectively in 1076 and 1078), the latter of which especially derived from a lengthy period of reflection and mental wrestling while seeking to encapsulate divinity, and suddenly ended by a revelation which he considered divinely provided. In this tradition, logical deduction had a place, but was fundamentally unnecessary: it was God who revealed, who gave the desired answers by intuition. Questioning and detailed analysis in search of answers was almost inappropriate: the search began with acceptance of orthodox belief, in recognising that the act of questioning was itself faulty, so that orthodoxy and an understanding of why something so inappropriate as questioning could occur would together provide the foundation on which to resolve the uncertainty. As Anselm himself put it, 'I do not seek to understand so that I may believe, but I believe so that I may understand; and what is more, I believe that unless I do believe I shall not understand'.[18] Faith precedes reason, and provides the parameters within which reason can operate.

This monastic tradition was already under threat when Anselm wrote. Indeed, that he wrote almost acknowledges the threat. While he can be treated as the culmination of the tradition, he was in some respects outside it. His own early life and late conversion to monasticism meant that he was not part of the inherited pattern of vocations and generational transmission of monastic culture. His education, first in the schools of northern Italy, and later at Bec, set him in a different intellectual category from most monks, one more used to analysis and disputation. That he wrote when his career had also taken him outside the monastic milieu, into the power politics of the Anglo-Norman realm, into the Investiture Contest, and into the academic debates provoked by Roscelin, was also non-traditional. Moreover, although Anselm's career represents the culmination of a tradition, it also marks its supersession, as conflicts became more overt, and the search for answers required not tradition and a return to authority, but investigation, and the settling of issues not so far considered satisfactorily resolved. Anselm himself offered answers to such questions, with his *Cur deus homo* (*Why God Became a Man*, written 1095–8) explaining the necessity for the Incarnation as part of the process of human redemption, in a way which was influential for centuries. His proof of God's existence, the Ontological Proof, based ultimately on the argument that the logical need for there to be a God means that God must exist, still taxes philosophers.

The essential stability of the monastic theological tradition was challenged by two critical forces, derived from the changes in the intellectual and institutional structures which occurred after 1050. First, there was the application of philosophical method, and greater insistence on application of the rules of language. Whereas ambiguity was a useful tool for circumventing uncertainties, allowing sleight of mind to elide inconsistencies and internal contradictions, an insistence on precision, on the application of formal rules, tied ideas down more firmly, making uncertainties into issues. The second evolution was the rise of the non-monastic schools, where theology could evolve unconstrained by tradition, against a background of dispute and competition. This created

18 In his *Proslogion*, ch. 1: *The Prayers and Meditations of Saint Anselm*, trans. Benedicta Ward (Harmondsworth, 1973), p. 244. See also p. 251: 'O righteous and compassionate God, whose light I seek, help me to understand what I am saying!'

a kind of free market approach, where daring theological speculations were among the attractions offered by masters in their search for pupils, and where rivalry and the need for pupils pushed thinkers to the intellectual extremes. That theology would be of little real utility for many of the pupils was unimportant: as a science it became embroiled in the world of the schools, forcing it forward. Old theology, old masters, had a built-in obsolescence. It is little surprise that, in Paris, theology as a discipline acquired stability and consistency precisely when the masters were transforming themselves from competitive individuals into a monopolistic self-perpetuating guild.

The clash of cultures reflected in the emergence of academic theology is often exemplified by appealing to the conflict between St Bernard and Abelard, part of which Abelard records in his *Historia calamitatum*. More intriguing is the career of Rupert of Deutz (d. 1129), a Benedictine who had begun his career as an oblate, and known no life other than that of a monk. He should stand for the old tradition, but breaks all the stereotypes. His early location at Liège brought contact (probably indirect) with the city's schools and their arguments; he was not averse to going out on a theological limb (and consequently faced heresy accusations); he was prepared to challenge and amend the received exegetical tradition, even to upbraid Augustine. Biblical commentator and theological analyst, he became embroiled in numerous controversies, at one point leaving his monastery with the intention of engaging in formal debate with Anselm of Laon and William of Champeaux. Yet, although he was an astonishingly prolific writer, he wrote in relative isolation: few of his works entered the new mainstream. That needed closer engagement with academics, involvement with the schools.

As the context for theological investigations changed, new and real questions arose about the science itself. As a science based on words, how should it be expressed? If theology was Queen of Sciences, who should be its courtiers? As old verities were challenged, how was theology to respond to the new questions?

The attempt to deal with theological issues in words raised the basic issue of the feasibility of the task. Here problems were both practical and theoretical. The precise linguistic analysis of mystery is necessarily difficult, because language confines human thought. That problem may be compounded when debate is conducted in a second language: as clerical Latin was necessarily a second language, to some extent constantly translated from the words and thought patterns of the first, the question of whether opponents were actually talking about the same thing might be a real one. More basic was the issue of applying human language to God: could a divinity defined as illimitable and indefinable really be confined and described in human language? Could human language (which meant Latin: vernacular theological languages were not even considered) undertake that task? This was debated: Hugh of St Victor commented on the issue, and Alan of Lille pointed out the paradoxes and the feebleness of human language and intellect for the purpose. Yet, ultimately, language was the only means available: if knowledge of God was to be communicated, then language had to be used, even if incoherently. Hence Alan's use of paradox and contradiction in an attempt to pin down God:

> language, since it fails to reach the essence of God, grows senseless when it tries to express things divine ... He is the just without justice, living without life, beginning without beginning, end without end, measureless without measure, strong without strength, powerful without force, directing all things without movement, filling all places while free of all places, lasting without time, abiding without abode, in possession of all things at once without holding them, speaking without voice, in repose without resting, shining without renewal of brightness, aglow without light.[19]

Language became particularly contentious when tackling doctrinal complexities. It was therefore necessary to ensure that meanings were actually shared, that theological discussion was confined to a single language (Latin), that the rules for the use of language were agreed. Unfortunately, in the early stages, there was no commonly accepted terminology, and none appeared until Peter Lombard produced his *Sentences* in the 1150s. Many early attempts to construct a systematic theology fell at this hurdle by failing to define terms adequately, or to use them clearly and consistently; while the lack of agreed meanings for the technical terms gave many opportunities for misunderstanding and misrepresentation and, admittedly, for vigorous debate. Even after Peter Lombard had produced the definitions, theological jargon was an acquired skill, creating the possibility of miscomprehension even among the Latinate when the terminology leached beyond the schools. Hence the doubts about the Lombard's conceptual Trinitarian doctrine raised by Joachim of Fiore, when (applying more traditional allegorical inter-

---

19 Alan of Lille, *Anticlaudianus, or the Good and Perfect Man*, trans. James J. Sheridan (Toronto, 1973), pp. 141–2.

pretations) he misconstrued him as arguing for a fourfold God. This charge was laid to rest only by a dogmatic statement of the Fourth Lateran Council of 1215, which accepted the Lombard's definitions.

The need to comprehend the jargon, the evolution of a specific technical theological language (including terms like 'transubstantiation'), clearly made the subject itself more esoteric. At the same time, there was growing interest in the topics which theology claimed as its preserve: Christian spirituality was unavoidable in western Europe; people seeking salvation had to be instructed, had to receive the message and inter-pretations of the theologians (even if in a very watered-down fashion) to ensure that they were on the right path. Access to theology therefore became an insistent issue, especially when the formerly remote possi-bility of heretical contamination became by 1200 an insistent reality even at the heart of the schools. The perception that popular heresy might derive from the spread of bad academic theology is shown in the pursuit of the alleged followers of Amaury of Bène in the early thirteenth century.[20]

The issue of language impacted on the intellectual communities. When were people sufficiently trained to move on to theology? As theology became more complex, was progression automatic once the appropriate skills of language had been acquired, or was a further period of training needed – in how to 'think like a theologian' – before access was granted?

Abelard's somewhat impromptu transition from philosopher to theologian epitomised the problem, especially when he faced accusations of heresy because his skill with words got the better of the doctrine. His assumption that he was qualified to analyse the Bible theologically showed the dangers in letting an 'untheological' mind loose on such matters. His case also pointed towards issues which arose later in the century: if those who used the Latin Bible might err, what of laity claiming direct contact with God through a vernacular Bible? That situation – which confronted Pope Alexander III in 1179 when the Waldensians claimed the ability to preach doctrine on the basis of their understanding of a translated Bible, and which Pope Innocent III also had to address in dealings with the bishop of Metz in 1199 – raised the issues of the reliability of translations, which might be faulty or impose a precision not in the Latin, and of the control of understanding, as untrained minds might misinterpret and reach the wrong conclusions.

The problem of controlling the development of theology extended beyond dealing with Abelard: the almost unrestrained speculation at

20 Below, p. 125.

Paris in the first half of the century created an atmosphere ripe for allegations of heresy. The complex Trinitarian analyses of Gilbert of Poitiers led to such accusations at Rheims in 1148; but he managed to avoid formal condemnation by declaring that he did not wish to deviate from orthodoxy. While the masters debated, little is known of how their students, or wider audiences, reacted. Yet there was wider dissemination, and the case of Amaury of Bène (d. 1206) revealed worries about the impact. His ideas were tinged with pantheism, and had been proclaimed in lectures and further broadcast by his adherents at sermons in city churches. Heresy accusations followed, and formal condemnation of Amaury's ideas and adherents at Paris in 1210 and at the Lateran Council of 1215. Investigations around Paris also discovered people who apparently had similar views. There is no demonstrably direct connection between Amaury and these alleged followers, yet a connection was made (not for the last time): academics were undermining the people's faith with their heretical ideas. Possibly a 'common-sense' application of Christianity to the surrounding world had stimulated the popular ideas, but that was not considered. The apparent transition reinforced the need to keep theology a controlled and disciplined science, in Latin, and with only orthodoxy being broadcast.

Construction of an orthodoxy was a hard task. The search for an adequate summary of systematic theology was the great challenge to the early academic theologians. The labour was accomplished in Peter Lombard's Four Books of Sentences, the final version of which dates from a few years before his death in 1160: sufficiently late to survey the key debates of the early twelfth century; sufficiently early to become (with the Bible) the basis for theological instruction during the rest of the middle ages. This first successful, coherent, and complete attempt to construct a systematic theology became the standard textbook, defining both the appropriate questions and (while still subject to some discussion) the appropriate answers. This was the text which every student of theology had to confront, and every aspiring academic theologian to lecture on, for centuries to come. It was not fully authoritative; but had it been so there would have been nothing to discuss and develop later.

Differing approaches legitimated a distinction between theologians working in the secular academic sphere, and their monastic counterparts. Yet academic skills were absorbed into the monastic milieu, as Rupert of Deutz showed, and the separation of monastic and scholastic theologies cannot be rigidly maintained. Growing monastic intellectualism was most evident among the Cistercians, who had initially rejected the academic discipline, and led by St Bernard derided the linguistic approach to theology. But not even Bernard could stem the tide: by 1200 the Cistercians were themselves contributing to the intellectual debates, although sometimes only because of late conversions. Alan of Lille died a Cistercian (c. 1203), but wrote most of his major works before joining the order.

The prime monastic contribution to theological change in this period was the evolution of a more mystical approach to God. The leading centre for this was the abbey of St Victor in Paris, whose Augustinian status encouraged an emphasis on pastoral care, on taking doctrine and instruction to the people. Its contemplative tradition emphasised the mystical, through analysis of the sacraments and their effects, and a concern to produce a structure which would make God more accessible and guide Christians towards Him. The strong academic tradition of St Victor's early years reinforced the need to be sure of authorities and language, stimulating concern to authenticate the text and meaning of the Bible by contacts with Parisian Jews, and sometimes producing charges of Judaising. St Victor's monastic tradition empha-sised the Bible as the focus of theological attention – the Victorines were masters of the sacred page rather than speculative theologians – developing and refining the process of biblical analysis by use of all four levels of understanding. Their contribution also merged back into the academic tradition as they also became authorities and so contributed to the growth of the pastoral and mystical traditions of later centuries.

As linguistic philosophy became more complex and self-assured, the application of its rules to theology became more appealing. This seemed to offer a chance of comprehending the mysteries of faith by reason and analysis. The risk was that the processes might prove incompatible, especially when addressing doctrinal matters which had already been decided, and when (as in the Creed) the terminology already existed, but without formal definitions. Since the conclusions had already been reached without the aid of reason, argument might find itself lost in the convolutions of arguing towards them. In some areas, doctrinal development could occur without too much distraction: for instance, the evolution of the ethic of intention, the idea that guilt and punishment should reflect the intention of an act rather than its outcome, produced a significant shift in attitudes to penance. Once sin was identified as willing consent to an act which was known to be sinful, rather than just an external event, a less rigid penitential stance became possible. While stressing personal responsibility, this insisted that contrition and confession were more important than the process of satisfaction. The shift in emphasis was doubtless aided by the theologians' adoption of Purgatory as a place where incomplete penances could be worked out *en route* to Heaven, thereby legitimating more popular beliefs about the existence of an intermediate status between Heaven and Hell which had circulated for centuries. Other issues were less easily resolved. Application of linguistic reasoning to doctrines of the Trinity, the mass, and the union of the divine and human Natures in Christ, was especially dangerous. Here the application of the language of universals, and specifically divisions on the possibility of the separation of substance and accidents, lay at the heart of bitter debates. On the Trinity the formal doctrinal position was clear, even if expressed in the turgid (and to modern ears peculiar) repetitions of the Creed of St Athanasius. Yet the idea of the Trinity, of God (as a singularity) consisting of the three Persons of Father, Son, and Holy Ghost, each distinct but inseparable from the others, had the potential to be a major stumbling block, and intellectuals accordingly stumbled. The doctrinal statement had not precluded the clash between Roscelin and Anselm, nor Roscelin's condemnation; Trinitarian teachings continued to cause problems, providing the tinder for the initial attacks on Abelard, and later for challenges to Gilbert of Poitiers. Abelard's repeated attempts to explicate the Trinity also show its centrality to contemporary academic debate. As for the mass and the effect of the words of consecration, the imprecision of the 1050s retreated before the gradual consolidation of the idea and doctrine of transubstantiation. The debate on the Natures in Christ also became entangled in the nets of academic argument. The influx of Greek theology in the century (notably the works of John of Damascus) fed into the discussion, especially over the meaning of critical Greek words in translation. The Aristotelian influx also had an effect, playing a positive part in the development of Christology in the early thirteenth century by providing language which allowed the resolution of the relationship between the two Natures in Christ. The question of Christ's Natures also became prominent in the response to heresy, when the Cathars effectively denied Christ's human materiality and insisted that his Incarnation was merely in a spirit form.

Disputes between faith and reason were not confined to ethereal issues. Individual theologians, seeking to reconcile the received faith with the dictates of the new philosophical investigative procedures, could not avoid occasionally bizarre conclusions. Yet the aim was reconciliation. As the highest of sciences, theology had to be the ultimate reconciliation of all sciences. If authorities were authoritative (and even if, as the cliché had it, 'authority has a nose of wax', and was therefore malleable), they too could be reconciled. Until around 1100 old arguments could be rehearsed in a fairly static context, making the problem relatively minor. But as new knowledge first seeped and then poured in, as institutions changed, as the tenor of intellectual life became more forceful and competitive, so the issues became more insistent. In a sense, there never could be an accepted authoritative reconciliation: that would defeat the object of the exercise. Everything that seemingly approached that goal in turn became the object of further analysis and debate. Peter Lombard's *Sentences* appeared to be the last word; within a generation they were just the starting point for theological education, themselves commented and debated. It was not just a matter of reconciling Plato and Aristotle (and, in time, incorporating the latter's Arabic commentators). The issues at stake were fundamental and cosmological, affecting understanding of the soul, the body, the world, time, and God.

Other factors also had to be considered. The twelfth century was one of Christian expansion, most notably in the south, where the general advance gained extensive territory from the Muslims in south Italy, Palestine, and particularly Spain. This led to increased contact with non-Christian faiths; and in turn made Christianity's rivalry with those faiths, and the need to respond to them, highly important. While conflicts with heresy were undeniably formative (as with the need to respond to Catharism's doctrinal challenges), they were essentially over the internal definition of Latin Christendom. The credal statement of Lateran IV, with its dogmatic resolution of various issues raised by heretics and academics over the preceding century, is part of this process. Outside western Europe, the need to respond to the presence of Orthodoxy and other Christianities in Palestine should also have provoked a response; but if it existed (apart from simple hostility) it has left no trace. The distance from the western intellectual centres perhaps made the debates seem irrelevant, if they were known. There were attempts at conversion, with the Maronites accepting union with Rome and being represented at Lateran IV; but the aim in the east was seemingly to overwhelm rather than persuade, demanding subjection rather than acknowledging different traditions (although some recognition was offered in 1215), a stance which was often counter-productive. The opportunities for reconciliation and reunion offered by the conquest of Constantinople in 1204 – if there were any, given the fact of conquest – were frittered away, and within decades popes were calling for crusades against the Greeks as heretics. Analysis of the faith in western Europe was therefore to an extent

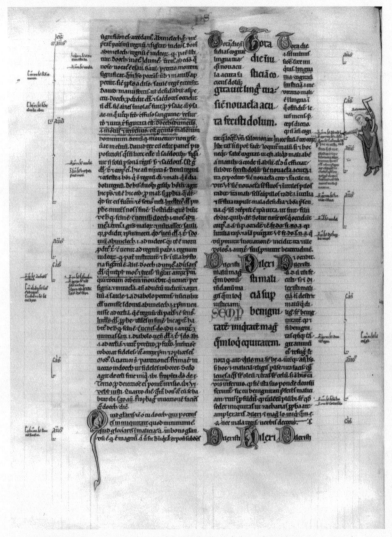

2] *'Published' glosses and the new theology*: Herbert of Bosham's revised version of Peter Lombard's gloss on the Psalms, in a formal presentation copy given to Christ Church, Canterbury, written 1172–7. Herbert checked the Lombard's quotations: the small figure of Solomon points to a misquotation, saying *Non ego*: 'Not me!'

provoked not by variant forms of Christianity, but by the religions which formed part of 'the Other': Judaism and Islam. A third religious 'Other', paganism, survived among the north German Slavic tribes; but was largely ignored. Jews were scattered across western Europe, with significant communities in Italy, Spain, and several French cities. The Muslims were more obviously 'Other', and could more easily be portrayed as monstrous and diabolical, if the *Song of Roland* reflects widespread attitudes. That portrayal owes much to ignorance and presumably lack of contact; and attempts to excuse the misrepresentation by seeing in it a transference to Spain of 'reminiscences of the earlier threat of northern and eastern paganism', as confronted in Scandinavia and the Slavic northeast,[21] seem inappropriate for the region from which the text derives. In contrast, the *Poem of the Cid* often treats Muslims as equals, who could be more honourable than Christians. The key issue was how these two religions related to Christianity. Judaism was part of the Christian tradition, which had adopted the Jewish Bible, taken over Jewish history for its own, and had to acknowledge its roots in a religion which it claimed to have supplanted. Paradoxically, Christianity's relationship with Islam almost matched its own to Judaism, in reverse: Jesus was an Islamic prophet, and Islam claimed to replace Christianity much as Christianity claimed to supersede Judaism. Towards both, therefore, Christianity had to be defensive: it had to justify its replacement of Judaism, and the assertion that Jesus was the Messiah; it had to deny the claims of Islam and assert its own status as the ultimate revelation. Yet there were differences. Judaism was considered a valid if misguided religion; Islam had no right to exist, and as an enemy had to be eliminated by force or argument, or both.

The twelfth century saw increasing tension between Christianity and Judaism, as Christians became more assertive. Anti-Jewish violence, perhaps motivated primarily by economic and social hostility, but justified by appeals to religion, was part of that assertiveness. The Rhineland pogroms of the First Crusade, charges that Jews ritually murdered Christian children (first noted after the death of 'St William of Norwich' in 1144), massacres in England in 1189 (notably in York), and French moves to expel Jews from the royal domain, were stages in a cumulative process.

Against such a background, intellectual contacts between the two religions seem less important; yet they provided a channel for the

---

21 Joseph J. Duggan, 'The epic', in *A New History of French Literature*, ed. Denis Hollier (Cambridge, MA, and London, 1989), p. 22.

transmission of thought and theological evolution. In Spain, Jewish bi-
(or tri-) lingualism played a part in the translation movement. More
important culturally was the fact that Judaism and Christianity shared the
Old Testament. Indeed, by retaining the Hebrew Bible Jews were closer
to the original texts than Christian theologians, for whom Hebrew was
usually an unknown language. Contact with the original Old Testament
text through the Jews accordingly offered a way to check readings, and
amend interpretations. One thing appreciated by twelfth-century theologians was the potential for the corruption of the Latin Bible in manuscript transmission, and the vulnerability of their own texts. This weakness was even more significant when dealing with the New Testament.
An early spat between Abelard and Bernard centred on the version of the
Lord's Prayer used at the religious centre established by Abelard at the
Paraclete. Abelard used the text in Matthew, which mentioned
'supersubstantial bread' (Matthew 6.11), against the more normal 'daily
bread' in the version given by Luke (11.3).[22]

Scholars concerned about the textual accuracy of their Old Testament therefore turned to the Jews, with some (like Herbert of Bosham)
even learning some Hebrew. The late twelfth and early thirteenth
centuries saw a flourishing of Hebraic studies, not matched until the later
Renaissance. As a result of the contacts, interpretations were affected as
well as readings. No one suggested replacing Jerome's Vulgate text with a
fully new translation (although Psalters translated into Latin from
Hebrew survive from the thirteenth century), but the meaning could still
be checked with reference to the Hebrew original. Moreover, interpretation, exegesis, could be affected by drawing on Jewish scholarship.
Here lay a chink in the Christian armour; for Jewish traditions were
arguably more authoritative for Old Testament understanding than the
new Christian versions. The Christians' fourfold scheme of interpretation of the Bible, and the belief that the Old Testament functioned partly
to offer prefigurations of the New (as Abraham's near sacrifice of Isaac
prefigured the Crucifixion), meant that their readings of the Old
Testament would always be tinged with that comparative hindsight.
Here lay the tension: the Jewish exegetical tradition did not need such
mental baggage; it therefore emphasised the historical and literal
meanings of the text. A Christian exegesis based on Jewish traditions
would also emphasise the historical and literal, at the expense of the other
readings. Any scholar doing that was open to charges of Judaising, of

22 The difference exists only in the Latin of the Vulgate, and is not retained in post-
    Reformation English translations.

undermining Christianity. Perhaps unsurprisingly, some of the Victorines faced such charges, notably Andrew of St Victor. Yet he overcame the obstacle, and the Jewish contribution to Christian exegesis and understanding, acquired through the Christian Hebraists of the late twelfth and early thirteenth centuries, provided a significant boost to biblical studies.

A final notable aspect of the twelfth-century contacts between Christianity and Judaism is the sudden upsurge of 'debate literature'. As a genre this was not solely concerned with the relative validity of Judaism and Christianity: other works discussed Christianity in relation to Islam, and to a naturalistic philosophy which had no place for God. Thus, Gilbert Crispin wrote a dialogue between a Christian and a Jew, while a tract by Abelard portrayed a debate between a Christian, a Muslim, and a Philosopher.

The purpose of the Christian–Jewish debate material is uncertain. It used to be treated precisely as debate material, produced as part of the Christians' attempt to persuade Jews that Christ was the true Messiah, that Judaism had therefore been superseded, and that they should convert. That remains, indeed, a valid reading of some of it. There were actual debates, which presage the one-sided disputations of the thirteenth century, like that at Barcelona in 1263 on the authority of the Talmud. Sometimes Jews took the initiative in issuing the challenge: Herman (later abbot of Scheda) recorded in his account of his own conversion to Christianity that he had demanded the debate between himself (then still a Jew) and the Benedictine theologian Rupert of Deutz at Münster early in 1128. Anti-Jewish polemic was also adapted for use in other contexts. Alan of Lille's *Against the Heretics* draws on Gilbert Crispin's *Disputation between a Jew and a Christian*. Crispin's work was clearly part of at least a textual debate between the religions, some of it being translated into Hebrew in the anti-Christian *Wars of the Lord*, written by Jacob ben Reuben c. 1170.

The writing of Jewish anti-Christian polemics and the convert Herman's stance against Rupert of Deutz suggest that the status of some of the debate material is rather complex. Despite the traumas of the First Crusade, the Jews of western Europe were perhaps becoming more self-assertive, certainly more conspicuous, during the early twelfth century. Meanwhile, as Christianity sought to make sense of itself through the academic development of doctrine, its own weaknesses became more obvious. The literal and historical Jewish approach to exegesis was basically more 'rational'; the stirrings of heresy blatantly revealed Christianity's inconsistencies. In such circumstances, some perhaps found Judaism more attractive than Christianity. A substantial drift from Christianity to Judaism was inconceivable, but conversions happened.

(However, the most high-level conversion, of Andreas, archbishop of Bari, c. 1078, was presumably of a Greek Orthodox prelate and not a Latin Christian.) Later allegations of Judaising against some intellectuals, and the highly dramatic response to some conversions (as in 1210, when an English deacon was burnt for apostasy) show continuing concern at the challenge of Judaism. In such contexts, the Christian–Jewish debating tracts were perhaps meant not to convert Jews, but to reassure Christians. Some tracts seem to preach to the converted: there is no evidence for their use against Jews, and every indication that their only readers were Christians.

Yet some Jews did convert, adding a final ingredient to the potent mixture which produced concerted anti-Judaism. To be fully effective, conversion for such people required a total cultural break; indeed an actual and radical rejection of their old religion. They would keep the Old Testament, but even there understanding would be affected by the change. Some elements of traditional Jewish exegesis might be retained, but acceptance of Christ as the Messiah invalidated all historical evolutions in Judaism since the Incarnation. Here were the seeds of the most significant feature of Jewish–Christian intellectual relations in the thirteenth century, the Christian assault on the Talmud, engineered originally by the convert Nicholas Donin. The Christian Church now assumed to itself the role of guardian of Jewish orthodoxy, an orthodoxy which it itself defined, and which could not legitimately have evolved beyond the Judaism of the time of Christ because the transfer of God's favour from Israel to Christianity required Judaism to be a static remnant religion, a fossil reminder of what the Incarnation had invalidated. Jews had to be tolerated precisely as such reminders, and so that their ultimate mass conversion could provide a sign of the approaching Last Judgement; but toleration could only be on Christian terms.

Latin Christianity's encounter with Islam was more problematic. The crusades and conquests in Spain and southern Italy made Christian intellectuals aware of the Islamic challenge; but their response was limited. There was talk of mission and conversion, but not much happened. The reality of the contacts – across a significant linguistic divide, with Christians assaulting a religion which considered itself irrefutable, and conversion from which was anathema – was probably very limited, and opportunities to seek converts few.

Yet attempts were made. This required Christians to accept the impossibility of debating specifically religious issues (perhaps, also, to accept that as Islam claimed to supersede Christianity, its claims and doctrinal clarity might also make it attractive). Debate material exists, but here formulated to make Christianity appealing almost despite its theology: Islam's invalidation had to be much more radical than the attack on Judaism, yet had to leave Christianity as the intact survivor. As with Judaism, there is no proof that the arguments advanced were actually put to Muslims. As most of the relevant works are known only from northern France, it seems most unlikely. Yet awareness of the religious divide, of a need to understand Islam in order to secure its invalidation does occasionally appear (moving significantly beyond the travesty in the *Song of Roland*, where Islam is a debased parody of Christianity). In 1142, for instance, Peter the Venerable, abbot of Cluny, had commissioned the first translation of the Qur'an into Latin. This was done in Spain, where the Cluniac order was itself spreading its roots, and was therefore in contact with real Muslims. The translation was probably undertaken to provide ammunition against Islam: Peter the Venerable certainly produced an anti-Islamic tract, the *Book against the Sect or Heresy of the Saracens*, which he had hoped to see translated into Arabic. (It was part of an overall policy of defending Christianity: Peter also produced a tract *Against the Inveterate Stubbornness of the Jews*.) But Cluny was not Paris, and the translation was virtually unknown. Islamic–Christian contacts were marginal to the evolution of Christian theology in the twelfth century; but that they did exist, that Islam's challenge was recognised and built into Christian perceptions, was important, and was to bear further fruit in the next century, when questions of mission and conversion received much more attention.

All these forces and tensions combined to produce a new type of theology, very different from the former tradition. Recognition that the faith needed further definition, and that authoritative declarations were lacking, had led to uncertainty and questions about its precise content. That they were voiced in the schools added to the vibrancy: debate and competition produced not only academic theology as a discipline, but (eventually) a new theological orthodoxy. Histories of heresy usually focus on individuals and movements which experienced dramatic repression or gained a widespread adherence: in the twelfth century, people like Henry of Lausanne and Peter of Bruis, and movements like the Waldensians, Humiliati, and Cathars. The appearance of heresy charges against academics was just as significant, and for the long-term development of the faith arguably more formative. No one can say how Catholicism would have evolved if Berengar of Tours had triumphed over Lanfranc; but speculation can run riot. Among academic theologians, at every stage responses to ideas (especially if accepted into the mainstream) opened and blocked routes for Catholicism's future development. Moreover, academics were not just formally arguing towards conclusions which opponents could then rebut: heterodoxy almost had to be invented to be rebutted. The new academic techniques, notably the confrontational disputation, set the debate between orthodoxy and unorthodoxy at the heart of academic theological life. The supporter of the accepted view had to face an opponent defending erroneous propositions (and also, necessarily, attacking orthodoxy). Some questionable views might be advanced merely as debating points. That dilemma confronted theologians for centuries, yet established the basis of claims to some sort of 'academic freedom', as the debaters often restated opinions already officially condemned. The points still had to be argued; and even if orthodoxy had to win, it had to win by argument. Furthermore, although the theological disputation was an academic exercise, it also provided valid combat training.

One contributory cause to the appearance of academic heresy was the impact of new philosophical ideas, and the need to fit them into the existing models. Aristotelian naturalism and secularism here led the field. Challenges on the nature of creation, on links between form and matter, or accidents and substance, the problem of time and eternity, all fed into questions which theologians then had to address. Secularism – using the word here in its modern sense – was also a threat, but perhaps not one of great significance. Nobody in the twelfth century sought to eliminate God, even if they tried to redefine Him. Yet attempts to limit the Church's sphere of activity and clerical privileges (including those of academics) might evoke responses couched in theological language: whether Becket's reply to the Constitutions of Clarendon and their threat to clerical immunities, or outbursts of papalist hierocracy which sought to put the world well and truly in its place. Such statements, while responses, were not refutations. The challenges could not be eliminated; indeed they would grow as the implications of Aristotelian ideas were explored and elaborated, and as princes sought to re-establish their pre-eminence within their realms against the quasi-separatist claims advanced by ecclesiastics in their own interests.

As the variables increased so a paradox developed. While there was greater precision in defining the faith, there was also greater imprecision about what the definitions meant. Ambiguity went to the heart of the system. It was perhaps less evident in the twelfth century than later, mainly because theological debate was concentrated in a small geographical area, mainly northern France, and primarily at Paris. The doctrinal definitions and programme of pastoral reform decreed at Lateran IV in 1215 in many ways mark the imposition of a Parisian programme on the rest of the Church. But once the debates spread beyond Paris, with the foundation of new universities and the mendicant *studia*, differing theological interpretations could evolve, based on the twelfth-century ambiguities. The growing doctrinal precision of the twelfth century was more apparent than real, an umbrella for variety. Conflict could be glossed over, but not eliminated, as debates between faith and reason, between seculars and regulars (especially the mendicants), re-emerged in the thirteenth century.

Although caveats apply, over the century theology – the study of God, or of the language about God – had become a real academic discipline. Yet, while it generated numerous texts, and stimulated considerable debate, theology was always a minority subject. Leaving aside questions of cost (being essentially a 'postgraduate' study), academic theology was, bluntly, not necessary for most clerics. Some theological awareness would be gained from sermons, perhaps even by reading: but the amount must not be overstated, especially in the twelfth century itself. Some clerics gained fleeting contact with academic theology through short periods at the schools, but that would be patchy and variable. There was no concerted policy to widen access until the thirteenth century. The decrees of Lateran IV required cathedral chancellors to arrange theological lectures for their diocesan clergy; and thirteenth-century diocesan synods sought to improve local clerics' theological awareness by setting minimum standards of knowledge. Whether such schemes could work would depend on the assiduity of the cathedral chancellor and the size of the diocese, and on the willingness of the diocesan administration to enforce the decrees.

Most academic theology developed in something of a vacuum. Its impact outside the restricted audience of the schools cannot be properly tested, encouraging a concentration on masters and ideas rather than the overall development and significance. There were geographical constraints as well. Despite the magnetic pull of Paris, the audience was mainly located in northern France and southern England (but was not absolutely confined to people from those areas, and might then disperse as their careers distributed students throughout the Church). The activities of Anselm, at Bec and Canterbury, are almost the exception which proves the rule; and that he secured his audience through writing is significant. Many Parisian academics remain obscure precisely because they were simply teachers, speakers rather than writers. For the wider world, the declamations of an Abelard might go unheard: Salisbury cathedral built up a major collection of books between 1100 and 1150, but it reveals almost no awareness of the developments across the Channel.

Although abstruse academic theology commanded only a limited audience, the cause it served was that of salvation, which affected everyone. Salvation required primarily faith rather than reason; most of Europe's population, perhaps most of Europe's clergy, needed help towards that goal not from analyses of the Trinity and the intricacies of Christology, but from practical instruction and assurance. Even among intellectuals, engagement with the demands of pastoral care led to a massive shift in focus. This, too, is an aspect of the changes in twelfth-century theology, where distinctions between 'monastic' and 'scholastic' approaches become less significant, and where the regulars made a considerable and valuable contribution. (The search for a 'twelfth-century renaissance' in Germany, perhaps especially in Bavaria, might be formulated in terms of the impact of this practical regular pastoral care, witnessed in the distribution of works by Rupert of Deutz and Honorius Augustodunensis.)

As the Church's jurisdictional and administrative structures con-gealed in the parishes and dioceses over the long twelfth century, the concern with pastoral care became more explicit. Dealings with parishioners had to be straightforwardly instructional and disciplinary, without causing confusion or uncertainty (the priests were considered personally responsible for the souls of their subjects, and at the Last Judgement would be accountable for any failure to provide adequate care and instruction). A frequent comment was that the laity required easily digested but sustaining sops: others could chew on harder matters. Preaching became more important, with many of the leading thinkers leaving sermons, and with evidence that even more were produced and delivered either generally or to specific social groups (the *ad status* collections which appear from the end of the twelfth century). Hand-books for preachers, although drawn up as an aspect of the *ars dictaminis*, also conveyed doctrine. Alan of Lille produced a tract on preaching, while Stephen Langton (d. 1228) – later famous for his dramatic political career in England – was so renowned as a preacher that his name was punningly transformed to 'Stephen of the ringing tongue' (*Stephanus de lingua tonante*). The appearance of *exempla* collections – anthologies of snappy little tales to illustrate moral points, often in terms reasonably close to the experiences an audience might have had – also fits into this concern with preaching and instructing.

Other instruction emphasised discipline. The sacramental analyses of the academic theologians determined what was needed for salvation; the parish priests had to ensure that the laity knew, and obtained the benefits. Here an emphasis on confession and communion became paramount, established as an annual obligation at the Fourth Lateran Council in 1215. Penance also became a major concern, as a personal obligation. The production of new confessional handbooks was an outcome in the twelfth and early thirteenth centuries. Their contents reflect a significant change in the penitential system, from one of hard immediate demands which if unfulfilled meant damnation, to one in which the penances imposed in this life were relatively light, but leaving the main period of penance to the post-mortem pains of Purgatory. Ultimately, this change amounted to a shift in the awareness of the possibility of salvation. Hitherto, only monks had been assured of salvation; for others damnation seemed more likely. Over the twelfth century, the net spread more widely: even the laity might be saved; indeed, even the married laity might be saved. Laypeople (or, to be more precise, non-noble laypeople) might even become saints. In 1199 Pope Innocent III formally canonised the first merchant saint, Homobono of Cremona. Later canonisations would make sainthood something which others could imitate, even if it was beyond their aspirations.

With these considerations the borderline between a possible intellectual renaissance and a medieval Reformation here grows indistinct. The fuzziness shows that the academic developments cannot be quarantined off from the rest of history. There was a world beyond the schools in which the intellectuals' ideas would apply: getting the theology right was a matter of eternal life and death, not argument for its own sake.

The twelfth century had laid foundations and ground rules for theology; but in 1200 academic theology was still in its infancy. Maturity came only in the next century, with greater academic institutionalisation, and with the emergence of the mendicant *studia* as intellectual hothouses producing giants like Albert the Great and Thomas Aquinas. By then the initial enthusiasm had passed, and the theologians, as specialists, settled down to a process of nit-picking to identify questions and seek answers, that almost unavoidable outcome of academic evolution. Scholastic theology was now truly a discipline, in marked contrast to the relative indiscipline, but more appealing drama and vitality, of the preceding century.

Humanism and the individual

In addition to these intellectual transitions, the twelfth century has also been credited with a significant psychological transformation: the appearance of humanism, and 'the discovery of the individual'. Just what this means, and whether the changes really happened, are matters of debate.

The prime difficulty with the concepts of humanism and individuality is that the terms are anachronistic to the period. They therefore tend to be tackled somewhat retrospectively: the terms seem to be defined to suit modern minds, and the historical record is then examined to see whether anything appropriate can be found. This process is obviously dangerous: it assumes that twelfth-century writers would express themselves in ways that allow the similarity to be deduced; it demands real empathy to ensure that modern preconceptions are not imposed on the evidence to distort conclusions. The process also demands consensus over the terms themselves. Yet 'humanism' (to consider just one of them) remains a singularly ambiguous term. As Sir Richard Southern has pointed out:

> One of the main difficulties with the word 'humanism' is that it has two distinct, though related meanings ... The most general meaning of the word according to the Oxford English Dictionary is 'any system of thought or action which is concerned with merely human interests, or with those of the human race in general'. It is in this sense that this word is now in popular use, especially among those who call themselves humanists. This meaning ... associates humanism with the extension of the area of human knowledge and activity, and consequently with the activity of limiting (or abolishing) the supernatural in human affairs. ... [T]here is also an academic view [in] which ... the essential feature of humanism is the study of ancient Latin and Greek literature.[23]

Both versions of humanism now have their advocates for the twelfth century. The first has perhaps been the slower to gain ground, yet is fairly widely adopted, especially with reference to the cosmologists of the first half of the century, and their concern for Nature. It may also appear in the search for signs of a more clinically scientific endeavour in the same period, linked with the same people. The second, perhaps more traditionally Renaissance approach to humanism, is exemplified, for instance,

---

23 R.W. Southern, *Medieval Humanism and Other Studies* (Oxford, 1970), pp. 29–30. Very similar phrasing is used in R.W. Southern, *Scholastic Humanism and the Unification of Europe, vol. 1: Foundations* (Oxford, 1995), pp. 17–18.

in Hans Liebeschütz's discussion of the humanism of John of Salisbury, and the emphasis on the classical tradition and the revival of Latinity.[24] Whichever definition is adopted, neither seems to leave much room for the ineffable. Yet just as discussions of later Renaissance humanism now accommodate a variety of 'Christian humanism', so arguably must the search for twelfth-century humanism. Here again, Southern provides the working definition which allows God a place in the total picture:

> there can be no humanism without a strong sense of the dignity of human nature ... Along with this ... there must go a recognition of the dignity of nature itself ... Finally the whole universe appears intelligible and accessible to human reason: nature is seen as an orderly system, and man ... understands himself as the main part, the key-stone, of nature.

A link with God is, however, central to this whole construct:

> we may expect a humanist to assert not only that man is the noblest of God's creatures, but also that his nobility continues even in his fallen state, that it is capable of development in this world, that the instruments exist by which it can be developed, and that it should be the chief aim of human endeavour to perfect these instruments.[25]

More recently, Southern has called this 'scholastic humanism', a label which Renaissance and modern humanists might well consider a contradiction in terms. Firmly based on reason, which

> testifies both to the autonomy of nature and the necessity for that which is above nature ... It is as far removed from the elitism of Renaissance humanism as it is from the godlessness of modern secular humanism; but ... it has a good claim to be considered the most important kind of humanism Europe has ever produced.[26]

While the precise content of this scholastic humanism remains open to refinement, it emphasises human free will and responsibility for actions. It stresses the period's growing concern with ethics and morality, especially in a twelfth century set within fairly precise chronological limits, and perhaps before the switch in emphasis to pastoral theology in the later part of the period. Even this definition has limitations: it blurs

---

24 Hans Liebeschütz, *Mediaeval Humanism in the Life and Writings of John of Salisbury*, Studies of the Warburg Institute, 17 (London, 1950). Despite the title, the book is extremely reticent about providing a definition of humanism: the word itself appears sparingly in the text, and rarely with any precise connotations.

25 Southern, *Medieval Humanism*, pp. 31–2. Cf. Southern, *Scholastic Humanism*, pp. 22–3.

26 Southern, *Scholastic Humanism*, p. 44.

the distinction between humanism and the broader developments in philosophy and theology. Moreover, whether twelfth-century human- ism can be confined within this definition is also open to question. Against it can be put Panofsky's comment on the intellectual changes of the period. Reserving the term 'proto-Renaissance' for the artistic changes (as 'a Mediterranean phenomenon, arising in Southern France, Italy and Spain'), he puts the intellectual movement in northern Europe under the umbrella of 'proto-humanism'. This, however, comes with a proviso that:

> the term 'humanism' is not considered synonymous with such general notions as respect for human values, individualism, secularism or even liberalism but more narrowly defined as a specific cultural and educational ideal ... based on the conviction ... that it is necessary to preserve – or to restore – that union between clear thought and literate expression, reason and eloquence, *ratio* and *oratio*, which had been postulated by the classics.[27]

The differences between this definition and Southern's encapsulate the problem, but cannot eliminate it. At least these are definitions, for 'humanism' often appears in discussions of the twelfth century as a somewhat disembodied term, whose meaning becomes almost a matter of choice. Not to use it, however, is not necessarily to deny a greater human focus in the intellectual concerns of the period. That focus certainly appears in the concern to analyse human relations, and in the stress on the search for salvation which appears in the pastoral theology.

The search for the 'discovery of the individual' suffers from similar terminological problems. It takes in a wide range of material, among which the personally produced records are most evocative. The twelfth century is notable for the revival of autobiography as a genre, in works like Guibert of Nogent's history of his own times, and Abelard's *Historia calamitatum*. To these works can be added various of the letter collections of the period, in particular the correspondence between Abelard and Heloise, and collections like those of Peter of Blois and Peter of Celle. Less immediately personal, but still valuable sources, are some of the lives written at this time (that of Christina of Markyate being commonly cited), and the fictional construction of personalities in some of the romances. Clearly these reflect a different type of record and recording:

---

27 Erwin Panofsky, *Renaissance and Renascences in Western Art* (London, 1970), pp. 55, 68–9.

autobiographies and letter collections are exercises in self-revelation and self-construction (temporarily setting aside the problem of 'self'); biography and fiction entail a creative depiction, a construction, which may be a reflection of personality as externally displayed rather than a revelation of personality as something interiorised.

However, that the twelfth-century changes equate with 'the discovery of the individual' has been disputed. The main criticism is that what the writings reflect is discovery not of 'the individual', but of 'the self'; that people did not internalise their identities, but defined themselves through the various roles they adopted (either singly, or in combination). The sense of role-playing, of adopting a persona, thus replaces the sense of being a truly individual and discrete personality. It may, indeed, carry overtones of constraining the personality. The classic role model was Christ, and a key theme which develops in twelfth-century spiritual life is the imitation of Christ. Imitation may be more, however, that mere copying: the major psychological thrust was perhaps more towards conformity, a training of the person, mentally and behaviourally, to match the model. This practice of *conformatio* need not be confined to the spiritual sphere: something very like it has been suggested as a key feature of education in the cathedral schools before 1100. The process of training obviously requires a restriction of self (as a negative), but also an awareness of each human as a separate being, capable of adopting characteristics and of following guidance to create a new personality.

Application of the ideas of role-play and *conformatio* to the career of Abelard, for instance, makes him dissolve into the various characters which he assumes at different times: the peripatetic philosopher, Jerome advising holy women, perhaps even Christ. But interpretation rests on recognition and acceptance of the models as valid and applicable, which leaves room for ambiguity, especially when dealing with some of the autobiographical material. Abelard's roles change considerably in his *Historia calamitatum*; they seem also to overlay a more general tension. Abelard, as philosopher, recounts his life almost as that of a knight. He himself admits to having chosen between the two careers, yet his tale assumes elements of a chivalric quest, in which he, searching, faces repeated trials and tribulations. Precisely what the quest is towards remains obscured, but the parallel may not be too far-fetched. It is, though, a parallel constructed from within the text, rather than any explicit statement. Other people in the period gain their identities through the accumulation of characteristics explicitly provided by named models, the creation of an identikit persona which perhaps validates

claims that the medieval Latin Christian personality 'is seen in quantitative terms of the number of desirable and undesirable characteristics,
rather than in modern terms of qualitative assessment of the personality
as an organic whole'. This quantitative approach means, for instance,
that 'Abelard expresses his individuality in terms of being better than
others rather than substantially different'. Particularly in autobiographical accounts, therefore, 'feelings of uniqueness can be expressed only by
indicating that they possess a special genius, have more and greater
talents than others'.[28]

At the same time, however, people often created their identities by
membership of a group, rather than wishing to stand out. Although this
following of models, adoption of roles, and sense of group (rather than
individual) identity carries implications of stereotyping and uniformity,
this need not follow. Variety was clearly accepted. In the Church, for
instance, new role models were fully accommodated, as shown by the
creation of the new regular orders and the appearance of canons regular
and friars, despite some teething problems (and, admittedly, some long-
lasting rivalries). The slogan of *diversi, sed non adversi* – 'different, but not
opposed' – was a suitable umbrella here. Moreover, some of the models
were very vaguely defined: the *vita apostolica* (the 'apostolic life') had
many variants, and assumptions about what it was changed over time
from a monastic life to one where poverty and preaching were basic
components. The vagueness of many monastic customs means that
assumptions of uniformity and conformity within houses are often
misplaced. Most monastic orders were Benedictine, in claiming to follow
that Rule, but their interpretations of it varied markedly. The so-called
Rule of St Augustine remained remarkably amorphous, but nevertheless
gave an anchor which those claiming to follow it could use to validate
their lives.

Twentieth-century formulations lie at the heart of the problem of
twelfth-century individuality. Guibert, Abelard, Heloise, and others
certainly invite (and often now receive) an emotional response from
readers, which may be why they wrote. The task is to separate the
response from the stimulus: are these people truly 'individuals', do they
know 'the self'? The writing of autobiographies need not mean much:
Augustine's *Confessions* were a precedent which was clearly being

28 Chris D. Ferguson, 'Autobiography as therapy: Guibert de Nogent, Peter
    Abelard, and the making of medieval autobiography', *Journal of Medieval and
    Renaissance Studies*, 13 (1983), pp. 206–7 and n.58.

followed at times. Moreover, the standard type of life-story was that of the saint, battling against the odds, which could also be adapted. Within their texts, the authors could construct themselves by using a combination of confession and hagiographical motifs.

The problem with the question of the individual/self is that it may not adequately address the real issues, since the terminology employed rests on anachronism and imposed meanings. It is twentieth-century commentators who judge whether 'the individual' or 'the self' has been discovered, and establish the grounds on which that self-identity is judged. The leap of centuries, and the subtle changes of meaning which can occur in translations, increase the problems. The shift in focus from 'the individual' to 'the self' seems to occur with little real focus on what 'the self' actually is. The modern concept of a psychological 'self' is seemingly primarily something shared among Anglo-Saxons and Americans. For psychologists, its history begins with John Locke in the seventeenth century; a transition from a focus on the soul to a recognition of 'self', and from a use of the word 'self' which was largely pejorative and negative – a self being essentially selfish – to one which was much more positive and conscious. However, self-focusing clearly occurred before 1700: here the linguistic problems of English become important. The word 'self' is almost unavoidable, but its use may impose interpretations. The demand for annual confession issued at Lateran IV in 1215 has been called the 'most important technology of the self introduced by Christianity';[29] while a key tag of the period is 'Know thyself', perhaps most widely encountered as the alternative title for Peter Abelard's *Ethics*. At least, 'Know thyself' is the usual translation of the Latin, which effectively short-circuits discussion. But *Scito te ipsum* might also be rendered as 'Know what you are', which is less prescriptive about what is to be known. Twentieth-century concerns, and twentieth-century jargon, may also misrepresent the past by not considering it in its own terms.[30]

What those terms were is elusive. The key question may be not whether the period knew the individual, but whether that awareness could actually be communicated. This is at heart a linguistic and conceptual problem; it is quite possible that it is ultimately insoluble.

---

29 K. Danziger, 'The historical formation of selves', in *Self and Identity: Fundamental Issues*, ed. Richard D. Ashmore and Lee Jussim, Rutgers series on self and social identity, 1 (New York and Oxford, 1997), p. 150.

30 See e.g. S. Spence, *Texts and the Self in the Twelfth Century*, Cambridge studies in medieval literature, 30 (Cambridge, 1996), which seems to be driven more by its own theoretical and jargon-laden agenda than by the texts which it claims to analyse, and whose broad historical context is barely considered.

Philosophically, people may have been aware of individuals. For intellectuals accustomed to debating universals and the relationship between substance and accidents, that goes almost without saying. Abelard, for instance, remarks that 'all men differ from each other as much in matter as in form'.[31] Yet the inexactitude of some of the philosophical and theological language of the early twelfth century suggests that it would have been rather difficult to convey 'individuality' as a difference in the essential make-up of a person: Abelard has been described as 'a logician who tried to account for the validity of universal knowledge with no metaphysical doctrine about the constitution of the individual'.[32] In contrast, Gilbert of Poitiers's view of humanity does seem to have recognised individuality, or at least a very strong form of particularity. His definition of a human person as a union of body and soul which constitutes a *res per se una*, 'a thing which is one on its own', and insistence elsewhere in his linguistic analyses on the substantial singularity of humans, suggests advocacy of some kind of individuality. Nevertheless, his formulations did not receive unqualified acceptance, even among his own followers.

The problems surrounding the metaphysical doctrine of individuality do not necessarily entail inability to recognise an individual; but they may affect the way in which the sense of human particularity was conveyed. The self-describing individual may be recognised externally, as in modern responses to the autobiographies. But how is recognition of another's individuality to be recorded, and communicated? The ability to do that is arguably what the debate on the individual is actually about, not the initial recognition by contemporaries. Given the linguistic problems, and the tradition of analogy and allegory which permeated twelfth-century society, a catalogue of accidents, or distinguishing characteristics, might be the only effective means of communication. That would have to operate in terms already known, which suggests models, and the listing of attributes which could be identified by references to a shared precedent which was often biblical. The language of particularity and identity had to be constructed by pointing to discrete characteristics, recorded (and thereby communicated) in terms of recognisable cultural models. Yet the sum total of those characteristics may still be an 'individual'. There is clearly an awareness and an acceptance of human particularity, of separateness, of subjectivity, both physical and emotional; whether it carries other psychological baggage remains indeterminable.

31 F. Wade, 'Abelard and individuality', in *Die Metaphysik im Mittelalter: ihr Ursprung und ihre Bedeutung*, ed. P. Wilpert, Miscellanea Mediaevalia, 2 (Berlin, 1963), p. 165 n.5.
32 *Ibid.*, p. 171.

In the search for the twelfth century's awareness of personality, the role of friendship has attracted some attention, especially as revealed and constructed through correspondence. Letters and letter collections raise issues of self-consciousness, especially when some of the texts were clearly altered for later circulation. How much can be read into such activities? When Peter of Blois revised texts and so altered the record of his activities, was he deliberately trying to construct a new 'image', or simply altering a stylistic pattern? Some letters do reveal emotions and personalities, like those of John of Salisbury and (to cite a female case) Hildegard of Bingen. The best-known series of surviving correspondence, the letters apparently between Abelard and Heloise, is the most problematic of all. Although the two lovers are among the archetypes of twelfth-century individuals, the doubts expressed about the authorship of the letters almost make them unusable as evidence – unless the doubts are simply ignored, given the inconclusive state which the challenge to the letters' authenticity has now reached.

For all their vitality, letters are not always convincing as expressions of friendship. Most of the letters in existing collections were not intended as private correspondence, but public statements. They were composed to make an impact, but not necessarily to reveal innermost feelings or convey any sense of individualism. Building on the Roman rhetorical tradition of friendship – albeit Christianised – they can appear not merely idealised, but formal, constructed, even artificial and calculating, if not empty. Indeed, their dependence on a classical tradition is itself a source of problems. The rhetoric 'is often sterile epistolary convention that cannot be taken at face value ... One may detect a sincere expression of friendship in medieval epistles more often than not *in spite* of such [Ciceronian or Senecan] formulas.'[33] This, though, raises questions of how one detects such sincerity, and how it is to be proved. Some subjectivity is unavoidable here, which may transform the character of the relationship quite profoundly.

In any case, the focus of the friendship is often ambiguous. Frequently expressed in contexts which presume a relationship with Christ as well as the friend (most obviously within a monastic community), the friendship is normally a spiritual and moral rather than affectionate connection. Yet affection does shine through at times. Overt expressions of friendship within a closed community like a monastery also provoked displays of

33 R. Hyatte, *The Arts of Friendship: The Idealization of Friendship in Medieval and Early Renaissance Literature*, Brill's studies in intellectual history, 50 (Leiden, New York, and Köln, 1994), p. 40.

envy and jealousy at the exclusiveness (and, perhaps, favouritism?) of the relationships which evolved. Aelred of Rievaulx (c. 1110–67) stands as a leading proponent of spiritual friendship in the century, his *De spirituali amicitia* (*On Spiritual Friendship*) providing classic guidance on how a friend should be chosen and a friendship quite deliberately cultivated and constructed. He openly reveals his emotional dependence on a junior monk, in terms which have been considered homosexual. His comments seem individual, certainly personal, and appear to reflect real self-awareness. According to Aelred's biographer, Walter Daniel, others resented the exclusiveness of that relationship: their jealousy might be considered equally self-revealing.

A concern to express friendship is a short step away from a recognition of sexuality, and sexual identities. Here psychohistory has claimed a voice in dealing with twelfth-century individuality. Abelard and Heloise clearly express and respond to issues of sexuality in their letters (Abelard's comments being overshadowed by the humiliation of his castration and its traumatic effects). Guibert of Nogent can be read as a case of sexual repression. The strident concern with clerical celibacy during the century is linked with a growing antifeminism which is generally labelled misogynistic (although some aspects of it may have been misinterpreted). The linkage between friendship and eroticism – expressed or imposed – has encouraged a view of the early twelfth century as a time of homosexual liberation, when acceptance of sexual identity marched with proclamation of personal identity. The existence of homosexuality in twelfth-century Europe cannot be denied; but its ready acceptance is questionable, and the language of friendship – necessarily rhetorical and hyperbolic – has probably been misconstrued. To see the period as one of toleration sits ill with the contemporary evidence for rejection of homosexuality (at least, of its male variety) as the sin of Sodom, and of deliberate persecution and exclusion.

Self-awareness has also been seen in the tendency for authors to insert themselves into their works (here particularly emphasising their appearance in fictional works), as an assertion of possession and personal control. This certainly occurs in several troubadour songs, with the assertive subjectivity of the singer at their core, allegedly buffeted by the emotional demands and physical dangers of courtly love. This awareness of subjectivity and possession has been linked with the increasing number of depictions of authors and artists, an endorsement of a 'performing self', which occurs during the period. However, that the sculptors Gislebertus and Giraldus are named over the doors of churches at Autun and St Ursin at Bourges is very different from the obscure identification of others on column capitals, where they would be barely visible. Similarly, the naming of scribes and artists in books is scarcely a public proclamation of individual awareness, especially if it occurs in a volume intended solely for private use, like a private prayer manual. Moreover, any real sense of identity remains elusive. Very few authors and craftsmen proclaimed their responsibility for their products; most remain obscure and anonymous. The pride and self-identity of a creator or patron may shine through in some contexts, such as Suger's obvious delight in his work at St Denis, but many authors and artisans launched their works anonymously, leaving them prey to deliberate or unintentional misattribution. The prolific productivity of Honorius Augustodunensis (c. 1075/80–c. 1156) is revealed only late in his life, in his autobiographical cataloguing of his works (which may not be complete). The texts often circulated anonymously, their identifications to be conjectured or elucidated by later scholars from Honorius's descriptions of their contents. While some writers proclaimed their authorship, the attitude of others is put succinctly in the preface to the *Liber derivationum* (a massive etymological dictionary) produced in the 1160s. The authorship (and perhaps authority) of the work was ascribed to God; the writer, Huguccio of Pisa, claimed for himself only the status of an 'instrument' in its production.[34]

Although the changes often appear tentative, something new was definitely happening to increase 'self-awareness'. The very fact of academic and intellectual contention presupposes self-reliance on the part of the contenders. The emphasis on reason and argument rather than authority forced thinkers to defend themselves and their ideas, and to be willing to strike out independently. This sense of independence is clear from the career of Abelard. It also appears with Rupert of Deutz: despite his monastic status he forcefully defended his own views against the world, engaged in intellectual battles, and challenged Augustine. Without that self-reliance, that self-assurance, there would have been none of the intellectual debates, and probably none of the intellectual advances.

But the penetration of a sense of personality, which may be individualism, might have gone further. Here we have to look sideways, at that medieval Reformation which has so far been left out. One of its

---

34 Wolfgang P. Müller, *Huguccio: the Life, Works, and Thought of a Twelfth-Century Jurist*, Studies in medieval and early modern canon law, 3 (Washington, DC, 1994), pp. 36–7.

key features is its involvement of the laity, and the promotion of a sense of choice reflected in the idea of conversion. The element of choice, of personal responsibility for moral and spiritual decisions, presupposes the ability to make such choices. It is hardly surprising that the twelfth century revived the old problem of free will against predestination as an aspect of the search for salvation. For many debaters this might have been merely an intellectual exercise, especially for monks who were by definition among those almost guaranteed salvation. For others the problem of salvation was more intense. Free will forces choices; choices entail responsibility and accountability; improper choices may merit punishment, even damnation. In the twelfth century the laity began to voice a real concern for a personal salvation. Guibert of Nogent's mother, nameless as she is in his autobiography, represents this movement of anxiety about a salvation which was achievable by making the right choices. Several of the changes in practical Christianity which occurred during the long twelfth century can be fitted into this process: the emphasis on sin and confession (and, as a necessary corollary, absolution); a stress on works as a means to salvation; the alleviation of the old rigour of penitential satisfaction for sin and its replacement by a more manageable process; the theologians' adoption of Purgatory; the spread of indulgences (notably the plenary indulgence of the crusades); and the movement for annual lay communion. As the thirteenth-century pastoral revolution took hold, so the ground was prepared for that strand of late medieval religion which is sometimes labelled semi-Pelagian, a label which by definition requires personal awareness. If the focus of attention lies with the soul, and its movement towards God and away from a preceding state of sinfulness, that may be an implicit rejection of the self (or, at least, of its selfishness). Yet it still asserts an awareness of human particularity, and of a personal and to some extent private relationship with God. Such awareness of personal responsibility does not automatically produce a positive outlook, especially when the responsibility is for sin, and the outcome determines eternity. Some twelfth-century writers certainly were positive in their hopes for humanity: Alan of Lille wrote with confidence and expansive erudition in his *Anticlaudianus*, anticipating the creation of a new man (possibly a new mankind) who would overcome all vices. The period also saw the emergence of a strand of pessimistic writing, best exemplified in a work of Lothar of Segni, the future Pope Innocent III. His *De miseria condicionis humane* (*On the Misery of the Human Condition*, also known as *De contemptu mundi*) was meant to be paired by another work on the delights of the human condition, but it may be significant that the treatise on misery was written first, that the work on dignity remained unwritten, and that Innocent's tract was among the most reproduced works of the middle ages. Whether it can be taken to mark the inception of a 'guilt culture' which afflicted Europe through to the eighteenth century is less certain,[35] but it shows an awareness of the human condition, and the need for each individual to provide an appropriate response to it.

At the external level, the acceptance of particularity and personality is most effectively demonstrated in changing attitudes to marriage. If the imposition of annual confession in 1215 was a crucial recognition of the personal conscience, of interiority against exteriority, then the insistence that the partners' declaration of mutual consent was the constitutive act in a marriage also recognised and supported the choices of the particular human against the pressures and demands of membership of a wider group, in this case the family. Christina of Markyate's determined refusal to marry, against the equally determined insistence of her family that she should, nevertheless points to a tension in attitudes. Such choices, and insistence on particularity, could operate in other ways, between religions, and in choosing heresy (this being not the simple choice of a wrong belief, but a persistent refusal to change back to conform to the beliefs of the Church). If the key issue of salvation was the problem of evil, and personal responsibility and accountability for evil, then people might choose between solutions to that problem. Part of Catharism's appeal may have been that it offered a less demanding and more mechanistic solution to the problem of evil than the very personal responsibility imposed by Christianity.

Despite what has been said about group identity and role models as ways of creating personal identity, clashes could occur between insistence on particularity and participation in a broader group. Where that entailed rejection of the group – whether family at its smallest, or Christianity at its largest – recrimination and exclusion, a denial of the right to particularity, would result. To some extent the creation of a persecuting society, in the discriminatory attitudes adopted to various minorities during the period, acknowledged that society consisted of people aware of, and asserting, their particularity, their ability to make choices and to live accordingly.

† † †

35 Jean Delumeau, *Sin and Fear: the Emergence of a Western Guilt Culture, 13th–18th Centuries* (New York, 1990).

Insofar as these disparate strands can be drawn together, the changes of the long twelfth century amount to a fundamental reconstruction of the intellectual and perhaps psychological foundations of western Europe. Beginning among a relatively small group, the intellectuals, the changes in philosophy and theological thought were to remain mainly the preserve of intellectuals, although a watered-down version of the theological demands would be more widely distributed as the pastoral revolution of the thirteenth century took hold. The psychological changes are more problematic: they clearly appear among a wider group, which included at least members of the religious orders. A more popular impact is harder to determine, at least specifically in the short twelfth century, simply because of the lack of personal statements from the laity. Yet the evidence of spiritual ferment among the laity suggests that there was a broader acceptance of the changes, again a recognition of the responsibilities and obligations (both personal and communal) of particular people. However, the group mentality also remained strong, especially in the family. The emergence of a new lay spirituality in the thirteenth century, with a growing emphasis on private devotion and personal accountability, nevertheless shows that the psychological changes had found a broader base. The lines of intellectual and spiritual development which would affect western Europe until at least the sixteenth century had now been established.

6

The arts, vernacular literature, and music

T HE preceding chapters have unashamedly focused on matters Latinate, whether literary or intellectual, while largely ignoring the vernacular and the non-textual. That emphasis can and should be questioned. The long twelfth century also saw extensive change in other spheres. The development and proliferation of poetry and romances in vernacular literatures signals a major cultural breakthrough. Alongside, the prominence ascribed to painting, sculpture, and architecture in the traditional Renaissance, which makes it for many a period in art history rather than in literature or thought, virtually commands some consideration of artistic aspects of the twelfth century. Yet, aside from general comments on Romanesque style and the rise of Gothic, art, architecture, and sculpture rarely receive much detailed attention in discussions of that century. Music also changed, but it is usually comprehensively ignored. Incorporating these areas into the present survey is problematic. Haskins cited 'the complete development of Romanesque art and the rise of Gothic', and 'the full bloom of vernacular poetry, both lyric and epic', as likely constituents of his twelfth-century renaissance,[1] but gave them no detailed attention (and missed out music). For Panofsky, in contrast, art history defined the 'proto-renaissance'.[2] Art historians appear to have made most effort to tie developments to the renaissance label; literary historians seem less concerned overall, perhaps because of the very different issues which arise in their field. Even for art history, integration creates problems: in relation to a classical tradition, for instance, attention has been drawn to the 'structural differences between *borrowing* from Antiquity in the visual arts and antique *tradition*

1 Charles Homer Haskins, *The Renaissance of the Twelfth Century* (Cambridge, MA, 1927), p. 6.
2 Erwin Panofsky, *Renaissance and Renascences in Western Art* (London, 1970), pp. 55–68.

in other areas of intellectual life'(although the extremism of the contrast might be hard to sustain in practice).[3] Different rules and constraints do apply; there are particular technical issues, different questions about relationships with the past and the evolutions which occurred. It can, accordingly, be argued that to include the arts under the renaissance umbrella 'makes sense only if the term "renaissance" is used in the loosest sense of a "flowering", a quickening of pace, a concentration of creative effort'.[4]

Disciplinary frontiers conspire with other factors to make a co-ordinated and comprehensive survey almost impossible. The only viable approach must be a blunt division: a discussion of the visual arts (where architecture takes pride of place), followed by a comment on the vernacular writings. The treatment is unavoidably somewhat sketchy and perfunctory; yet here, perhaps more than in any of the other chapters, there arises one of the major issues in the identification of a 'renaissance': is it a movement which necessarily borrows from the past (however it uses those borrowings), or is it one where what really matters is a seismic shift in cultural foundations to provide the basis for a new period of development?

Visual arts

The logistics of survival mean that the extant art of the period available for comment is primarily architectural: the buildings themselves, sculpture, and associated decorative works; though the earthquakes in Italy in 1997 showed that even their survival is fortuitous. Among the gaps, no tradition of 'portable painting' (in the sense that we would now consider something a painting) can be assessed until the thirteenth century. While chairs, saddles, and chests might well be decorated with pictures, most painting survives as wall-paintings. The only really portable paintings appear to have been icons, which certainly existed in Italy, and were treasured. These, however, were mainly of Greek origin (but might be repainted or copied). An equivalent to portable paintings might be book illumination, which was a vital and expanding area of artistic activity. Equally important was work in precious (and non-precious) metals:

3 Willibald Sauerländer, 'Architecture and the figurative arts: the north', in *Renaissance and Renewal in the Twelfth Century*, ed. Robert L. Benson and Giles Constable (with Carol D. Lanham), (Oxford, 1982; reprinted Toronto, Buffalo, and London, 1991), p. 671.

4 Ernst Kitzinger, 'The arts as aspects of a Renaissance: Rome and Italy', in *Renaissance and Renewal*, ed. Benson and Constable, p. 637.

notably gold, silver, and bronze objects produced mainly (but not exclusively) for religious purposes. The surviving works, taken alongside references in texts (like the description of the new shrine constructed at Bury St Edmunds under Abbot Samson) show that there was no lack of artistic production; discussion is hampered only by the loss of the objects themselves, and by the intellectual difficulty of unifying discussion of works as disparate as the Isle of Lewis chessmen, the Bayeux Tapestry, and the shrine of the Three Kings at Cologne.

One other important consideration must also be mentioned. The artistic development, at least for ecclesiastical art, has to be set against a background of debate over the very validity of art, especially in a monastic context. That art had to be used carefully, with two-dimensional works serving a didactic purpose and a ban on free-standing sculpture (other than a crucifix) lest idolatry result, was a long-standing precept. The twelfth century gave more precise expression to a sense of unease that art might distract rather than teach. To prevent this, the Cistercians advocated a rigid anti-artistic asceticism, reflected in the stark architecture of their early foundations (as at Sénanque, in southern France) and the lack of gold decoration in their texts (as in the extant works from the house at Sticna in Slovenia). The Cistercian legislation, and the statements of St Bernard, proposed a course of ecclesiastical cultural evolution which, if adopted, would have produced a very different art history in western Europe.

Against such asceticism stand many of the surviving monuments. How far there was a real debate about art in the twelfth century is not clear; but Abbot Suger at St Denis certainly felt obliged to respond to Bernard's strictures. His justifications gave not a mystical but a practical defence of art; of art *per se*, not of any particular new style which might have been evolving in his abbey. Suger's defence also dealt explicitly with monastic art: an art of symbolism for the educated to decipher (he specifically mentions that it would be fully comprehensible only to the *litterati*;[5] in fact the complexity of the St Denis decor perhaps soon made some of it incomprehensible even to them). That the Cistercians lost the battle was important; but their defeat does not mean that the battle can be ignored.

Simply because the buildings still stand, architecture takes priority in any discussion of the twelfth-century arts. The accidental role of twelfth-century buildings in the later Renaissance also validates its consideration

5 Conrad Rudolph, *Artistic Change at St-Denis: Abbot Suger's Program and the Early Twelfth-Century Controversy over Art* (Princeton, NJ, 1990), p. 61.

here. The fifteenth century's search for the antique was notably side-tracked precisely in terms of architecture. The baptistry at Florence, constructed in the twelfth century, provided the architectural precedent for the reconstructed Romanness sought by Brunelleschi, being considered too good to be a product of so recent a time. (In Brunelleschi's defence, it has to be admitted that even current commentators are not certain whether the baptistry was a completely new building, or the restoration of an Early Christian edifice.)

That said, the sheer range of architectural achievement in the long twelfth century once more raises a basic question about labelling this a period of 'renaissance': how far was there one single, coherent, and cohesive movement? Artistic production in all periods (at least up to the twentieth century, and in some respects still) has been notoriously regionalised, responding to different physical requirements and resources, different intellectual and emotional stimuli. To agglomerate all the varying regional styles which appear in the twelfth century under a single umbrella may be invalid.

Nevertheless, the architectural history does seem to fall into two broad swathes. North of the Alps the trend is generally summarised as a move from Romanesque to Gothic. Yet Romanesque reached its peak during the late eleventh and twelfth centuries – notably in the churches of Anglo-Norman England – and so must be viewed as a movement in its own right, not just an obsolescent style. Its ripple effect was still apparent in the second half of the twelfth century, as the French architectural style imported into Britain with the Norman Conquest worked its way north. A major Romanesque building, the cathedral of St Magnus at Kirkwall in Orkney, was begun probably in 1137. Romanesque parish churches – like that whose apse survives at Leuchars in Scotland – were probably being built even later. Further north, to bring Scandinavia into the net, several Romanesque cathedrals were erected during the twelfth century. Scandinavia indeed highlights the question of regional styles, since numerous Norwegian churches of this time were built entirely of wood – 'stave churches' – often using motifs also found in stone buildings. That at Urnes, dated to c. 1160, is effectively Romanesque in wood, probably influenced by recent work at Trondheim, although the carving on the capitals fuses in the inherited Nordic style. Scandinavian churches were also built in stone (which was perhaps replacing wood in places by the end of the century), and building in brick also began to appear around 1200. Initiated with Abbot Suger's architectural experiments at St Denis, Gothic had established itself as the increasingly fashionable style by 1200, but while gaining ground in France had not yet swept the board. Yet

Gothic had burst out of its French heartland even in the twelfth century, occurring as far north as Trondheim and Orkney by the 1190s. Its expansion was not universal: while it moved into Spain in the 1220s, what might be called 'pure Gothic' made little headway in Italy south of Lombardy.

Artistic trends would obviously follow colonists, and the transmission of new styles in the twelfth century owed much to the plantation of new religious orders. The 'traditional' Cistercian monastic plan, for instance, could be imposed whatever the location. Internationalism, participation in a broad cultural community, would also permit the exchange of ideas, to allow some homogenisation of taste over relatively long distances, from the crusader states of the Holy Land to the west of England. But taste could never be totally homogenised. Gothic in Tuscany and Umbria fused with earlier architectural styles to create a distinctive hybrid form in which old Roman influences were highly important. Most Italian Gothic dates from the thirteenth century, like the cathedral at Siena, begun in the 1220s. Southern Italy – the Norman kingdom – had its own tradition, affected by its Byzantine heritage. In the Iberian peninsula, despite the French influx which carried Gothic in its train, the Islamic architectural inheritance was not eradicated. To hide such disparate architectural histories under one label is clearly improper.

But if regional styles and identities are to be retained, how should they be tackled? How can they be placed under the heading of 'renaissance': as revival, rebirth, or new birth? Here, a separation of the antiquarian and the new styles – the Romanising and the Gothic – makes debate about the content and identity of a 'twelfth-century renaissance' especially concrete.

The possibility that a Romanising tendency existed revives all the issues encountered earlier about continuity, dependence, and the desire to re-establish a classical past. It also raises questions about how historians impose ideas on those whom they discuss. The use of the term 'Romanesque' implies a conscious tradition, which is at least implicitly deliberately Romanised. The tradition may be conscious; its Romanness may not. Most extant Romanesque buildings are churches. Their stylistic similarity is established by their rounded arches and their apses, and they may once also have been covered with whitewashed plaster. Of these features, the rounded arch may just reflect a technological necessity: if the mechanics of the pointed arch were not understood (although they were in Burgundy, even as part of the region's Romanesque architecture), there were few other options when using stone. Romanness would be an irrelevant issue. The apses and plaster may suggest a more conscious

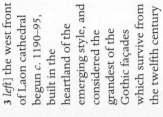

The new Gothic architecture:

3 *left*] the west front of Laon cathedral begun *c.* 1190–95, built in the heartland of the emerging style, and considered the grandest of the Gothic façades which survive from the twelfth century

4 *right*] the south side of the nave of Laon cathedral, looking east. Built *c.* 1175–90. The style is still to some extent transitional from Romanesque, but still manages to convey a sense of structural lightness.

adherence to traditions, possibly more consciously Roman. However, they might be even more consciously ecclesial: by tradition churches had apses, were covered with painted plaster; for buildings to look like churches, they had to match the model. The builders' style might, accordingly, be more consciously Christian than Roman. That said, however, a new stylistic pattern was being imposed on some churches of the period: the eleventh-century chronicler Ralph Glaber (d. c. 1046) commented on the widespread rebuilding of churches which took off in the early 1000s, beginning in Italy and France. The multitude of white-coated churches which he refers to – some rebuilt even though the preceding structures were still perfectly usable – clearly reflected both novelty and fashion. As the movement took hold in more northerly areas, the main novelty might be in the fact that the churches were now stone-built, rather than wooden. In England, plaster-covered basilicas (like the first post-Conquest version of York Minster) were certainly new. Some at the time – among them the historian William of Malmesbury – perhaps saw the stylistic innovation as one consequence of conquest, as the imposition of a kind of Norman architectural yoke, rather than showing the revival of a classical heritage.

The one region where consciousness of the classical past almost certainly did affect architectural practice was Italy. There the Roman legacy was unavoidably visible, and still being maintained. Certainly architectural continuity persisted in Rome itself: St Peter's had the antiquity of its Constantinian origins, an antiquity shared with many other churches. The pagan Pantheon was now a church; baths and basilicas had been converted. If anywhere should have had a sense of 'heritage' in the twelfth century, it was Rome. Other parts of Italy would have been equally conscious of the past, but the assertion of continuity there was probably less of an imperative.

At Rome, the urge was to be 'Roman'. For the popes, continuity with the past was critical: the tradition – the 'handing on' – had to continue. The successor to St Peter and Silvester I (the latter being invoked here because he was the alleged recipient of the Donation of Constantine) had to assert that continuity. Old churches had to be kept up, and augmented, to ensure that the papal message was constantly restated. Artistic patronage in Rome was the most immediate and durable weapon for papal propaganda, used for example in the frescoes depicting imperial humiliations in the struggles of the reform period. Roman precedents were accordingly followed even when new churches were constructed, as at S. Clemente, where the rebuilt church of c. 1125 retained the shape and character of a Roman basilica, and reused some components of its sixth-century precursor. It cannot be assumed that this following of models was always (or even normally) a conscious adherence to antique patterns. They might be followed because they were the norm, and reflected an ideology rather than being merely an architectural heritage.

Unquestioning continuity was sometimes supplemented by conscious restoration, although exactly how people looked back to the architectural past is hard to fathom. In Provence, for instance, although Roman-style motifs and features appear, they are scattered rather than integrated, seemingly copied with little care for stylistic coherence or original purpose. Incongruously combined with non-Roman features, they suggest an eclectic rather than antiquarian view of the past, creating a sense of pastiche rather than classicism. On the other hand, Abbot Desiderius at Monte Cassino used columns from Rome in his rebuilding of the abbey, and the reuse of old material was naturally not uncommon in Rome itself. Farther afield, there are some suggestions that the past was appreciated for being classical: Henry of Blois, bishop of Winchester (d. 1171), reportedly carted Roman columns back to England for his buildings. Suger also planned to transport columns from Rome, but in the end turned elsewhere, to suggest other impulses from the past: his building reused Merovingian columns which were already on site, and drew on Merovingian motifs in the carving. The use of local leftovers also occurred at Canterbury, where columns from Roman ruins were transferred to the rebuilt Christ Church.

While the role of the classical heritage remains somewhat problematic, the northern transition from Romanesque to Gothic appears to offer a case of real novelty. Perhaps here, if anywhere, 'renaissance' should mean birth rather than rebirth, although the deliberate and conscious building programmes also make this a time of renewal. The architectural history is, however, more than just a process of transition: the years to c. 1150 also witness the fruition of Romanesque as a style which, because of the adoption of Gothic (or the totality of the switch), never had the time – or perhaps the complexity – to become stale and decadent. The lengthy stability of Romanesque architectural style in continental Europe, going back almost to the Carolingians, often means that its continued vitality into the twelfth century (and, indeed, into the thirteenth) is overlooked; but it should not be. In the new major buildings of Anglo-Norman England, notably the castles and cathedrals, Romanesque was actually a regional novelty. Arguably, though, Romanesque reached its stylistic peak in England, much as contemporary intellectual traditions culminated in the encyclopedic compilations of the mid-1100s. For most of the period

Romanesque architecture was the dominant form north of the Alps. Gothic usurped its place eventually, but slowly. Gothic's great efflorescence came after 1200; until then most major ecclesiastical buildings were Romanesque in style, unless deliberately rebuilt. The architecture of major secular buildings in England was also Romanesque during this period; the equivalent of the new monasteries and cathedrals appears in castles like the Tower of London, or in surviving stone houses like those in Lincoln.

On the available evidence, Gothic architecture is northern Europe's most significant contribution to the artistic changes. Nevertheless, it poses some difficulties. Just where the impetus towards the new form came from remains unclear. Clearly it reflects technological advance: the move from the round to the pointed arch, and an awareness of the need to deal with the changed flow of forces thus created within a building; the reduction in the building's mass by changing the thickness of pillars and increasing the area of the windows; the increased height of the buildings, and the introduction of vaulting. This could result from trial and error, the successful experiments setting a widespread fashion, the failures collapsing in unrecorded catastrophe. The problem of origins is matched by that of transference, of explaining why Gothic became so popular. That, though, is a very different issue, which involves questions of fashion and patronage, of the spread of building techniques and technologies, and of the availability of funding for new projects.

Such matters cannot be addressed here. More important is the nature of the changes, and their cultural significance for the period. Here, Suger's reflections on his innovations at the abbey church of St Denis – the archetypal, and effectively the prototypical Gothic church – are extremely important. These comments stress the spiritual and religious significance of a new way of building, which would increase the light, especially through stained glass (this certainly made the church's interior more jewel-like, but not necessarily any lighter). The idea that architecture could transform a church into a miniature heaven on earth, a foretaste of the celestial Jerusalem, was a prime stimulus. Much is made of the possible influence of the light-based mysticism of the pseudo-Dionysius as a defining idea in Suger's schemes (pseudo-Dionysius being mistaken for Dionysius the Areopagite associated with St Paul, and conflated with St Denis as apostle and martyr of the Gauls to produce the patron saint of Suger's abbey). However, the validity of the Dionysian label is questionable in terms of what Suger actually said and did. Perhaps more important was a rather mundane concern: in a pilgrim church like St Denis, the pilgrims had to be impressed. The new techniques of building and decoration offered new opportunities to do that, in art which 'functioned

5] *The spread of Gothic*: The architect Villard de Honnecourt's view of the interior of the chapel choir at the newly built Rheims cathedral, *c.* 1235. The comments (in French) suggest that the drawings were also to serve as architectural patterns.

visually as part of a sensory saturation of the holy place which combined with the liturgy and the proximity of the sacred to overwhelm the visitor'.[6]

Building to get closer to God gave the new Gothic a very specialised purpose: this was a style whose transference to secular buildings would need its own justification. The search for an explanation, however, remains no more than guesswork: perhaps an appreciation that larger window areas increased the amount of light available internally; possibly a kind of inertia, as masons became used to working to patterns which had ecclesiastical origins; or simply a matter of fashion. Gothic features did make the cross-over, but a specifically Gothic style of secular architecture is rare before the late thirteenth century. Perhaps the fact that most secular architecture which survives from the time is military helps to explain that. While Romanesque provides an identifiable style for castle building, this may be largely coincidental, because that was the current style when stone fortifications began to be built. Later castle building, while evolving to face changing military needs, and creating impressive structures like Krak des Chevaliers in the crusader County of Tripoli, is more reticent about changing to an explicitly Gothic style (partly because the decoration was obviously superfluous). Gothic style may have been more visible in the domestic quarters which rarely survive, and pointed arches were used internally.

The architectural styles of the long twelfth century often developed in conjunction with ancillary arts which had architectural functions: notably sculpture, stained (or painted) glass, and mosaic. Sculpture and buildings are effectively inseparable: free-standing stone sculpture is unknown from before the late twelfth century (unless some tomb sculpture counts as free-standing). Indeed, a significant evolution of the period is the gradual movement towards recreating free-standing stone sculpture, and the erosion of the ban on statuary in all materials lest it provoke idolatry. The first moves towards the revival of stone figure sculpture (leaving aside an insular tradition in Britain which appears anomalous) occurred in southern France, around 1000. The abbey of Moissac lays claim to be the place where the revival first began, the early works appearing almost like murals in stone. Thereafter, a process of ever-increasing relief, and ever-decreasing contact with the building, allowed for more effective representation. A defining moment in the shift from Romanesque to Gothic was the appearance of figures attached to columns, as in the portals at St Denis and Chartres. (But at St Denis Suger did build within

6 Rudolph, *Artistic Change*, p. 65.

the recognised constraints: his church contained no free-standing images of saints.) From column-statues it was a short move to figures which could stand independently in niches, as some did by the late 1100s; but the architectural setting and function remain important, and perhaps the fact that such niche statues are not isolated artefacts. It would be worth knowing who had the audacity and temerity to produce the first free-standing stone image to provide an independent devotional (or other) focus: this was a change of considerable potential and implications, yet it seemingly occurred without comment.

Architectural sculpture occurs predominantly in capitals and corbels, and in the use of figure sculptures in portals and columns. The art is often lively, showing a wide range of human activity with considerable naturalistic flair, notably on capitals and corbels. Much of this carving is small scale, indeed almost invisible in the normal confines of a church. Its status as 'public art' is therefore questionable: it becomes almost decoration for its own sake, addressed to no one. The vitality of the carving is often striking, as is the elaboration. How far this was really a new movement of the twelfth century is not clear: the Cistercian insistence on architectural and decorative austerity suggests that earlier sculpture was equally elaborate but has left little trace. Some certainly suggests continuity in a non-Roman style. The masks on the capitals at Leuchars in Scotland, and the strange sculptures around St Andrew's church at Pershore in Worcestershire – both twelfth-century in date – seem almost anachronistically Anglo-Viking in appearance, suggesting a marriage of heritages rather than a consciously new pattern.

The figure sculpture is sometimes linked to the debate about individualism, the carving being considered increasingly realistic and suggesting attempts at real portraiture. Such deductions are not wholly convincing: assessment of individuality is usually a subjective response produced by the eye of the beholder, perhaps particularly when dealing with the barely visible capital and corbel sculpture which is now often considered 'marginal' (and by extension more 'popular' and 'unlearned'). There is a danger of circularity in the argument here: the scuptors of these 'marginal' works are usually unknown, but because current reactions to the works consider them more naturalistic, it is assumed that the carvings (at least of appropriate craftsmen) are self-portraits; and only 'individuals' would produce self-portraits. The argument cannot, though, be applied to other, more prominent, works (apart, possibly, from tomb sculpture). The elongated figures in the portals of Chartres cathedral are certainly different, from each other and from what preceded them. Their separateness perhaps conveys particularity; but the serenity of their features, and their shapely incongruity, prevent them from being mistaken for real people. There is little which is immediately 'emotional' in the representations. These figures appear, indeed, more unreal than some slightly earlier English figure sculpture, the statues of Moses and John the Evangelist once in St Mary's abbey, York.

Equally, there may have been greater awareness of the artist's role, as the maker claimed credit for his work.[7] Some artists and craftsmen doubtless had widespread reputations; and leading masons did move around to fulfil commissions. But artistic self-proclamation remained limited; for all artistic production the patron remained 'the maker', the one who caused it to be made. As with the writing of the book produced by Huguccio of Pisa,[8] the craftsman was merely an instrument of the creative process. The notion of 'the artist' did not exist. Equally, while teams of masons moved from site to site – like the group from Durham who moved up to Scotland – their individual identities are unrecorded.

Among the other 'architectural arts', development varied considerably. Wall-painting, possibly the most significant aspect of interior decoration in Romanesque churches, remained a major form, but the growing use of glass in Gothic buildings obviously reduced the wall-area available for such work. The production of stained glass was one of the most dynamic of the architectural arts, stimulated by the rise of Gothic building with its larger windows, and the massive building programmes of the period. The glazing programmes at places like Chartres and Canterbury were major artistic and technical endeavours. This was a change of form and function: in some ways Gothic glass functions like murals in a new medium. However, the nature of the message also altered with the shift to glass. Perhaps because their translucence could be exploited, the windows became more intricate than murals had been, serving a complex didactic purpose which made them more clearly 'books for the unlearned'. Complex iconography also allowed the various levels of reading the Bible to be transferred to glass, as in the windows in Canterbury cathedral, or at St Denis. However, as with sculpture, much of the detail would have been invisible from ground level (as much of it still is); and to understand the stories required either an expositor or prior knowledge about how to crack the code. Such visualisation of biblical interpretation places glass alongside equivalent manuscript productions, notably the moralised Bibles of the early thirteenth century. Yet, with the

7 Above, pp. 147–8.
8 Above, p. 148.

many foci for attention within a major church (images, shrines, and so on), with the likely numbers of people present, perhaps also with the constant distraction of building work, how many people would take time to read the windows? How much of the real appreciation would be lost in the 'sensory saturation of the holy place'?[9] The jewel-house of light would impress, but might not improve, its viewers; although the impact may have been considerable on those who did use the windows to aid contemplation. Medieval visions owed much to external visual stimuli, and the new images in glass would have provided an obvious source.

Less complex, and less discussed, is the use of mosaic as an art form, especially in church decoration. This is perhaps because the focus on the shift from Romanesque to Gothic is a northern phenomenon, and mosaic (or, at least, ceiling and wall mosaic) was almost exclusively confined to Italy. (Suger, ever exceptional, installed a mosaic in a portal of his new church at St Denis, but this seems to have been a unique northern instance.) The Italian evolution was a conscious revival of an old art, owing much to the popes of the mid-twelfth century. However, it was not a total novelty at that point: the tradition, perhaps in this case more Byzantine than truly Roman, had continued in Venice, and had recently been implanted in southern Italy. Its establishment can be ascribed to Abbot Desiderius of Monte Cassino when he rebuilt his church in the late eleventh century. Although initiated with Greek craftsmen, Italian mosaics soon developed their own style, and their own uses. Particularly important was the use of mosaic by the reform popes to recall early Christian Rome when redecorating Roman churches (as in the work commissioned by Innocent II for Sta Maria in Trastevere).Not all mosaic adopted the new forms. The major schemes at the Capella Palatina in Palermo and the cathedral of Monreale in Norman Sicily used imported Byzantine craftsmen, and Byzantine models, even where the architecture was not Greek in style.

Alongside the reintroduction of mosaic, Desiderius's floor pavement at Monte Cassino also reputedly revived a tradition lost for centuries. At least, the tradition had been lost in central Italy: mosaic floors were apparently more common further north, and were perhaps more traditional, with examples still extant at Aosta and St Denis (but the latter is fragmentary, and is an oddity in using materials normally encountered only in wall mosaics). The complex iconography on these northern floors contrasts with the geometric patterns of the pavements of major Italian churches of this time, showing a different inheritance. By 1200, northern

9 Above, pp. 160, 162.

mosaic floors were generally being replaced by tiles, often (as in several Cistercian churches) used to create a new form of mosaic with shapes being produced in fired clay as a kind of jigsaw puzzle of patterns.

There is also carving in other materials, notably ivory and wood. The wood might well be painted, or covered with gold leaf; stone figures were likewise painted. Even if little free-standing sculpture was created, antique survivals could be appreciated: besides carting columns from Rome to England, Henry of Blois, bishop of Winchester, supposedly collected other antiquities from the city. His activities are among the small amount of real evidence for a clear interest in the classical artistic past as specifically classical: Rome's main use for marble antique statuary was as a raw material for other purposes. Some examples were appreciated, and perhaps deliberately salvaged. Visitors might be especially impressed: the English 'Master Gregory' who produced a treatise on *The Wonders of the City of Rome* in the second half of the twelfth century was enraptured by one particular statue of a naked Venus. The fate of Henry of Blois's collection once back in England is unknown; it leaves no trace, unless reflected at second hand in fragments of capitals carved for his building projects.

Although direct connections are rarely evident, the twelfth century's awareness of the past perhaps encouraged a concern among others to exploit Rome. Some surviving carvings seem to be copied or derived from Roman models. How direct the link is is uncertain; or indeed whether it is real rather than assumed. Moreover, for every carving which suggests classical influence, many more do not. The dependence appears at its greatest in non-stone works, most strikingly in ivory work (often using walrus ivory rather than elephant). However, more likely derivations are either a continuity with Anglo-Saxon traditions, or (more probable in continental cases) a link with Byzantium, and only thence to Rome. Of course, contacts with Constantinople also affected regional traditions: across large areas of Italy, and perhaps the crusader states, the Byzantine link with Rome permitted the unconscious continuance of a classical tradition, now most evident in somewhere like St Mark's in Venice. Yet a propensity to see Byzantine influence has to be kept in check: the Greek impact on western art, although seemingly clear, is often elusive. It is perhaps best summarised as 'essentially a midwife service'.[10]

10 Ernst Kitzinger, 'The Byzantine contribution to western art of the twelfth and thirteenth centuries', in Ernst Kitzinger (ed. W. Eugene Kleinbauer), *The Art of Byzantium and the Medieval West: Selected Studies* (Bloomington, IN, and London, 1976), p. 377.

Stylistic similarities can be shown, and direct dependence established in some cases, especially in Italy. There the influence of icons is visible in the thirteenth century with the appearance of paintings of the Virgin and of other saints. More broadly, and further back in time, links are postulated more than proved. Given the distribution of Byzantine works in the west, influence is quite likely, but stimulating local evolutions rather than encouraging dependence. What has been called 'parallelism' seems a more plausible outcome.[11]

Moving from the architectural works which often survive in situ, or at least in close proximity to their original sites, to the more portable types of art, new issues arise. This material is often highly mobile, and extremely uncertain in survival. While much can be labelled 'Romanesque' or 'Gothic', attempts to clarify connections and influences often rest on flimsy evidence. When many of the surviving works lack full provenances, have erratic distribution, survive only as fragments, or have been changed by restoration and remodelling, firm conclusions are necessarily elusive. Artists, artefacts, and influences were mobile, as even the architectural arts show: English artists painted murals in the Aragonese monastery of Sigena in the late twelfth century; craftsmen from Verona perhaps travelled to Magdeburg c. 1153 to cast the bronze plates which were to form the doors of the cathedral at Płock in Poland.

Moreover, attitudes to works of art were highly variable. Precious metals could easily be converted into bullion if need arose, and frequently were. Remodelling, additions, and relocations were frequent, as shown in many of the surviving works. This could happen also with artefacts which had survived from the past, or had been recently acquired from different cultures. At St Denis, for instance, Suger added new gold mountings to an old porphyry vase, transforming both the vase and its purpose; other vessels, including recent imports from the east, were similarly transformed, as he sometimes acknowledged in added inscriptions. A similar problem of remodelling, and therewith uncertainty about attitudes to and awareness of the past, also affects some illustrations (and texts) of the period. Classical gods are often shown as twelfth-century characters. Such anachronistic modernity is most obvious in religious works. The Bible moralisée, a thirteenth-century text which unites illustrations and French text in a summary of several Old Testament books, makes the past all but contemporary. The Philistines become Saracens, soldiers knights, and the Temple a mosque.

11 For parallelism, Kitzinger, 'The Byzantine contribution', p. 371.

6] *Vernacular scriptures and anachronistic history*: The Bible as a French picture book, with modernisation and allegorised meaning, from a copy of the *Bible moralisée*, produced c. 1215–30. In this summary of 1 Kings 5.2–6.5 the top six roundels depict the events, summarised in French alongside (the Philistines being called Saracens, the Temple a 'mahommeri' (mosque), and the idol Dagon a 'mahomet'). The bottom two roundels and attendant commentary allegorise the biblical text as an attack on avaricious and sodomitical prelates who are eventually brought to repent and abandon their sinful ways.

7] *'The Cloisters Cross'*: English walrus ivory, possibly from Bury St Edmunds. The back of the cross, showing prophets and the symbols of the Evangelists, with the Lamb of God at the centre. There is no consensus about when in the twelfth century it was made.

Similar anachronism occurs in other contexts, as in the Spanish *Auto de los reyes magos* (a fragment of a play dealing with the visit of the Three Kings to the Infant Christ), where one of Herod's rabbis swears by Allah. The main problem affecting artworks during this period is the lack of secure provenances, which bedevils analysis. When connoisseurship at best supplements hard evidence, at worst substitutes for it, the room for debate only increases. The 'Cloisters Cross', a crucifix in walrus ivory which is almost certainly English, and may come from Bury St Edmunds (but this is not absolutely established), has been ascribed dates scattered across the twelfth century. Attempts to establish its place in the stylistic evolutions accordingly provoke debate, over 'whether the cross anticipates changes of style from Romanesque to Gothic, is a mutation of the two, or is a late manifestation of Romanesque verging on the regressive'.[12] Problems of a slightly different kind arise towards the end of the century, when Nicholas of Verdun appears as the artist responsible (it seems) for a significant artistic shift, his new style of drapery in enamels for a pulpit at the abbey of Klosterneuburg near Vienna (completed in 1181). This was widely adopted over the next half century in several other media, including glass and manuscript painting. Much is made of Nicholas, and of a significant change which has been traced in his work over time. However, caution seems appropriate when his identity – and with it the construction of his whole career – rests only on two brief inscriptions separated by twenty-four years and some 500 miles.

These more portable arts are virtually impossible to deal with in a coherent pattern; although there are stylistic interconnections, each has its own history as a result of technical and other changes.

Book illumination remained a significant art form, in the way it could convey a message sharing many characteristics with contemporary glass. Localism was a significant factor: individual scriptoria had their own styles of illumination as well as of script, although there are general characteristics which mark the products as being from the period as a whole. The most important change was perhaps the growing availability of texts, partly the result of the appearance of vernacular works, and the extension of illumination beyond the liturgical sphere within which it had hitherto mainly been confined. As literacy increased, and as devotional practices spread among the laity, so the demand for illustrated texts also grew. An increasingly literate and literary culture could

12 Elizabeth C. Parker and Charles T. Little, *The Cloisters Cross: its Art and Meaning* (London, 1994), p. 238.

particularly use book illustrations as devotional foci. The emergence of the Book of Hours in the thirteenth century – small portable devotional miscellanies, used by individual readers as a private stimulus and source of prayer – effected a major shift in the demand for books, and their illuminations.

Developing techniques and changing demand (in quantity and quality) also affected evolutions in other art forms. Enamels became a prominent form over the course of the century, with the technique perhaps being imported from Spain into southern France, and then spreading north. Limoges gained a particular reputation as a centre for production. While there are major works in enamel, it is the small-scale production which perhaps best reflects the changing demand of the time, as in the little reliquary boxes linked with Becket and his cult. Enamel could be treated as a branch of metalworking, which in general became more refined, perhaps even audacious. This audacity is shown in the greater depth in relief in shrines and other works, and also in the production of what are effectively the first free-standing works, of which the most famous – despite being lost – must be the massive bronze lion cast for Duke Henry the Lion of Saxony. There are also masterpieces like the head reliquaries of St Alexander and John the Evangelist, the latter of which is often taken to be a representation of Emperor Frederick I. Such works might be considered in breach of the traditional ban on figure sculpture, but head reliquaries were known in earlier centuries, and possibly their function as mere containers for holy objects (and therefore no different from other containers shaped like arms or other body parts) obviated worries about idolatry. Concurrently, social demands also had an effect. Coins were relatively unimpressive, although the portraiture improved slightly, and the gold coins minted during the thirteenth century were prestige products. Seal engraving became more intricate. The mass production of pilgrim souvenirs in base metals at major shrines is another change which can be considered artistic, even if some of the products are rather crude.

The different types and potential markets for pilgrim souvenirs might provide the basis for a debate about the evolution of distinct 'high' and 'low' cultures during this period, but the available evidence is too sparse to justify that. Yet changes at all levels and in all types of artistic production (including those for which there is extremely scant evidence, like textiles) must be included in the analysis of the period's cultural transformations.

Most of this art, despite the existence of some prominent secular objects, served religious purposes, in an ecclesiastical setting, to stimulate and record devotion. It therefore also stands as a record of changing patterns of spirituality and devotional practice, something which links it in with the intellectual and theological changes of the period. In registering those changes, the central image is that of the crucifix. At this focal point of Christian devotion, significant changes in the nature of the depiction raise major issues in art history, and for the history of emotions. Over the long twelfth century the standard form of the Crucifixion changed in every art form. Although it caused considerable comment, even anguish, the move from depictions with four nails (one for each hand and foot) to those showing three (a single nail through both feet) is relatively unimportant. Much more critical was the shift from a Christ triumphant on the Cross to a Christ who suffers. Until *c.* 1150 carved crucifixes (but not necessarily manuscript illustrations) normally showed Christ crowned on the Cross with a royal diadem, obviously alive, not in torment. The Cross serves almost as a backdrop to the figure. Images of a Christ in pain existed earlier, but only between 1100 and 1250 did a general shift occur. With increasing frequency, Christ was shown in agony, crowned (if at all) with thorns, slumped close to death, humiliated and suffering. The Cross ceased to be a podium, and became the cause of the pain. The suffering Christ demanded an emotional response because of the agony, because of the humanity, because of the personality and emotion in the carving. (Similar emotions are also elicited in manuscript illustrations.) In stark – very stark – contrast to other contemporary carving, the new-style crucifixes transform the debate about the recognition of personality and individuality, and the rise of humanism as the appreciation of human experience, into key issues. The new crucifix invites cross-reference to other novel strands of contemporary spirituality, especially the changing theology of the Incarnation, and the search for answers to the question of 'Why did God become Man?' It points towards the highly Christocentric and emotional spirituality of the thirteenth century which is often labelled 'Franciscan', but which clearly grew out of changes which had occurred before 1200.

The overall picture suggested by an admittedly broad survey of the visual arts is one of change and evolution in all spheres, sometimes dynamic, often steady and relatively unremarkable. Some changes might be interpreted as rebirth, others as marking a renewal or a new start; but overall, and making allowances for what has been lost over the centuries, the long twelfth century was undeniably one when artistic production reached new heights of technical excellence. There were massive quantitative and qualitative changes, although these often reflected specific opportunities and priorities. Insofar as the developments were facilitated by changed social conditions, notably the development of a money economy and the establishment of relative peace, which perhaps allowed for a broadening of the market and wider access to works which were in turn specifically produced to satisfy that greater demand, some of the production must also reflect those structural changes, and the potential which they unleashed.

Vernacular literature

Alongside the manifold developments in the visual arts, which challenge any idea of a twelfth-century renaissance that relies primarily on retrospection, a change in the verbal arts also occurred which was potentially the most important cultural change in the whole period; one whose implications, worked out over later centuries, could not have been anticipated. The stress on a Latinate culture which provides the basic parameters for assessment of medieval intellectual life constantly threatens to marginalise the non-Latin cultures in which everyone (including the Latinate elite) shared. This vernacular world rarely impinges on that of the twelfth-century intellectuals, unless they voluntarily demean themselves to participate in it, mainly by preaching. It was, however, clearly irrupting into the world of the literate. The emergence of vernacular texts, the creation of a literate vernacular culture, was one of the main legacies of the long twelfth century. In the long run it offered an effective challenge to Latin's pre-eminence, so that where works from the time are known to have existed in both Latin and vernacular versions, in some instances only the latter have survived. This applies with the lives of Olaf Tryggvason, king of Norway, composed in Latin in Iceland by Oddr Snorrason and Gunnlaugr Leifsson, who may have overseen their almost immediate translation into Icelandic.

The rise of vernacular literatures was a giant step in western Europe's cultural history. The nature of the change, however, varied considerably, and it would be misguided to cram all the different genres into a single bundle. Moreover, it is important not to focus exclusively on novelty, and thereby ignore continuity. Old Norse had been a literary language before the period began, and functioned as such after its end, notably in the sagas. It could therefore import influences to affect the style of its literature, rather than emerge in 'new' forms. Signs of a 'courtly love' tradition accordingly affect the Norse poetry produced in Orkney from the 1160s.

Continuity also applies to a non-Latin language which was geographically most widespread, and arguably had the longest history, but whose existence in western Europe is usually ignored and still (it seems) little studied: Hebrew. While it was a learned language, and a fundamental component of Jewish identity, most Jews were presumably bilingual so that they could function in their surrounding societies. Yet Hebrew may also have been a first language, at least for purposes of writing, as some texts survive in other languages transliterated into Hebrew characters. Most Hebrew works would have been biblical and rabbinical texts, with polemical anti-Christian texts also being produced during the twelfth century, and old texts rewritten (of these the Talmud was the most important for present purposes, given the major Christian assault on its religious status in the thirteenth century). Hebrew was also used for business contracts and bonds, with many minor documents and miscellaneous jottings surviving from the period. A 'fictional' Hebrew literature remains elusive, although there is evidence of a flourishing poetic tradition, at least in Spain.

Other languages revealed different patterns of emergence rather than continuity. The emergence of English, as distinct from Anglo-Saxon, from the shadows of the Norman Conquest was a slow process. That England had a living tradition of written vernacular in the twelfth century, whose scale is inadequately revealed by the surviving material, is shown by the continuation of the Anglo-Saxon Chronicle at Peter-borough through to 1154, by the existence of an Anglo-Saxon version of the *Elucidarius* of Honorius Augustodunensis, and by the inclusion of works like *Solomon and Saturn* in twelfth-century manuscripts. Such texts show that Anglo-Saxon remained a viable language used for reading, writing, and composing for some generations after 1066. The *Elucidarius* even suggests the continuity of an 'academic' Anglo-Saxon. By 1200 something more obviously 'English' had emerged, although exactly when is debated. The twelfth-century dating of *The Owl and the Nightingale* is now challenged, meaning that the first surviving Middle English works may derive only from the first years of the thirteenth century, in Layamon's *Brut* and the peculiar *Ormulum*.

The appearance of texts in Anglo-Norman and French follows a different course, with its own features. (A further nuance here is that contemporaries referred to 'French' as 'roman', which may be suggestive of the self-perception of those using the language.) There is a difference between totally new composition, like the work of Chrétien de Troyes, and a process of writing down (even if this entails altering) an oral tradition, as with the *Song of Roland*. French vernacular works date back into the eleventh century; and French material from the long twelfth century establishes many of the literary genres applied to study of the period, from *chansons de geste* to romances and *fabliaux* (short comic tales, which quite often stray into obscenity). For French literature this was a time of change and instability, which it might indeed be inappropriate to call evolution. This situation continued in the thirteenth century, a time 'characterized by extensive experimentation with generic forms. Preexisting literary genres are fused, deconstructed, and recombined in a dazzling array of hybrids, which in turn give rise to further innovations ... [a] vital process of generic transformation.'[13]

Developments in other areas were also nuanced. The close similarity of Italian and Latin, which possibly made them interchangeable in practice, has been used to explain the lack of Italian vernacular Bibles before *c.* 1200: they were produced only when the linguistic divergence made them necessary. The writing down of Provençal troubadour verses records an oral tradition, yet also reveals conscious composition. Meanwhile, Provençal was also used for academic works, the legal text *Lo codi* being a prime example.[14] The first recognisably Spanish vernacular texts appear at the turn of the twelfth and thirteenth centuries, although documents in a hybrid Latin from the 1100s may indicate attempts to create a written vernacular. The first major identifiable Spanish writer is Gonzalo de Berceo, who lived through to the 1250s. His work was primarily religious in nature, dealing with hagiography, the signs of the Last Judgement, and the mass.

The slow evolution in Spain contrasts with the early appearance of German works, in the eleventh century. These usually have religious connotations, ranging from a commentary on the Song of Songs (the *Hohes Lied*), and summaries of books of the Bible, to poetic laments for sin (*Sündenklagen*). The appearance of epic tales like the *Alexanderlied* (completed in two stages between *c.* 1135 and *c.* 1170) and *König Rother* (*c.* 1150) marks a new stage, soon followed by versions of French romances, and a notable flowering of German production in the early thirteenth century.

For all the vernacular texts, the question of survival is highy important. Linguistic evolution meant that many early texts might be discarded as they became incomprehensible. Even popular texts might have a poor survival record: they would rarely be treated as historical curiosities, or be left forgotten at the back of a cupboard. The most widely distributed vernacular texts of the twelfth century were probably saints' lives and scriptures, but their survival is patchy. Some were, indeed, deliberately

---

13 Kevin Brownlee, 'Generic hybrids', in *A New History of French Literature*, ed. Denis Hollier (Cambridge, MA, and London, 1989), p. 88.
14 Above, p. 171.

destroyed. The Paris council of 1210 which condemned the alleged heresies of the Amalricians (the supposed adherents of Amaury of Bène) also demanded the surrender of vernacular theological works and copies of the Creed and Our Father, proclaiming that their retention would automatically mark the possessors as heretics. Only vernacular saints' lives were to be tolerated. These religious texts were obviously highly important writings, causing more heart-searching (in many senses) than the romances or 'literary' works. The reading (or hearing) of a translated life of St Alexis inspired Peter Waldes to change his life, and so led to the emergence of Waldensianism. Waldes's desire for access to comprehensible scriptures, and the debate about their use in Metz *c.* 1199, stimulated discussion among clerics about allowing such translations, and their control. The role of a vernacular literate culture in creating a context on the one hand for heresy, on the other for the early stages of Franciscan spirituality, perhaps receives less emphasis than it merits. Such vernacular religious works also offered a controlled medium to disseminate 'correct' theology. The verse translation of Genesis begun by the otherwise unknown Evrat at the request of Countess Marie of Champagne in 1192 (which exceeds 20,000 lines), incorporates extensive additional material giving symbolic and moral interpretations, treating the text at several levels, and in depth, to ensure that it was read in the approved way.

Also worthy of consideration are the scattered references to vernacular religious drama, in surviving texts like the Anglo-Norman *Mystère d'Adam* (of *c.* 1160), and the Spanish *Auto de los reyes magos*, and in the occasional notes of performances in other sources. As in other obscure fields, absence of evidence is not evidence of absence. It is impossible to assess the scale of this dramatic tradition, or its audience and impact, but the early date of these plays suggests a growing awareness of the content and import of Christianity's spiritual message, and a desire to convey it in an accessible manner.

The limited size of the medieval audience has to be taken into consideration when dealing with this literary production. Every extant text is now read far more than it ever was in the twelfth century; it is extremely difficult to make the leap of imagination which deprives these works of their current academic environments and canonical status, and their wide circulation and easy access. Much twelfth-century English spiritual writing – the so-called 'Katherine group' of texts – originated in nunneries, and has an extremely sparse manuscript tradition. If texts had only limited readership, in an audience already converted, their cultural significance for contemporaries (but not their historic importance for studies of literature, language, and spirituality) is much reduced.

As so many of the major literary genres first appeared in French versions (the *chansons de geste*, saints' lives, verse histories, romances, troubadour verses, and *fabliaux*) analysis of 'French' literature (which includes material in Anglo-Norman and Provençal) tends to dominate discussion. This dominance can be domineering: it certainly works to the detriment of the equally vital Germanic literary tradition, which is often described as more derivative from and dependent on French precedents than was really the case. This is not, however, to deny the importance of the French transitions, which were trendsetting novelties. Most important were the production of romances (the development of the Arthurian and related cycles) and the emergence of the troubadours. The two strands converge in the debate on the meaning and significance of the 'courtly love' tradition, recently given new nuances by its integration into the debate about the status of women in medieval society.[15]

The elaboration of the Arthurian legend and the legend of the Holy Grail owes much to Chrétien de Troyes (d. *c.* 1183). The sudden appearance of such refined works is puzzling: where did the tradition come from; where did Chrétien acquire his skills? The Arthurian tradition – or parts of it – was not itself new; Chrétien was probably exploiting a core of stories which had circulated orally, but which he refined and augmented for his own purposes. Whether he actually 'invented' the vernacular romance is less certain: other texts, anonymous and undatable, challenge his claim. Yet he was a prolific producer, whose influence was undeniably widespread. He was not just someone who secured a wide personal audience; he also established a new and lasting genre, continued by imitators and successors, which introduced an element of fashionability into literary production. The creation of a primarily courtly tradition (assuming that these romances, like those of his female counterpart, Marie de France, were written to entertain comital and royal households) established a new audience for written texts. How it changed court life is debatable: it may give a new veneer of 'civilisation', but whether the new literature actually increased refinement is to be doubted. Perhaps it contributed to changing attitudes towards women: but identifying those new attitudes depends on how the texts are currently read.[16] Certainly it created a new kind of relationship between producer and audience, with the emergence of literary patronage for specific authors (and competition between authors to secure such patronage). However, the links between the producers and patrons of this vernacular material are debated,

15 Below, pp. 202–3.
16 *Ibid.*

especially for romances. The old view that a newly civilised knightly class encouraged production by lay writers is challenged: before 1200 most romance writers were clerics (taken in the broad sense of 'the educated', but including Marie de France as an 'honorary cleric'), not laymen, perhaps writing with the deliberate intention of using romance to spread a moralising and civilising message. Only later did the writers acquire patrons: 'patrons did not make courtly romance; courtly romance made patrons'.[17] Yet there clearly were patrons around, some prominent and active. The court of Henry the Lion in northern Germany produced the German version of Honorius Augustodunensis' *Elucidarius*; while the epic *Rolandslied* and *König Rother* probably derive from the court of Henry Jasomirgott, duke of Austria (although there are arguments to link them with Henry the Lion).

However read (and whoever did the reading, which is a real issue, since at the time reading was often associated with women and clerics), vernacular literary traditions were established, and spread. It comes as no surprise that there is no sign of a specifically English romantic literature at this time: being courtly, romances in England had to be in the courtly language of Anglo-Norman, and they therefore conformed to the continental French tradition. Vernacular literature in Germany perhaps penetrated to lower social levels. Late twelfth- and thirteenth-century texts, although dependent on the French traditions of *chansons de geste*, are very much rewritten, moving away from the genre's normal conventions and inserting a moral line which can be almost hagiographical. Wolfram von Eschenbach's *Willehalm* explicitly refers to its hero William d'Orange as a saint. Although many of the adapters were clerics, some were prominent laymen, apparently writing for a more bourgeois audience, albeit one aping courtly romanticism. At the same time, a clearly Germanic mythological and heroic tradition was validated in the anonymous *Nibelungenlied* (written down, but perhaps not composed, c. 1180–90).

In Italy things were different again. Although Italy was clearly influenced by the Arthurian tradition, traces of which appear in contemporary carvings, there are no texts comparable to the works in French. This absence may be partly illusory, as north Italy's vernacular was a form of Provençal, making it in fact part of the linguistic (and perhaps literary) bloc of Occitania. Regional emphases might also have been different.

---

17 C. Stephen Jaeger, 'Patrons and the beginnings of courtly romance', in *The Medieval opus: Imitation, Rewriting, and Transmission in the French Tradition. Proceedings of the Symposium held at the Institute for Research in the Humanities, October 6–7 1995, The University of Wisconsin-Madison*, ed. Douglas Kelly, Faux titre, 116 (Amsterdam and Atlanta, GA, 1996), p. 46.

Lacking major noble courts, there was little stimulus to develop a courtly tradition. Despite its sculptural vestiges, the Arthurian tradition had less local relevance at this point; maybe also the spread of Cathar and other heresies in the region encouraged spiritual rather than romantic writings. (The presence of vernacular heretical texts is well attested, raising issues which merge with the general one of the production of vernacular theological and spiritual works which ecclesiastical authorities wished to control even among the orthodox.)

Spain also leaves little 'fictional' vernacular writing, at least until the thirteenth century. The key vernacular text is the *Poem of the Cid*, written down around 1207 but clearly based on older material, which presumably circulated orally. Incomplete as it survives, it provides a verse biography of a heroic figure who by 1207 had been dead for a century. Stimulated by the struggle between Christians and Moors in the Reconquest, but with its own moral and political message, it suggests the vitality of literary production in a region which otherwise leaves sparse evidence, and which for the purposes of a twelfth-century renaissance is noted mainly for translations from Arabic into Latin. (None the less, those translations may presuppose the existence of Spanish literary language(s). As a vernacular could be the intermediary language in the translation process, Spanish texts may have been constructed for that purpose. Required only technically, and temporarily, their long-term survival would be unlikely.)

The *Poem of the Cid* is significant beyond being written in Spanish, and beyond its revealing a society in transition. It also reflects a new awareness of history in vernacular works, which characterises the period as a whole. The closest immediate parallel is the verse biography of William the Marshal, written in England (but in Anglo-Norman French) in the 1220s. This also glorifies a prominent military figure; again morality and chivalry are emphasised. Rather different is the evidence for the production of vernacular chronicles, or broader histories, most of which were produced in varieties of French. In England (setting aside the last stages of the Anglo-Saxon tradition, which died with the ending of the Peterborough Chronicle in 1154), this tradition first appears with Gaimar's *Estoire des Engleis*, written in the 1130s. Germany leaves little of this type of writing, but there is the vernacular *Kaiserchronik*, produced *c*. 1150. The most significant writing of this sort, perhaps keying into a major cultural shift, is the proliferation of vernacular chronicles and histories in northern France and Flanders in the early 1200s. (Their historicity is less important than their language: a number of them are actually adaptations of romantic historical texts dealing with Troy and

Alexander the Great.) These works show both a widening of the audience for history, beyond the Latinate clerical class, and a concern to assert local historical identities against the expanding Capetian monarchy.[18]

The development of chivalric and mythological romances, and perhaps of vernacular histories, also suggests a deeper cultural evolution, although one which is highly problematic. Whatever their moral import, such works imply a reduction in clerical control. If Christianity, defined and codified by clerics, was the 'dominant ideology' of the twelfth century, these vernacular works could mark a rejection – or, rather, evasion – of that dominance, a search for a new ideological context. This may be considered secular, but the word is now a loaded term. Certainly it was 'non-clerical', worldly (which is how contemporaries would understand 'secular'). The validation of the non-clerical world represented by such writings (especially the historical texts) may also reflect a new type of audience, which could respond to new types of material. While dependent on earlier models (especially in those histories which incorporated translations of pre-existing Latin works), these works are not mere evolutions from the epic. Focusing on the recent past and the recently living, such texts may be a rejection of the epic, and a revalorisation of the present. However, talk of secularisation faces one massive obstacle: the problem of literacy. Most vernacular works needed a clerical writer for reproduction, or had clerical authors.

Writing in the vernacular also raises an even more basic issue: that of writing itself. Latin, as a standardised, learned, and grammatical language, was built on an inheritance of script which most vernaculars lacked before 1000 (Anglo-Saxon and Old Norse appear as oddities here, the latter certainly in its use of runes). As writing was a clerical, Latinate, attribute, the vernacular tongues almost had to be reinvented as writable vehicles of communication before the literature could be recorded or created. This essentially meant developing an orthography to reflect phonetics in a standardised and comprehensible way. That might actually be achieved more easily in Germanic languages, which were undeniably different from Latin, than in the Romance tongues, where the derivation from or similarity to Latin might well inhibit the recording of difference and distinction. An awareness of the desirability of standard orthography to ease communication appears in Iceland about 1150, where the *First Grammatical Treatise* (an imposed title) seeks to establish precisely such rules, and also lays down a canon of acceptable vernacular writings which includes law, history, genealogy, and religious instruction. All these

18 See also above, pp. 63–4.

genres are represented in surviving twelfth-century works written in Icelandic. The establishment of standard forms may actually mean (given the many dialects in the spoken tongues) that even the written vernaculars are artificial languages, the realm of the learned. This is especially likely when they have a standard form over wide areas, like the generic categories of Anglo-Norman or Provençal. Recent discussion of Anglo-Norman literature certainly suggests that written insular French had reached that position by 1200.

Unmentioned so far, except in passing, is the one strand of vernacular literature which is almost invariably associated with this period: troubadour poetry. Just where and how these works fit into discussions of cultural change is uncertain. Some argue that the troubadours' verses derive from Spanish Arabic models, being thus another import from Muslim culture; but this claim is not universally accepted. The troubadours' regional focus – in Occitania, which retained a strong and distinctive cultural identity – is also significant. Although clearly within a courtly tradition, and often dominated by 'courtly love' (although readings have found more, including biting satire, in their verses), the works seemingly had limited geographical distribution, and the troubadours' reputations may owe more to historians and literary scholars than to contemporaries. Yet they did have renown in their time – or shortly after – because the poems were collected and transcribed, together with biographical information about the writers (although this is of little independent worth, usually being derived from the verses themselves). An added piquancy comes from the fact that some of the writers were women, the *trobairitz*.[19]

Despite the problems they pose, the troubadours and the tradition of courtly love with which they are linked cannot be ignored. Yet, disconcertingly, they seem less significant the more they are set in context. The works survive in limited numbers, their attributions often uncertain or doubtful. The surviving corpus can be only a fragment of the original output: does that mean that only the best was saved, and the rest was dross? Frequently only one copy of a song exists, raising all kinds of problems when assessing cultural significance. The troubadours of Occitania may be only a localised phenomenon, which had little widespread impact. On the other hand, they epitomise a much wider practice (witnessed by both Latin and vernacular texts) of small-scale poetic writing, perhaps commissioning, which the prominence given to this particular group has overshadowed. Vernacular love poetry also

19 Below, pp. 191, 200.

circulated in northern France, produced by the *trouvères*, with a style of its own. Germany, too, saw a similar development, in the poems of Friedrich von Hausen and others at the time of Emperor Frederick, and the works of the *Minnesänger* in the next century, headed by Walter von der Vogelweide (*c.* 1170–*c.* 1230). Their adoption of the conventions of courtly love gives their works greater kinship with those of the southern troubadours than their closer northern neighbours (a connection occasionally proved by 'contrafacts', whose German words are linked to a pre-existing troubadour tune). All of this love poetry – and other verse works, especially the *chansons de geste* – emerges from a shadowy world of popular entertainment, of jongleurs. Here again arise questions of high and low culture, about the transmission and preservation of works, and the identities of the performers, which make attempts at an integrated overview and analysis almost impossible. In addition, there are problems about using terms like troubadour in a specialist sense which did not really apply in the twelfth century itself. Qualms on this score mean that 'It might well be profitable to abandon altogether the use of the terms "troubadour" and "trouvère": for when used in their original sense, they are so vague as to be useless, and when restricted to their modern connotation, they give a misleading and stereotypical impression of this period of musical history.'[20] They may also give a 'misleading and stereotypical impression' of contemporary poetry as well.

Music

Whereas the visual and literary arts are fairly widely acknowledged as possible aspects of a 'twelfth-century renaissance', music is usually ignored: its history seems even more esoteric, technical, and arcane than art history, its terminologies more complex and off-putting. Musicologists, for their part, seem to operate in a world of their own devising, in which debates about – even mention of – a twelfth-century renaissance have no place. Paucity of sources, and massive technical problems in understanding those which do survive, create an introspective focus on the music itself rather than its broader context. Fundamental uncertainties persist: musical notation in this period, before the use of the stave (which emerged in the thirteenth century) to fix individual notes at specific pitches and intervals, was recorded in 'neumes'. While visually akin to later notation, their interpretation is still a matter of debate. This has

---

20 L.M. Wright, 'Misconceptions concerning the troubadours, trouvères and minstrels', *Music and Letters*, 48 (1967), p. 39.

created a situation in which, for instance, most historians treat the troubadours' works as poems rather than songs; as texts for which the existence and significance of the music is not really addressed even when the fact of performance is acknowledged. Yet the period's music cannot be totally overlooked. Its history offers an obscure undercurrent to many artistic and literary developments of the time, and may also be a significant contributor to the psychological changes. Music's seeming self-containment and particular evolutions and periodisation also question the terms on which any search for a twelfth-century renaissance might be based.

This 'music history' embraces many genres. At one extreme is the specific Church music of the liturgy, inextricably linked with Latinity. Here the tension between Cistercian artistic asceticism and growing luxuriousness encountered when dealing with the decorative arts reappears: Cistercian legislation complained about the abandonment of the sobriety of plainsong, replaced by elaborate melody and increasingly intricate singing. These complaints may have come late: such polyphony (known as *organum*) had existed since the ninth century, but it was certainly becoming more complex in the twelfth century. The Cistercian complaints were initially directed against other monastic observances, but after 1100 could also apply (as John of Salisbury applied them) to cathedral liturgies. The emergence of a more complex polyphony in twelfth-century Paris, sometimes with four voices, was a major development, although it is ill-recorded, as is its spread beyond the city. Although linked specifically to two composers, Leonin and Perotin, they are little more than names. This Parisian material is novel in its complexity, but its status for the debate about renaissance is problematic: somewhat like the cosmological analyses which came to a head in the early twelfth century, this is an end-product, not an innovation. 'Traditionally, the first phase of medieval polyphony has been seen to culminate in the Parisian repertory of the late twelfth and the thirteenth centuries.'[21] This Parisian phase seems to have been short-lived: although the material penetrated outside Paris, older traditions of two-part *organum* survived throughout the later middle ages, with the more complex arrangements giving way to the motet form from the middle of the thirteenth century.

Nevertheless, polyphonic singing was an acknowledged skill by 1200, probably taught more by example than by text. (The twelfth

21 Sarah Fuller, 'Early polyphony', in *The Early Middle Ages to 1300*, ed. Richard Crocker and David Hiley, New Oxford history of music (2nd edn), 2 (Oxford, 1990), p. 553.

century leaves little sign of musical instruction or theory as something conveyed by texts: there is a major hiatus between the work of Guido of Arezzo in the early eleventh century and the musical theorists like Jerome of Moravia and Johannes de Grocheio of the later thirteenth century.) In this polyphonic practice of the twelfth century lie the foundations of later evolutions in liturgical celebration and choral performance as a specialised craft.

The evolution of polyphony from the ninth century included new kinds of work, notably 'sequences', rhythmic prayers which often had an accompanying tune (although the words themselves carry a rhythm, so they could be recited as well as sung). The thirteenth century saw the addition of *conductus*, sacred songs which were not explicitly associated with the divine office. Many twelfth- and thirteenth-century sequences and conducts mirror the contemporary growth in Marian devotion. Liturgical music probably drove the most significant change in the period, a musical equivalent of the shift 'from memory to written record'. The rise of polyphony required new ways of writing music to ensure that the desired co-ordination of voices could be adequately recorded. This duly changed attitudes to composition, and to the reading of music.

At the other extreme, distinct from the clerical and Latinate liturgical developments, but fully capable of feeding off them (and feeding into them), lie the evolutions in more secular and lay music. The borderline between ecclesiastical and secular is highly fluid: clerics certainly acted as minstrels, and as the ecclesiastical careers of the first recorded polyphonic singers appear very insecure, their ability to switch to a lay mode, taking clerical skills and traditions with them, might even be a necessity. This might also extend to the process of recording, although changes in the noting of secular music presumably occurred more slowly than with liturgical works, there being less need for it to be written down. The overlap between secular and clerical musical repertoires is reflected in the thirteenth century in the rise of the ecclesiastical motet, a complex arrangement of singing for several voices, each with its own words, and sometimes bilingual. Here traditions of liturgical chant merge with more popular musical modes, derived from the northern French *trouvères*, and (more rarely) from the southern troubadours. Moreover, motets were often written in the vernacular. Their Latin contrafacts may postdate the French version; sometimes the Latin version is the earlier; often it is impossible to tell which came first. The emergence of a devotional musical tradition incorporating vernacular elements possibly stimulated regionalised evolutions: English thirteenth-century polyphony differs in some respects from that known in France.

One key lay musical tradition, perhaps constant throughout the long twelfth century, derived precisely from the vernacular and oral origins of the *chansons de geste*. These had been sung, and continued to be sung, by minstrels and jongleurs. Such practices may also underpin the vernacular poetic histories of the period, despite their being 'composed' by clerics. Gaimar records that Adeliza of Louvain had a copy of the verse history of Henry I of England by the otherwise unknown David which included the music for its first verse (presumably to be repeated in recital). If David's lost work was so treated, why not others? Songs of the deeds of princes were considered acceptable by contemporary moralists, and many vernacular verse chronicles could fit that description.

Yet clerics had reservations about other types of music and singing, often condemned as devilish in their effect. Here tensions between 'lay' and 'clerical' culture seem significant; but not, perhaps, tensions between 'high' and 'low', since participation need not reflect social status. There are problems about the cultural interactions connected with music (for example, whether written *chansons de geste* provided singers' texts), and the process of disseminating songs and their music is virtually irrecoverable beyond the bare record of performance. The problem is highlighted in Jean Renart's early thirteenth-century prose *Roman de la rose* (also known as *Guillaume de Dole*). Several songs are woven into the text, including some by known troubadours and *trouvères*. Renart seems to assume that his audience already knew these lyrics. As the work now survives, no music is provided; but the original intention may have been to include it together with the words.

A new way of writing music and a formal musical theory emerged fully in the later thirteenth century. Yet something was happening in the twelfth century, which must be integrated with the rise of vernacular texts, and with liturgical change. How this feeds into considerations of renaissance in the long twelfth century is uncertain. If Parisian *organum* of the late 1100s is a culmination, then discussions of birth and rebirth are inappropriate. However, the emergence of the motet, the integration of the vernacular into the sacred, and changes in lay musical practices, may justify treating the general process of transformation as a kind of renaissance. Clerical debates about the evolution of Church chant, and castigation of minstrels and jongleurs, reflected awareness of that shift. Despite such criticisms, the thirteenth century increasingly accepted that music was licit, even a valid art form. Novelty, and intricacy for its own sake, continued to arouse criticism, as did music to accompany lascivious dancing and dubious words; the distraction from spirituality offered by mere entertainment was also denounced. But there was greater clerical tolerance of the performing arts; partly because they were ineradicably integrated into a courtly culture, partly because music (like drama) was seen to have spiritual and didactic potential. The final step in the valida- tion of popular songs and music came in the thirteenth century when mendicant preachers used them as preaching aids in their sermons, reinterpreting the words to convey a spiritual message.

† † †

The cumulative significance of all these artistic changes remains some- what perplexing. Regionalism in developments, problems of intention, reception, and dissemination, and the disparities between the different forms, make a coherent and comprehensive summary and estimation impossible. All labelling is open to challenge. The melting pot of the crusader states, where many of the western evolutions also confronted strong Byzantine inheritance and influence, and numerous local traditions, encapsulates this issue, causing doubts to be voiced about the validity of identifying something which can be labelled 'Crusader Art'.

Yet, disregarding the caveats, what does impress is the constant vibrancy and vitality, no matter where attention turns. Interrelationships and interdependence are also striking: the conjuncture of words and music in liturgy and songs; the combination of words and image in texts. Indicative of the latter is the format of the thirteenth-century French *Bible moralisée*. Anachronism abounds in both words and pictures, under- standing being modernised with the addition of contemporary reson- ances when Philistines are transformed into Saracens, pagan temples into mosques, and biblical soldiers into knights. The general expansion of patronage and participation is also important, even if patronage's precise mechanics, and the degree of control which the supposed patron main- tained, remain obscure. Dedications in texts often reflect an appeal for patronage rather than its operation; how far any one court was a conscious centre of cultural production is debatable, and recent investi- gations have undermined some of the cherished patronage networks constructed by earlier commentators. On close examination even that of Champagne in the late twelfth century fails to match previous expectations. Yet courts did offer networks of contacts and sources of benefactions (in works of art or financial support) which functioned as patronage. Obviously important here is the sheer scale of investment now made possible by the rise of a cash economy. It would probably be wrong to treat works of art (however defined) as aspects of commodity production – although those with a bullion content could be treated as forms of wealth – but clearly fashion was beginning to rear its head in art and literature. What seems certain is that even if the disparate strands cannot be integrated, and the precise place of each in the overall cultural development remains elusive, the changes themselves bear witness to the broader European transformations which facilitated the concurrent evolutions at the more rarefied intellectual levels. Many of these cultural transitions thus reflect the bedrock of societal change which underpinned the superstructure of intellectual evolutions.

Ultimately, however, the links between these artistic and literary changes and the Latinate intellectual matters covered in previous chapters seem rather tenuous. There clearly are connections, notably in the use of varied media to disseminate current theology; but in other respects (particularly music) the trajectories seem very different. This revives the issue of whether the arts are part of a twelfth-century renaissance, and of the same movement as the other transitions. If they are to be incorporated, then the treatment of the movement in terms of birth, rebirth, or general cultural flowering, again becomes a significant point for debate.

7
A renaissance for women?

S o far, the discussion has been almost exclusively about men. They have been the chief actors, whether as academics, clerics, or 'politicians'. The debates and contests have been between men; the career structures open only to men. Whether the exclusion of women has been noticed, and raised eyebrows (or hackles) is a subsidiary issue; but the plain fact is that women have rarely appeared. They have not been 'written out' of the picture: it is very difficult to 'write them in'; nor can they be subsumed by a contention that 'male includes female'.

This absence provokes a question: did women have a twelfth-century renaissance? The question parallels one asked in 1977 of the later Renaissance, which received a negative answer.[1] If the response for the twelfth century is similarly negative, another question arises: could women have had a renaissance at that point? That, as put, is ambiguous. It could mean that the social and economic structures, and the existing system of gender relations, immediately denied women the opportunity to take a major role in the period's cultural changes; that their participation was out of the question. Alternatively, it can imply that the potential did exist, but the routes were accidentally or deliberately blocked. By implication, this was done by men. To deal with these issues first requires some consideration of the general problems which arise in locating women within the culture of the time, before the extent of their involvement can be considered.

Women are certainly not absent from twelfth-century history. A good deal of recent work has dealt generally with nuns, but includes

---

1 Joan Kelly, 'Did women have a renaissance?', in Joan Kelly, *Women, History, and Theory* (Chicago and London, 1984), pp. 19–50 [reprinted (writing as Joan Kelly-Gradol) from *Becoming Visible: Women in European History*, ed. R. Bridenthal and C. Koonz (Boston, MA, 1977), pp. 137-64].

specialised work on Hildegard of Bingen (who shows every sign of becoming a cult figure), Heloise, and several other individuals. Women can now be considered in many contexts, but men and their actions and mentalities still dominate the record. This situation reflects three major problems associated with women's history in general. First is that of social expectations and suppositions regarding women. Contemporary twelfth-century assumptions, justified partly by biblical statements, but perhaps derived from deeper motivations and older social structures, considered women inferior to men. Men were the controllers, the primary actors. To condemn such stances as misogyny serves no useful purpose, other than to allow the venting of anachronistic spleen: to understand the mentality, and its contemporary significance, is more important. In general women were confined to a non-public role. Their primary function was generative, to secure successions and create family alliances through marriages (particularly at higher social levels, where inheritances were important). Patrilinearity, and the associated need to ensure succession and avoid cuckoldry, therefore imposed control, restricted women to a sphere which excluded them from most of the visible careers of the period, and marginalised their actions, their world, by making both relatively invisible.

At the same time, women's lack of visibility and activity creates a circular limitation. As women were not expected to act in certain ways, it was considered unnecessary to give them opportunities to do so. This lack of provision, especially of educational provision, limited the contexts in which women could appear as active: it is significant that many of the prominent educated women of the long twelfth century are religious, and that the only group of women generally treated *en masse* are the nuns. (This remains the case into the thirteenth century: then individual women visionaries usually provide most of the evidence for analyses of the lives of women as individuals, often emphasising their religious and spiritual activity.) Yet while women were excluded from some contexts, they did act in others. Women could be politically important, as associates of rulers, as rulers in their own right, as governors during the absence or minority of a husband or son: women like the Empress Matilda, Eleanor of Aquitaine, Queen Melisende of Jerusalem, or the Countess Matilda of Tuscany, to cite only obvious examples. They are, however, notably absent from judicial matters. Women were necessarily active in economic life in town and country, especially in the latter, as co-workers (even if there was a gendered division of labour) to ensure family survival. Whether urban or rural, we still know remarkably little about individuals of either sex, beyond generic labels as 'artisan' or 'peasant'.

Although women were not inactive, the sources often conceal their activity (or, perhaps, do not identify it clearly as female rather than male). This raises the general problem of the survival and biases of the source material. For the topics traditionally included in the 'twelfth-century renaissance', most extant material was produced by and for men, and reflects their lives and concerns. As most sources derive from contexts where women were not active – the schools, monasteries, legal and bureaucratic systems – women generally lacked a voice. They may appear elsewhere (in literature, for instance), and there are occasional hints of their offstage activity; but usually they are overwhelmed by male production. The presumption that writings were produced by men rather than women has its own inbuilt bias: in a century when the authors of many texts are unknown it is always possible that some were produced by women rather than men, and that women's contribution to the intellectual and cultural developments is undervalued. However, the balance of probabilities makes the risk that this creates a serious imbalance fairly slight. The only area where imbalance is a real possibility – even a probability – is in cultural patronage. Women may have commissioned texts (perhaps mainly vernacular and devotional works) on a scale which cannot now be recovered. Nevertheless, while women might pay for works to be produced, their control over the content is questionable, as this would often have been clerically directed.

Given these considerations, and the limitations they impose on any visible contribution by women to a twelfth-century renaissance, just how involved were women in these developments? Certainly there were prominent women, who merit attention. How far, though, do they reflect a broader trend? How far do they exemplify a larger but concealed group? Are the recorded women known precisely because they were extraordinary, their activities saying little about female involvement in general, even being actually misleading? Despite the continuing re-evaluation of women's role in medieval society, very few stand out for their involvement in the broad cultural movements associated with this period. This may be because they have not been hunted out yet. Recently, for instance, Elizabeth of Schönau (1129–64) has attracted attention, regaining a status perhaps lost since the sixteenth century. A visionary nun, she produced several works which circulated widely in later centuries. Yet her dependence on her brother Ekbert to produce the record of her experiences raises the issue of independence and control, and the question of how far words were being put into her mouth, or censored out.

Usually (as will have to happen here), discussions of twelfth-century women focus attention on a very narrow spectrum. The best known is undoubtedly Heloise. Her illicit affair with Abelard, and the subsequent letters between them when he was a monk and she an abbess, have given her a particular place in twelfth-century history. Yet, aside from the correspondence with Abelard and a few other letters, she was not a prolific writer, and her real influence is questionable. For women of long-term importance, we must turn to the likes of Hildegard of Bingen, or Marie de France. The former demonstrates female involvement with theological concerns and prophecy (something shared with Elizabeth of Schönau); the latter made a significant contribution to the rise of vernacular literature. She, too, is not unique: other women likewise wrote in the vernacular, producing saints' lives (Clemence of Barking), or love poetry (the *trobairitz* – female troubadours – of southern France).

While research is slowly adding to the tally of female writers, it also raises occasional doubts. The status of the *trobairitz* is sometimes questioned; the very existence of the female medical writer known as 'Trotula', whose works are often invoked as the key (and almost only) evidence of women's involvement in medicine as a learned science, is now disputed. (It looks as though a 'Trotta' did exist, who produced a medical work; but not the texts which have been assigned to 'Trotula' since the thirteenth century. Nevertheless, the testing of 'Trotula''s existence has reaffirmed the tradition of female medicine around Salerno in the eleventh and twelfth centuries.)

One significant and substantial way to expand the number of women participating in the cultural and intellectual changes of the twelfth century would be to incorporate nuns *en masse*. Their inclusion would certainly result in quantitative and qualitative expansion. Quantitative, simply because so many new female houses were founded during the long twelfth century, increasing the number of female religious by several thousand. Women gained a status to match men, notably in the Gilbertine order and that of Fontevrault, which either had explicitly double houses (among the Gilbertines) or government by an abbess over monks (at Fontevrault). If the women in less strict religious establishments are also included, like the beguines who appear in northern France and Flanders from the late 1100s, or the female anchorites who (like Christina of Markyate) were sometimes prominent figures, the numbers increase further.

Increasing the number of women involved in the twelfth-century changes by including all religious women would also lead to a qualitative change in their contribution to those changes. Many of these women had some education, and could cope with texts at least in the vernacular; those in nunneries might well also be Latinate. This expands the potential for readership; possibly also the potential for authorship. Moreover, including female heads of religious houses would increase the number of women who exercised real power, whether political, seigneurial, or spiritual.

However, to increase the number of female participants by including all religious women, without also including all male religious, merely remedies one imbalance by creating another. The religious expansion of the long twelfth century affected men as well as women, and more of them. It may not have increased the number of educated men in the Church: many intellectuals entered a religious order as the final stage of their mental quest; many others who became regulars would presumably have become priests anyway, especially among the Augustinian canons. However, for a while the monastic life had a new attraction, although this in part reflected changing opportunities: the existence of lay brethren in orders like the Cistercians increased the number of monks, but by allowing the illiterate to join in. For present purposes, such people make no positive contribution to the debate. In any case men, like women, sought religious opportunities outside formal religious houses, in structures which seem less organised than those for women (there is nothing immediately comparable to the beguinages). The growth of heresy in the late twelfth century (notably Catharism and Waldensianism in southern France and Italy) was clearly linked to expanding lay literacy, especially in the vernacular. This increase in religious opportunities suggests a quantitative and qualitative expansion in male as well as female participation in the broader cultural and intellectual changes. Taking this expansion for men into account immediately works against the effect of highlighting the growth in religious opportunities for women, and again pushes them into the background. Moreover, and despite older scholarship, it seems unlikely that heresy appealed more to women than to men: if anything, aspects of Catharism might be repellent to women. Evolution among the orthodox also generated hostility to the expansion of female religious opportunities by 1200, which might justify adding religious women to the generic victims of an increasingly 'persecuting society'.

Since few individual women of the period have left really detailed evidence of their lives, it seems appropriate to examine a selection of this small minority to test the possibilities for generalisation reflected in their lives.

The first such case must be Heloise (d. 1163/4), if only because of her fame, and the controversy surrounding her relationship with Abelard, essentially as recorded by him. As self-sacrificing victim taking the nun's veil to salve Abelard's conscience, or as assertive abbess ruling over the Paraclete, Heloise has attracted considerable attention. Her sexual relationship with one of the early twelfth century's major thinkers has given her a certain *frisson*. The continuing debate about her contribution to the surviving correspondence between herself and Abelard, and the search for her real voice, have prevented her from being marginalised.

For now, the most significant element in Heloise's career is not her love affair, nor her roles as an abbess and ruler, but the evidence of her education. Real questions arise from the account of this in Abelard's *Historia calamitatum*, and from the letters ascribed to her in the correspondence with him, some of which can also be viewed as her own record of calamities. The first question is the basic one of typicality: how far does Heloise's learning reflect the educational opportunities and attainments open to women of her social status and above? The second question concerns Heloise herself more directly: just how advanced was her education? Both issues feed into the link between education and Heloise's being a nun, but that is a minor element for now.

In his *Historia calamitatum*, Abelard portrays Heloise as his pupil, whom he was engaged to instruct in her own home. This in itself was not unusual: it was probably normal for masters to engage in private tutoring to gain funds, and John of Salisbury certainly did. It may not even be unusual that the pupil was a girl: other batches of correspondence survive between female pupils and male teachers, and a snatch of early thirteenth-century poetry suggests that girls were regularly taught their psalter and divine office in Latin by male masters. (It has been proposed that one of these anonymous letter collections, although surviving only in a fifteenth-century manuscript, is indeed between Abelard and Heloise, but this is unproven.) It is noteworthy that Heloise's lessons occurred at her home: there is little sign that girls received any 'public' or openly accessible education at this time. Nunneries provided some teaching, offering access to Latin for girls who were usually intended to become nuns themselves, and so paralleling the male oblate system in its purpose. Some of these women might return to the world without making a formal profession. Edith/Matilda of Scotland, the first wife of Henry I of England, was one notable early twelfth-century case. Her removal from Wilton to marry the king provoked murmurs because of suspicions that she had actually professed as a nun. Another case (this time provoking no known comment) was Heloise herself. She was first educated at Argenteuil, the house to which she returned as a nun following the affair with Abelard.

Precisely what Abelard taught Heloise is never detailed, but presumably entailed an expansion of her awareness of Latin classics, to reinforce her reputation as the most learned woman in France. Her letters to Abelard (assuming that she wrote them) reveal a good grasp of Latinity and several classical texts. She also knew the arts of composition well enough to produce correct and learned correspondence, and was fully capable of expressing her own opinion. She appears as a woman of considerable culture, who could operate in a milieu which regularly quoted ancient and patristic authors, where the past was cited to provide authority, where issues of individualism and 'humanism' were freely debated (as in the discussion on marriage in the *Historia*, where Heloise argues against Abelard's proposal as ill conceived), and where philosophy was constantly in the background. Abelard says that she knew Greek and Hebrew as well as Latin. If she did, she would be unique among recorded twelfth-century women, and indeed more knowledgeable than her master. She possibly had a smattering of both (that she knew Hebrew is repeated elsewhere), but real facility is unlikely, given the rarity of such linguistic knowledge in general. Her learning raises valid questions about the intellectual relationship between herself and Abelard, and her significance in Abelard's own intellectual development. Formative here may have been 'her imaginative understanding of the classics and, in particular, her passionate feelings about the pagan sages ... At the level of feelings, as much as of imagination, Heloise seems to have set the agenda which Abelard addressed in his theological writings.'[2]

There are difficulties in placing Heloise in the general picture of the twelfth century. Although there is growing evidence of women who could read and write in the period, it is significant that all those known are from a limited social range. There is no hint that literacy offered women opportunities for social mobility, or a means to change career. Among the small group of women who do express themselves, aspects of Heloise's experience, as separately identifiable aspects, are not uncommon. As a package, however, they do seem to be unique to Heloise: she was certainly not a 'typical woman'. Whatever her precise relationship with Fulbert, her guardian, his post as a cathedral canon marks him as someone with a certain social status. How high up (or down) the elite he and Heloise should be placed is debatable. It has been suggested that

---

2 M.T. Clanchy, *Abelard: a Medieval Life* (Oxford and Cambridge, MA, 1997), pp. 277–8.

Heloise was connected to one of the families which provided key courtiers and administrators to Louis VI of France. If so, she was certainly well placed. The educated Heloise was accordingly one of a very small minority among the women of twelfth-century France, even allowing for the fact that all the educated, male and female, were in a minority. The breadth of the group of educated women is hard to judge. Is their vocality due to their unusual possession of the appropriate abilities? Are they the stars, surrounded by a penumbra of women with some capabilities – who could read, and perhaps compose a basic letter – but untrained for greater intellectual heights? The closest secular parallel to Heloise may be the fictional Isolda, in some versions of the Tristan tale. She too is highly educated, and perhaps home-tutored. She knows languages, reads and writes, can compose, and is a skilled musician. Being a fiction, she may also be an exaggeration; but comparison with the attainments of Marie de France suggests that she is not beyond the bounds of credibility.[3]

Heloise's very oddity raises an important question. Why she was being educated is never revealed. What was Abelard's tutoring for? In 1405, Christine de Pisan's *Treasure of the City of Ladies* offered what has been described as 'part etiquette book, part survival manual' for women of varied social ranks.[4] Those who were to assist their husbands by governing estates in their absence (or rule on behalf of their offspring when widowed) particularly needed to be able to read and write, but not necessarily to quote classical authors. It is possible to project backwards from Christine's day to the twelfth century, when many lords were absent on crusade or for other reasons; when Eleanor of Aquitaine was responsible for the government of a major duchy; when the Countess Matilda was a significant player in north Italian politics; when Marie, countess of Champagne ruled in turn as regent for her minor son, during his absence on crusade, and again for another minor. But there is a real danger of anachronism, of imposing a static picture. Christine de Pisan offers a fifteenth-century picture, ideal rather than real. It cannot provide valid evidence for Heloise's intended fate. Although her education might reasonably seem directed towards her future as an abbess, she was not being educated in a nunnery, and had been removed from Argenteuil. If she was meant to become an abbess, why abstract her from the convent?

To ask how many shared Heloise's experience presupposes that the record of her experience is reliable, and somehow normative. There has,

3 For Marie, see below, pp. 198–200.
4 Christine de Pisan, trans. Sarah Lawson, *The Treasure of the City of Ladies* (Harmondsworth, 1985), p. 21.

however, been a long-running debate about the status of the letters between Abelard and Heloise, the views expressed ranging from outright rejection and condemnation as an elaborate forgery, to uncertainty about the amount of editing (and the identity of the editor) if the letters were retouched to transform them into a unit. If the correspondence was re-edited, by either Abelard or Heloise, this opens two avenues for comment.

If Heloise was the editor, then admiration for her is only increased; her status as an educated woman is confirmed and enhanced. What, however, if Abelard was the editor? Are we then presented with an artificial Heloise, constructed by him, making the educated woman of the letters ascribed to Heloise an illusion? With regard to those particular letters, the debate is not over. All that can be said here is that parts of the picture must be reliable. Heloise's writings were not restricted to the letters to Abelard: she also corresponded with Peter the Venerable at Cluny, in Latin, and had a wider reputation. Her governance at the Paraclete was apparently successful, confirming her administrative abilities. Even if the real Heloise was not exactly the woman of the letters (a statement which is highly speculative), she was still dynamic. As one abbess among others she may be less outstanding, and less forceful than others of the period, like the abbess of Las Huelgas in Spain whom Pope Innocent III reprimanded for exceeding the bounds of acceptable exercise of spiritual authority by women. Yet, as an abbess, Heloise joined a broad group of religious superiors in a brief period when, it seems, commitment to the regular life made individual gender less significant an issue than it usually was.

Hildegard of Bingen (1098–1179) offers a rather different picture. Like Heloise she was a nun, being abbess successively from 1136 at Disibodenberg and Rupertsberg. However, her career was markedly different. As her parents' tenth child she was offered to God as tithe, and placed with an anchoress from the age of eight. Despite these initially restricted horizons, Hildegard broke through the bounds of her profession and womanhood to claim a role in the contemporary external world. As a contributor to a 'twelfth-century renaissance', she is perhaps the one female polymath who emerges as clear equal of some of her male contemporaries. Indeed, her varied writings put her on a par with John of Salisbury. Her writing career began in the 1140s, continuing to her death. Best known as a prophetess – mainly for her *Scivias*, completed in 1151, although she wrote two other prophetic works – she produced explanations of the gospels, a tract on the Benedictine Rule, works on medicine and nature in the encyclopedic tradition, and saints' lives. Her numerous songs (for which she also composed the music, in a rather idiosyncratic style), have been called 'some of the most unusual, subtle and exciting poetry of the twelfth century'.[5] Her *Ordo virtutum* is often identified as the first morality play. She also left an extensive correspondence.

Despite her prolific output, Hildegard is problematic. A preacher whose prophecies were validated by Pope Eugenius III, and whose correspondents included Frederick Barbarossa, she did not claim her authority as a woman. Rather, she accepted the subsidiary status of womanhood. Her claim to be merely the voice of God in some ways cancelled out her own existence: it was not 'she' who was talking, although this might be seen as a subterfuge which allowed her to hide behind the authority of her voice, and legitimated selfishness. Perhaps the very fact that Hildegard undermined her own womanhood allowed her to establish her reputation, and her power: as an extraordinary woman who exceeded expectations she was more acceptable than an ordinary woman who overstepped the mark. Her fame certainly lasted: her prophecies were regularly cited in later centuries.

Hildegard is unlike Heloise in spending most of her life as a nun. She lacked Heloise's private tuition; her learning and intellectual attainments were accordingly confined by the resources available within her nunnery. Although she became a prolific writer, apparently thinking readily in Latin, her control over the language remained unrefined, and she depended on (male) amanuenses to record her works. Exactly whence Hildegard acquired her advanced knowledge is not known. Her works rarely acknowledge sources, and while many of her thoughts had obvious biblical origins, the derivation of other ideas is unrecorded. Her works suggest acquaintance with many of the texts normally available in a good monastic library of the period; but it is also suggested that many of her ideas were intuitive, rather than derivative (as is perhaps to be expected with the visionary material).

As an abbess, Hildegard necessarily exercised authority. Besides her administrative activities, she also intervened in other aspects of worldly life through her correspondence, and in her preaching tours. Her works, apart from their immediate content, show many traits associated with the 'twelfth-century renaissance'. Her letters allow her to be linked with the 'cult of friendship' which flourished in the period, notably in correspondence between monks. Certainly she was extremely deeply attached to the nun Richardis, whose decision to quit the Rupertsberg for another

5 Peter Dronke, *Poetic Individuality in the Middle Ages: New Departures in Poetry, 1000–1150* (2nd edn, London, 1986), p. 151.

house was a considerable emotional shock. Despite her attempts to hide behind the persona of divine mouthpiece, her letters also reveal hints of self-awareness. Her cosmological works associate her with the Platonism of the earlier twelfth century (it is perhaps significant that the general cast of her works often seems outdated when set against contemporary academic developments). Her frequent opposition of good and evil sometimes has dualistic undertones. There is a strong focus in her writings on human achievement, a view of mankind which is generally positive, and perhaps humanistic in twelfth-century terms. For Hildegard, therefore, 'man is the shadow of God ... the showing of the almighty God in all his miracles'.[6]

Hildegard's upbringing and life as a nun suggest that the educational attainments originally expected of her differed from those expected of Heloise. Heloise was presumably being educated as a prospective wife, and therefore for a life in the world. Hildegard was early committed to be a Bride of Christ; she therefore had less need for the more 'secular' and worldly aspects of education which Heloise received. Yet Hildegard was more assertive in her claims to authority, even while demeaning her own personality in the process. That, as a woman, she effectively had to deny her womanhood to justify and defend her claim to authority, may partly explain why so few women produced comparable work in the period: they could not provide adequate justification and defence, did not start from the right circumstances, and so lacked opportunities to express themselves in a manner which would be preserved across the centuries. Hildegard's reputation gave her status and power; but she was often on the defensive when dealing with the real world. She had male adherents and supporters; she had female correspondents. This female circle suggests one possibility for expanding the range of women participating in the twelfth-century transitions. Yet most of these female correspondents were nuns, and remained nuns. When Hildegard disappeared from the scene, no one emerged from her shadow to replace her. Hildegard was not alone, but she nevertheless appears as a loner.

With Marie de France, the third 'exemplary woman', the focus shifts dramatically. Virtually nothing concrete is known of her, yet she is the first woman for whom a reasonably extensive corpus of vernacular works survives, earning praise as 'perhaps the greatest woman author of the Middle Ages and certainly the creator of the finest medieval short

---

6 Quoted in Peter Dronke, *Women Writers of the Middle Ages: a Critical Study of Texts from Perpetua (†203) to Marguerite Porete (†1310)* (Cambridge, 1984), p. 175.

fiction before Boccaccio and Chaucer'.[7] Her works – the *Lais* (short narrative poems), *Fables*, and a French version of the experiences of the knight Owain in St Patrick's Purgatory in Ireland – were composed between 1160 and 1215, but dating is very imprecise. The accepted canon of her works may be incomplete: a Life of St Audrey has also been put forward as written by her. Although Marie may have ended her life as a nun (she is often identified with an abbess of Shaftesbury in England who died *c.* 1216) like Heloise she began life very firmly in the world. Her works are seemingly addressed to a courtly audience, probably in England. Her admission to a nunnery (if it happened) also lacked the drama of Heloise's flight, and was more a mature retirement. With both Heloise and Hildegard Marie shares a certain social status, perhaps higher than theirs if suggestions that she was a half-sister of King Henry II of England are reliable.

Where Marie differs most from Heloise and Hildegard is in the focus of her achievements. Her claim to fame rests on her role in the rise of vernacular romantic literature: her *Lais* offer a female contribution to the development of the Arthurian legends, setting Marie beside Chrétien de Troyes as a courtly writer, in French. In adopting the *lai* form from folk tales Marie was also being innovative, responsible for 'the first explicit canon revision in European literary history'.[8] The *Fables*, although derivative, also change the tales, offering a voice which is much more explicitly female. Given her social background, and the fables' moralistic function, it is no surprise that those stories offer social comment, and might even hold a political message. Marie certainly had education, and knew Latin; her claim to be using old texts extended to an Anglo-Saxon version of Aesop supposedly translated on the orders of King Alfred, which would make her at least trilingual; while the *Lais* suggest knowledge of Breton (or, possibly, Welsh).

The participation in a vernacular culture attested by Marie's writings and her alleged sources may exemplify the opportunities for women in the twelfth century. Their roles as audience and patrons may also be significant. Much is unknown about the addressees of vernacular texts in the period; but if the contemporary association of women with books is reliable (and the derogation of men who participated in such womanish

---

7 *The Lais of Marie de France*, trans. Robert Hanning and Joan Ferrante (Durham, NC, 1978), p. 1.

8 Stephen G. Nichols, 'Marie de France's commonplaces', in *Contexts: Style and Values in Medieval Art and Literature*, ed. Daniel Poirion and Nancy Freeman Regalado, *Yale French Studies*, special issue (New Haven and London, 1991), p. 135.

pursuits as reading), it may be that the literate courtly woman was more 'normal' than a literate courtly man. However, such women may not have extended their interests to Latinity; their cultural context would have been firmly vernacular. Even in nunneries the primary culture may have been non-Latinate (albeit French, not English), as suggested by the Life of St Catherine written by Clemence of Barking.

Although Marie de France wrote in French, her works are neither simple nor naive. The very novelty of her contribution to the Arthurian romances required access to sources, both those of the specific tradition (presumably contemporary continental French authors), and the broader classical heritage which underlies many of those texts. This might have been provided by some sort of cultural osmosis, just as French vernacular history-writing developed from an osmosis with older historical traditions; but Marie's Latinity indicates that she had been deliberately educated, perhaps along the domestic lines of Abelard's tutoring of Heloise, but possibly at a lower level.

Marie's audience also extends the possibility of a female role in the cultural evolutions of her time. Her works were read, perhaps chiefly by women (although there is nothing specifically 'feminist' about her approach, and it would be stretching the evidence to restrict her appeal to women alone). They show that the courtly tradition so often associated with men was not confined to them. Women could demonstrate compositional ability, at first hand in the cases of Marie and Clemence of Barking, or through an amanuensis (and probably translator) in the Life of Christina of Markyate.

Beyond the named few women writers, there were probably others unknown; possibly a broader tradition in which women wrote shorter verses, providing a route for participation in more ephemeral features of the emerging courtly society. The existence of female troubadours in southern France may offer a glimpse of that activity, although these women are very shadowy figures. Those who can be identified were mainly aristocrats, which creates an imbalance both with the male troubadours, and with other female entertainers. Female *jongleuses* remain anonymous, and their songs unidentified, unlike the songs of known male troubadours sung by their male counterparts. The *trobairitz* are less involved in courtly love, although they sometimes seem to be its rueful victims. Several of their songs create dialogues with men (sometimes themselves troubadours) and other women. Overall, their voice is somewhat different from that of the male troubadours; but the number of surviving songs is too few to construct a full 'female perspective' on contemporary courtliness.

The brevity of this comment on women's role in the twelfth century's cultural evolutions basically reflects the state of the evidence; but it need not mean that women were as passive as the record suggests. The question remains: does the imbalance in the historical record reveal only the tip of the iceberg? The answer must still be an admission of ignorance: we cannot tell. Certainly the Latinity of the nunneries suggests access to education, superimposed on an ability to deal with the vernacular. But this was not a speculative, academic, education; it focused on literacy, on the acquisition of reading skills. Nuns might also have acquired writing skills, but writing raises different issues: the mechanical skills needed to copy a text could be acquired without being able to read, while the ability to read and write was no guarantee of an ability to compose.

For those women not confined to a nunnery, home education by tutors, or even a generational transmission from mother to daughter (as later represented in images of St Anne teaching the Virgin to read) could have conveyed basic literacy, with an emphasis on reading above writing. But this would be to a limited end, to train a good wife. Women were excluded from the main areas of intellectual exploration, from the schools, and from the speculations of academic theology and philosophy. Being excluded also from the emerging professions – the law, pastoral care, and bureaucratic careers – they are absent from the areas which usually attract historians' attentions for the period. This marginalisation of women in some ways matches the marginalisation of the monastic educational system for men; but with the major difference that monks did integrate themselves into the new structures in the thirteeth-century universities. Such opportunities were closed to women, even to nuns.

In the secular world as a whole, aristocratic women would have had the best and most extensive opportunities to join in and be affected by the contemporary cultural changes; but the room for involvement was again limited. There were powerful women, but power is not the same as intellectual status, despite later suggestions that some women were more literate than their husbands. Women could also be a civilising influence on their menfolk, working with the clergy to promote new cultural and moral values. Women could provide an audience, even a market, for some of the new products of the period: some twelfth-century vernacular works were probably meant primarily for them; in the thirteenth their spiritual evolution was addressed by the appearance of Books of Hours, easing the development of a particularly domestic spirituality which was perhaps more female than male. That may have existed even before 1200, as suggested by the early emergence of the beguine movement.

Overall, the impression remains that women were not a major

directing force in the twelfth-century transformations. They were affected by them, especially by the broad social and economic developments; but in the precisely cultural sphere it is often hard to see any direct impact or involvement. Rarely can women be identified as instigators of change; and those whose activities do stand out remain exceptions to the general pattern. If there was a renaissance for women in the twelfth century, it is still invisible.

Meanwhile, alongside the issue of women, society faced a problem of 'woman'. A development which seems immediately antithetical to all the presuppositions associated with 'renaissance', but which is undeniably a feature of the times, is the appearance of a strident antifeminism in some texts, seen as either the birth or the confirmation of a misogynistic tradition in western Europe. In contrast, the long twelfth century also saw what was ostensibly an idealisation of woman in the traditions of courtly love which make woman an unattainable prize, and in the massive explosion of Marian devotion which was a transforming feature of contemporary Catholicism.

The traditions of woman as object of devotion, or of revulsion, initially seem incompatible. Understanding them, and working towards their reconciliation, has been a major concern of recent decades. The trouble here is that, as with the debate about individualism, the parameters are set by modern concerns and academic interests, which sometimes give the impression of predetermining the response. This particularly applies when dealing with a phenomenon popularly associated with the long twelfth century: courtly love.

Despite an assertion in 1968 that 'courtly love' 'is not a medieval technical term. It has no specific content ... As currently employed, "courtly love" has no useful meaning, and it is not worth saving by redefinition',[9] the term will not go away. Its appreciation remains extremely ambiguous. In some readings, women are elevated on a pedestal of unattainability, remote goddesses adored from afar. Other readings see women as debased by such attention, reduced to the role of commodities and sexual objects, victims and playthings of a misogynistic tradition which denied their claims to identity and personal worth. In this view, which has certainly become more strident in recent years, 'Misogyny and courtly love are coconspiring abstractions of the feminine

---

9 John F. Benton, 'Clio and Venus: a historical view of medieval love', in John F. Benton (ed. Thomas N. Bisson), *Culture, Power and Personality in Medieval France* (London and Rio Grande, OH, 1991), p. 120.

whose function was from the start, and continues to be, the diversion of women from history by the annihilation of the identity of individual women, hidden behind the requirement of discretion and the anonymity of the *domna*, and thus the transformation of woman into an ideal.'[10] Courtliness thus becomes 'a mode of coercion'[11] directed against women, which operates in effect as a form of misogyny.

That hostility to women is rife among twelfth-century male writers cannot be denied, nor that most writers automatically – indeed, instinctively – saw women as inferior to men. The task, however, is not to explain this situation, but to understand it. While it is evident that 'Courtesy was created by men for their own satisfaction, and it emphasized a woman's role as an object, sexual or otherwise',[12] to focus exclusively on the place allotted to women in the tradition may be unbalanced. To ignore the other players may impose misreadings. Thus, in troubadour lyrics, women are reduced to the status of stereotyped nonentities; but such treatment is no worse than that given to the other characters mentioned in the songs: 'the jealous husband, the guardian, the gossipers, all … reduced to a simple fictional function in a highly predictable lyrical situation'.[13] In these circumstances, only the lover has identity.

Here arises a significant problem when considering 'woman': 'man' is often ignored, except as oppressor. Yet it is increasingly clear that the twelfth century was a difficult time for men – and 'man' – leading one writer to make the long twelfth century central to a medieval *Herrenfrage*, a 'Men Problem', which saw a fundamental reconsideration and transformation of the status and role of men (or, perhaps more precisely, men of the higher social orders) in contemporary society. Another has mused that 'Perhaps the elevation of the lady was a major turning point in the history of men.'[14] Perhaps the real problem reflected in the texts is that of male sexuality and masculinity, a problem denied by formulations that sought to relieve men of responsibility for their own actions:

> Magic powers were often attributed to women in literature, and in life, as a way … of rationalizing the vulnerability men felt. That is, rather than admit the weakness of lust in himself, he focused on the power that

---

10 R. Howard Bloch, *Medieval Misogyny and the Invention of Western Romantic Love* (Chicago and London, 1991), pp. 196–7.

11 *Ibid.*, p. 197.

12 Benton, 'Clio and Venus', p. 118.

13 Paolo Cherchi, *Andreas and the Ambiguity of Courtly Love* (Toronto, Buffalo, and London, 1994), p. 56.

14 Meg Bogin, *The Women Troubadours* (New York and London, 1976), p. 16.

attracted him; if the power were magic, he was not responsible for giving in to it.[15]

Similar comment can apply to the emphasis on female sexuality and enticement in 'antifeminine' tracts of the time, notably those addressed to clerics who were now meant to be celibate, but whose masculinity could not be annihilated and had to be contained and controlled by emphasising an external female threat. It is notable that most of the works which explicitly denigrate women derive from a clerical context. There was, nevertheless, a broader antifeminism, partly ascribable to Christian tradition which made Eve's temptation the source of human misery and weakness; partly also ascribable to inherited patriarchal traditions of social organisation which, while supported and often validated by Church teachings, did not derive from them.

Concurrently, though, there was an acceptance of the validity of the feminine, and that 'women' did not have to be confined by the roles allowed to 'woman'. The elevation of women finds its peak in the escalation of Marian devotion over the twelfth century, perhaps most forcefully in a monastic context (all Cistercian houses were dedicated to Mary). The Virgin's role in the process of salvation was emphasised, being encapsulated in the reversal of the Fall as *Eva* (Eve) became *Ave* (the first word spoken by the Archangel Gabriel at the Annunciation). Mary as Virgin Mother, supreme intercessor, Queen of Heaven, became an increasingly prominent devotional focus. Just what Mary's elevation really meant for women is debated: interpretations are as ambivalent as those of courtly love. Mary possibly offered women a spiritual focus more accessible than the traditional God; but as role model she was so perfect, so inimitable, yet so to be imitated, that the demands of imitation further shackled the lives of real women.

Other signs of acceptance of the validity of the feminine have been seen in some men's use of maternal language to define spiritual roles, especially by heads of religious houses, and alongside an understanding of Christ which also stressed his maternal characteristics. (This should not be pushed too far: sometimes the maternal imagery is not overtly human, or feminine. In the sermons of Hélinand of Froidmont, for instance, the mothers are sometimes birds, allowing him to draw a parallel between Christ and a protective mother hen.) Nevertheless, appreciation of gender in terms of qualities rather than biology meshes in

15 Joan M. Ferrante, 'The education of women in the middle ages in theory, fact, and fantasy', in *Beyond Their Sex: Learned Women of the European Past*, ed. P.H. Labalme (New York and London, 1984), p. 30.

with a view of women which saw them as burdened by the weakness of their sex, but as capable of transcending those limitations by acting 'manfully'. Here a further paradox arises: because the social character-isation of the sexes was constructed and analysed primarily by male writers, the potentialities of the sexes varied. Women, as the lower sex, could always improve, by taking on characteristics associated with manliness as a virago; women's weaknesses were to an extent auto-matically excused by the nature of their sex (although women who stepped out of line and claimed a status which was not properly theirs faced strident criticism). Men, meanwhile, had the burden of maintaining their manliness; otherwise they risked the descent to effeminacy. Hildegard of Bingen, for one, strongly condemned her contemporaries for that fault, offering an intriguing reversal of roles. The ultimate aspiration was for a genderless status like that of the angels; but that was something reserved almost exclusively to clerics, perhaps chiefly members of regular orders. As they could not annihilate sexual identity, it was an aspiration extremely hard to achieve or maintain.

The long twelfth century was undeniably important in the overall history of women, whether those women were real (like Eleanor of Aquitaine and Heloise) or conceptual (the idealised creatures of courtly love). Yet it remains debatable whether women fit into the search for a renaissance. Women's status raises many issues, most of which interlock with social, political, spiritual, and economic developments, and cannot conveniently or convincingly be isolated as aspects of renaissance. Characteristic of the tense overlap between the forces at work is the change in attitudes to marriage, and the emphasis on free consent as its constitutive element. By giving women (and, incidentally, men) the right to say no, the new definition of marriage in theory offered women greater liberty. Some women did reject proposed husbands; but the most famous case, Christina of Markyate, was not really seeking her own choice of husband, but the right to reject marriage completely and become a nun. That wish gained her powerful ecclesiastical allies, against her family. Despite the canonists many (if not most) marriages were arranged between families rather than individuals, with the 'right to choose' usually being crushed by family and society expectations and obligations.

   Totally to deny a female place in the cultural and intellectual currents of the long twelfth century would be wrong; but in general women appear as acted upon rather than acting independently. The few who can be named as real contributors are exceptional rather than char-acteristic. If women did gain more prominence in the twelfth century, it did not last. The spread of the image of the Coronation of the Virgin in the thirteenth century has been taken to signify the end of Mary's period of elevation: iconographically she was no longer Christ's equal, being now more submissive. The growing restrictions on nuns' freedom and the imposition of segregation from men, likewise changed their status. Such restrictions, often responding to male hostility, aptly reveal the limitations which affected not only the scale, but the very possibility, of a twelfth-century renaissance for women.

8

Towards a conclusion

U NAVOIDABLY, this book has dealt with the transformations of the
years 1050–1250 in a manner both basic and generalised. Its coverage
has also been highly selective, providing nothing like a complete account
of all the changes of the period. Evolutions in other fields (notably in
economic and social developments, and changes in the organisation and
spirituality of Christianity) are crucial to any attempt to construct the full
context. The mental changes stimulated by these combined developments
may be particularly important, contributing to the justification for other
labels which can be applied to the same time-span, like 'The Medieval
Reformation', or 'The Formation of a Persecuting Society'.[1] The broad
context is also important for any evaluation of the wider significance of
the issues dealt with in preceding chapters. The Europe of 1250 was very
different from that of 1050, only partly because of the transformations in
education, politics, theology, and so on. Even if the broader swathe of
developments cannot be discussed here, they must be recollected, to
allow the debate about a twelfth-century renaissance to be set against a
wider background.

While aiming to offer a broad survey, several fundamental questions
have so far been deliberately evaded. How far was there really a
'renaissance' in the long twelfth century? If there was one when, if at all,
did it end: was there a clear cut-off point; did things settle at a plateau; or
was there a further lift-off to something different, with a marked change

---

1 Both of these obviously coincide in some respects with the changes which have
already been considered. The evolution of the persecuting society is especially
tied in, since the intellectual validations of the persecutions were often produced
by academics, and some of the formulations can be associated with the
insecurity which newly prominent clerics felt about their real place in the world
(especially as newcomers with little social status), and who therefore were
seeking to consolidate their own positions by attacking 'outsiders'.

of direction? Such questions can no longer be avoided.

The long twelfth century, from 1050 to 1250, undeniably saw extensive changes in all areas of western European cultural and intellectual activity. To apply the renaissance label to them all, indiscriminately, reduces the phenomenon to an amorphous mass. To impose a precise definition would necessarily exclude at least some of the areas which have been considered, although what would be excluded would depend on the definition itself. To require a revival of the classical past – especially if 'classical' excludes the patristic authors – would marginalise canon law, and much theology; yet both were major features of the period. Equally, to demand that any twelfth-century renaissance match that of the fifteenth also imposes inappropriate demands (setting aside the assumption that the later movement can itself be satisfactorily defined).

To deny the 'renaissance' label to the twelfth century seems equally inappropriate. If the term conjures up images of intellectual and cultural dynamism, it certainly applies. To abandon it, and therewith the historiographical tradition, leaves the transformations which have been considered disconnected and fragmented, perhaps still requiring a label to give coherence and definition. When 'twelfth-century renaissance' is the established term, validated by common usage even without common assumptions of content, why reject it?

However, to retain the label simply for lack of a better alternative still leaves open the question of content. In recent decades the idea of a twelfth-century renaissance has become less clear, as a single tag has been applied to a wide (and widening) range of content. The imprecision also reflects the greater sophistication of historical research, which, in penetrating below the surfaces of texts and institutions, has revealed their complexities more clearly. Moreover, as differing regional emphases have been clarified, separate strands have become more distinct and diffuse.

Assuming that the idea and label of renaissance are to be retained, it does seem necessary to apply them in a strictly limited manner, to eliminate the current imprecision. Yet that very imprecision, and the varying attitudes of historians, make it unlikely that any redefinition will (or can) gain universal acceptance. Any revised definition – one that is to work – must provide a working answer to the questions of how, when, where, and why.

Arguably, the renaissance must centre on the changes associated with the development of theology as an academic discipline. This gives a geographical focus on developments in northern France, England, and (less securely) parts of Germany. With theology as its focal point, the content of the renaissance then broadens out: theology provides a

8] *The charmed circle*: Herrad of Hohenburg, *Hortus deliciarum c.* 1180. This illustration from the compilation by a German nun points towards the problem of inclusion and exclusion for the content of any 'twelfth-century renaissance'. In the centre Philosophy sits above two philosophers (one of whom is identified as Plato), with the outer circle containing the arts of the *trivium* and *quadrivium*, shown as female in accordance with traditional iconography. Outside the composition sit 'poets' and 'magi' (all of them male), the small black birds whispering into their ears suggesting that their compositions are wrongly inspired. That the whole work was compiled by a nun also points towards the issue of female involvement in the intellectual life of the twelfth century. The original text was destroyed in the Franco-Prussian war of 1870; only a nineteenth-century copy survives.

pinnacle, but a pinnacle needs supports. The philosophical and educational transitions are therefore included, and the translation movement, thereby expanding coverage to Spain, and to Italy. However, this focus also excludes a great deal, notably the advances in law and political ideas. Although the personnel sometimes overlap, and the theological and canonical/political strands interreact (and indeed combine in the political theology of papal monarchy in the early 1200s), the canonical and political movement should perhaps be treated as separate and distinct. Its centre has a different geographical location, in Italy (although obviously there is wider diffusion, notably in England). Maybe the legal–political changes reflect a different renaissance altogether; although canon law can be reintegrated if it is associated with the revised penitential system arising from the new theology, and with the concern to complete the Christianisation of Europe by imposing ecclesiastical discipline and eliminating challenges and obstacles from heretics and others.

Wider cultural developments, in the arts, music, and vernacular literature, must also be excluded. This may again seem too rigid; but is justifiable. Those evolutions again attest a different renaissance; although a unifying feature is harder to identify. Northern evolutions in almost every one of these fields differed strikingly from those in Italy; while the numerous vernaculars, even if sharing genres, created different responses.

These revisions leave not 'a' twelfth-century renaissance, but several renaissances. Yet among these, the educational and theological renaissance remains as the central trend, defined in terms applicable to the period, and without the later and better-known movement looking over its shoulder. The semantic debate about rebirth, renewal, and new birth can be set aside. What matters is to examine the period for what it produced, to see the label for what it is: only a label, but one applicable to something recognisable (although perhaps not instantly) as a movement with profound repercussions and implications, and with a certain integrity. It is a movement restricted geographically, its avowed centre at Paris. Its core is education towards a specific goal, the study of theology as a defined academic discipline. It is in Latin, defiantly learned, necessarily elitist, limited in the number of active participants, almost exclusively male. It may be an arrogant movement in asserting the preeminence of theology, its arrogance gaining practical expression in the campaigns to eliminate rival and alternative theologies, even when they were produced by others among the educated elite. The movement's immediate impact was perhaps relatively limited: being focused on theology, an esoteric science with restricted appeal, there would have been few practitioners. Nevertheless, those who reached the foothills and then departed – who went through a version of the arts curriculum at the cathedral schools, and then used their new learning to other ends, including careers in the new bureaucracies – were still products of the same processes, and this considerably widens the influence. Here there is a link with the legal–political movement, whose participants required the same initial skills, and used them to the same effect. However, the ultimate aims of that evolution were different. The influence broadens when the emergence of academic theology is linked with the period's increasing pastoral emphasis, especially in the wake of Lateran IV.

One objection to this formulation is that acceptance of the idea of several concurrent renaissances makes the choice of which one should be identified as the central movement rather arbitrary. That charge cannot be adequately refuted; the only response can be a challenge to establish the pre-eminence of one of the alternatives. Equally disturbing could be the accusation that a Paris-centred renaissance falls into the familiar trap of medieval history, in seeing France (and particularly northern France) as normative and everywhere else as dependent, subsidiary, or deviant. The vitality and distinctiveness of the broad Italian experience must be stressed, alongside what was happening north of the Alps. England's involvement may also merit greater emphasis. In several respects (the development of canon law, emergence of administrative kingship, creation of an Anglo-Norman literature, architecture) England can challenge France. The activities of English intellectuals, among whom John of Salisbury is pre-eminent for his many and varied contributions, also question the French monopoly.

Setting a finishing point for these transitions is not easy. The preceding chapters have mainly highlighted developments before 1200: although the 'long twelfth century' extends to c. 1250, the comment has usually tapered off around 1200–1225. The search for an ending to the assumed renaissance must look more closely at the first decades of the thirteenth century, when earlier changes came to fruition. The external stimuli so necessary up till then had initiated processes of investigation and analysis which could now produce their own results internally. Although Aristotelian works continued to be imported and translated up to c. 1260, the twelfth-century accessions had been integrated, and generated a new intellectual tradition, even if it was a tradition treated somewhat circumspectly at first. As a theological movement encompassing many other branches of learning, this new intellectual tradition established its own organisation, developed its own tools (including ways to deal more effectively with its primary materials). The potent combination of the mendicant orders, greater concern with pastoral care, and precise doctrinal analysis, produced an efflorescence of novel ideas, but also some ossification, as debates and conclusions fell into a routine. Yet the influence of the changes was not confined to academe: as its ideas were distilled into a manageable form, to define obligations and modes of participation in the broader Church, the theology was disseminated via general councils and diocesan synods to the parish priests, and through them to the people. While universities as such emerged only slowly and tentatively, the renewed educational activity of cathedral schools, and proliferation of mendicant *studia*, allowed the thirteenth century to build extensively on the bases established in the twelfth. Here the expansion of literacy is important, as the development of vernacular devotions, and with them the capacity and need to express theology in those languages, challenged established Latinate structures. Possibly Italy's experience was different: starting from a more literate base, especially in the towns, the change in levels of literacy may have had a less radical outcome.

Yet the identification of a definitive and definable end to the twelfth-century renaissance remains problematic. The routinisation of academic activity, the shift from dependence on external stimuli to a process of self-generation which might become no more than self-replication, perhaps marked a sort of ending. Possibly the influence of the changes was gradually dissipated, or the sense of novelty wore off. Former innovations and challenges lost their edge as they became ordinary and orthodox, and to historians orthodoxy is always less arresting than change and challenge. Perhaps that too is important: the sense of intellectual change in the thirteenth century is diminished by historians' own changing concerns. As the range of sources expands after 1200 – with that onset of archives which is perhaps the most significant physical legacy of the twelfth century – so historians can turn to new areas, can look more closely at peasants, the economy, Church organisation, and other aspects of society. Changes in the types of source allow the questions to be reformulated, and facilitate new types of investigation.

Arguably, then, the movement which derives from the twelfth century had no clear-cut finish. Rather, it seems to fizzle out as the changes reach a plateau. The translation of Aristotle's *Politics* can provide a convenient termination; perhaps Thomas Aquinas can be invoked as a last manifestation, offering the convenient consummation which reconciled Plato and Aristotle and so achieved the aspirations of the early twelfth-century thinkers. Yet as one renaissance ends, another is hard on its heels. Some would argue that the thirteenth century can justifiably claim the renaissance label for itself, at least in some parts of Europe. Like many other intellectual and cultural movements, the twelfth-century renaissance both fades in, and fades out. When the label was first applied, no one could foresee the difficulties which it would cause. As with all labels, it remains necessary to look behind the mask, so that even if consensus is lacking on what the twelfth-century renaissance actually was, there is understanding and appreciation of the different approaches to a phenomenon which is often at the same time intriguing and infuriating, and which was of profound significance for the intellectual and cultural development of western Europe.

Further reading

The potential bibliography for a book like this is immense. This list, however, is deliberately not exhaustive, being concerned primarily to suggest works to supplement and expand the arguments advanced in the main text, without being too esoteric. The list is deliberately limited to works in English, although continental scholarship obviously contributes extensively to work on the themes which have been covered.

The layout requires some comment. I begin with wide-ranging general works which offer indispensable surveys, or contribute significantly to establishing the background and broad context. Then follow lists for the individual chapters. The original intention was to divide these to match the subheadings; but that soon proved artificial and confusing, when many works could not be allocated neatly to one segment. I therefore list simply by chapter, hoping that the titles adequately indicate the content and issues addressed. Most of the works deal with only one aspect: I have usually excluded books where just an odd chapter is relevant, other than collections of essays (for those, I have given only basic details where several articles are relevant to a single chapter). In recent years volumes of reprinted articles have proliferated: where I know of such reprints I give details of both the original and republished versions. The overall policy may mean that some points covered in the text are omitted here: I have sometimes broken my rule to avoid that, but gaps will remain.

A difficulty with a chapter-oriented booklist is that some of the more wide-ranging twelfth-century writers resist such neat pigeon-holing. I have given a brief list of biographies and other works on such people, but this is more an admission of defeat than an attempt at full coverage. I end with a selection of twelfth-century texts now available in English translation, which give more immediate and direct access to the period, and illustrate the issues discussed in the book. (Some translations also appear on the chapter lists, because of the importance of their introductory matter. These are marked *, to aid identification.)

General surveys and background

Robert Bartlett, *The Making of Europe: Conquest, Colonization, and Cultural Change, 950–1350* (Princeton, NJ, 1993).

Robert L. Benson and Giles Constable (with Carol D. Lanham), eds, *Renaissance and Renewal in the Twelfth Century* (Oxford, 1982; reprinted Toronto, Buffalo, and London, 1991). (Because of the importance of this collection I have also included relevant contributions in the chapter lists. The volume is there cited as 'Benson and Constable'.)

M.D. Chenu, *Nature, Man, and Society in the Twelfth Century* (Chicago and London, 1968).

M.T. Clanchy, *From Memory to Written Record: England, 1066–1307* (2nd edn, Oxford and Cambridge, MA, 1993).

Charles Homer Haskins, *The Renaissance of the Twelfth Century* (Cambridge, MA, 1927).

R.I. Moore, *The Formation of a Persecuting Society* (Oxford, 1987).

Colin Morris, *The Papal Monarchy: the Western Church from 1050 to 1250* (Oxford, 1989).

Linda M. Paterson, *The World of the Troubadours: Medieval Occitan Society, c. 1100–c. 1300* (Cambridge, 1993).

R.W. Southern, *Medieval Humanism and Other Studies* (Oxford, 1970).

—— *Scholastic Humanism and the Unification of Europe, vol. 1: Foundations* (Oxford, 1995). The final two volumes of this major trilogy have not yet been published.

Brian Stock, *The Implications of Literacy: Written Language and Models of Interpretation in the Eleventh and Twelfth Centuries* (Princeton, NJ, 1983).

Individual chapters

CHAPTER 1: DEBATES AND CONTENTS

U.T. Holmes, jr., 'The idea of a twelfth-century renaissance', *Speculum*, 26 (1951), pp. 643–51.

R.S. Lopez, 'Still another renaissance?', *American Historical Review*, 57 (1951–2), pp. 1–21.

J.L. Nelson, 'On the limits of the Carolingian renaissance', *Studies in Church History*, 14 (1977), pp. 51–69.

William A. Nitze, 'The so-called twelfth century renaissance', *Speculum*, 23 (1948), pp. 464–71.

Erwin Panofsky, *Renaissance and Renascences in Western Art* (London, 1970).

E.M. Sanford, 'The twelfth century – renaissance or proto-renaissance?', *Speculum*, 26 (1951), pp. 635–42.

Warren Treadgold, ed., *Renaissances before the Renaissance: Cultural Revivals of Late Antiquity and the Middle Ages* (Stanford, CA, 1984).

For material on background and context, see 'General surveys and backgrounds'.

CHAPTER 2: EDUCATIONAL STRUCTURES

Material on the debate about the School of Chartres is marked ◆. See also R.W. Southern, 'Humanism and the School of Chartres', in his *Medieval Humanism and Other Studies* (Oxford, 1970), pp. 61–85; R.W. Southern, *Scholastic Humanism and the Unification of Europe, vol. 1: Foundations* (Oxford and Cambridge, MA, 1995), pp. 61–101 (pp. 61–88 are a corrected version of the material in *Medieval Humanism*).

John W. Baldwin, 'Masters at Paris from 1179 to 1215: a social perspective', in Benson and Constable, pp. 138–72.

Julia Barrow, 'Education and the recruitment of cathedral canons in England and Germany, 1100–1225', *Viator*, 20 (1989), pp. 117–38.

M.L. Colish, 'Another look at the school of Laon', *Archives d'histoire doctrinale et littéraire du moyen âge*, 61 (1986), pp. 1–22.

◆Peter Dronke, 'New approaches to the school of Chartres', *Anuario de estudios medievales*, 6 (1969), pp. 117–40.

Jean Dunbabin, 'From clerk to knight: changing orders', in *The Ideals and Practice of Medieval Knighthood, II: Papers from the Third Strawberry Hill Conference, 1986*, ed. C. Harper-Bill and R. Harvey (Woodbridge, 1988), pp. 26–39.

Gillian R. Evans, 'The influence of quadrivium studies in the eleventh- and twelfth-century schools', *Journal of Medieval History*, 1 (1975), pp. 151–64.

Stephen C. Ferruolo, *The Origins of the University: the Schools of Paris and their Critics, 1100–1215* (Stanford, CA, 1985).

Valerie I.J. Flint, 'The "School of Laon": a reconsideration', *Recherches de théologie ancienne et médiévale*, 43 (1976), pp. 89–110.

◆Nikolaus Häring, 'Chartres and Paris revisited', in *Essays in Honor of Anton Charles Pegis*, ed. J. Reginald O'Donnell (Toronto, 1974), pp. 268–329.

J.K. Hyde, 'Commune, university, and society in early medieval Bologna', in *Universities in Politics: Case Studies from the Late Middle Ages and Early Modern Period*, ed. J.W. Baldwin and R.A. Goldthwaite (Baltimore and London, 1972), pp. 17–46.

K.S.B. Keats-Rohan, 'John of Salisbury and education in twelfth century Paris from the account of his *Metalogicon*', *History of Universities*, 6 (1986–7), pp. 1–45.

Jean Leclerq, *The Love of Learning and the Desire for God: a Study of Monastic Culture* (New York, 1961).

Constant J. Mews, 'Orality, literacy, and authority in the twelfth-century schools', *Exemplaria*, 2 (1990), pp. 475–500.

J.J. Murphy, ed., *Medieval Eloquence: Studies in the Theory and Practice of Medieval Rhetoric* (Berkeley, Los Angeles, and London, 1978).

James J. Murphy, 'The teaching of Latin as a second language in the 12th century', *Historigraphia Linguistica*, 7 (1980), pp. 159–75.

William D. Patt, 'The early *Ars dictaminis* as response to a changing society', *Viator*, 9 (1978), pp. 133–55.

Suzanne Reynolds, *Medieval Reading: Grammar, Rhetoric, and the Classical Text* (Cambridge, 1996).

—— '"Let him read the *Satires* of Horace": Reading, literacy, and grammar in the twelfth century', in *The Practice and Representation of Reading in England*, ed. James Raven, Helen Small, and Naomi Tadmor (Cambridge, 1996), pp. 22–40 .

H. de Ridder-Symoens, ed., *A History of the University in Europe, vol. 1: Universities in the Middle Ages* (Cambridge, 1992).

◆R.W. Southern, *Platonism, Scholastic Method, and the School of Chartres*, The Stenton Lectures, 12 (Reading, 1979).

—— 'From schools to university', in *The History of the University of Oxford, I: The Early Oxford Schools*, ed. J.I. Catto (Oxford, 1984), pp. 1–36.

◆—— 'The schools of Paris and the school of Chartres', in Benson and Constable, pp. 113–37.

Ralph V. Turner, 'The "miles literatus" in twelfth- and thirteenth-century England: how rare a phenomenon?', *American Historical Review*, 83 (1978), pp. 928–45.

Sally N. Vaughn, 'Lanfranc, Anselm, and the school of Bec: in search of the students of Bec', in *The Culture of Christendom: Essays in Medieval History in Commemoration of Denis L.T. Bethell*, ed. Marc A. Meyer (London and Rio Grande, OH, 1993), pp. 155–81.

John R. Williams, 'The cathedral school of Rheims in the eleventh century', *Speculum*, 29 (1954), pp. 661–77.

—— 'The cathedral school of Reims in the time of Master Alberic, 1118–1136', *Traditio*, 20 (1964), pp. 93–114.

Roger Wright, *Late Latin and Early Romance in Spain and Carolingian France*, ARCA Classical and Medieval Texts, Papers, and Monographs, 8 (London, 1982).

CHAPTER 3: PAST, PRESENT, AND FUTURE: LEGACIES, IMPORTS, MEMORIES

M.-T. d'Alverny, 'Translations and translators', in Benson and Constable, pp. 421–62.

Elizabeth A.R. Brown, '*Falsitas pia sive reprehendabilis*: Medieval forgers and their intentions', in *Fälschungen im Mittelalter: Internationaler Kongress der Monumenta Germaniae Historica, München, 16.–19. September 1986*, Monumenta Germaniae Historica, Schriften 33, 6 vols (Hamburg, 1988–90), 1, pp. 101–19.

P. Classen, '*Res gestae*, universal history, apocalypse: visions of past and future', in Benson and Constable, pp. 387–417.

Giles Constable, *Culture and Spirituality in Medieval Europe* (Aldershot, 1996).

—— 'Forgery and plagiarism in the middle ages', ch. I [reprinted from *Archiv für Diplomatik*, 29 (1983), pp. 1–41].

—— 'Forged letters in the middle ages', ch. II [reprinted from *Fälschungen im Mittelalter: Internationaler Kongress der Monumenta Germaniae Historica, München, 16.–19. September 1986*, Monumenta Germaniae Historica, Schriften 33, 6 vols (Hamburg, 1988–90), 5, pp. 11–37].

—— 'Dictators and diplomats in the eleventh and twelfth centuries: medieval epistolography and the birth of modern bureaucracy', ch. III [reprinted from *Homo Byzantinus: Papers in Honour of Alexander Kazhdan*, ed. Anthony Cutler and Simon Franklin (= *Dumbarton Oaks Papers*, 46), (Washington, DC, 1992), pp. 37–46].

—— *Culture and Spirituality in Medieval Europe* (Aldershot, 1996).

—— 'Past and present in the eleventh and twelfth centuries: perceptions of time and change', ch. IV [reprinted from *L'Europa dei secoli XI e XII fra novità e tradizione: Sviluppi di una cultura. Atti della decima Settimana internazionale di studio, Mendola, 25–29 agosto 1986*, Pubblicazioni dell'Università cattolica del Sacro Cuore: Miscellanea del Centro di studi medioevali, 12 (Milan, 1989), pp. 135–70].

—— 'A living past: the historical environment of the middle ages', ch. V [reprinted from *Harvard Library Bulletin*, new ser. 1/3 (1990), pp. 49–70].

P. Damian-Grint, 'Truth, trust, and evidence in the Anglo-Norman *Estoire*', *Anglo-Norman Studies*, 18 (1995), pp. 63–78.

John Gillingham, 'The context and purposes of Geoffrey of Monmouth's *History of the Kings of Britain*', *Anglo-Norman Studies*, 13 (1991), pp. 99–118.

Aryeh Grabois, 'The *Hebraica veritas* and Jewish–Christian intellectual relations in the twelfth century', *Speculum*, 50 (1975), pp. 613–34.

D. Greenway, 'Authority, convention and observation in Henry of Huntingdon's *Historia Anglorum*', *Anglo-Norman Studies*, 18 (1995), pp. 105–21.

Nicholas M. Haring, 'The Porretans and the Greek Fathers', *Mediaeval Studies*, 24 (1962), pp. 181–209.

T. Janson, *Prose Rhythm in Medieval Latin from the 9th to the 13th Century*, Acta universitatis Stockholmiensis, studia latina Stockholmiensia, 20 (Stockholm, 1975).

Janet Martin, 'Classicism and style in Latin literature', in Benson and Constable, pp. 537–68.

—— 'John of Salisbury as classical scholar', in *The World of John of Salisbury*, ed. Michael Wilks, Studies in church history, subsidia 3 (2nd edn, Oxford, 1994), pp. 179–201.

—— 'Uses of tradition: Gellius, Petronius, and John of Salisbury', *Viator*, 10 (1979), pp. 57–94.

M.B. Parkes, 'The influence of the concepts of *ordinatio* and *compilatio* on the development of the book', in *Medieval Scribes, Manuscripts, and Libraries: Essays Presented to N.R. Ker*, ed. M.B. Parkes and A.G. Watson (London, 1978), pp. 115–41.

G. Pollard, 'The *pecia* system in the medieval universities', in *Medieval Scribes, Manuscripts, and Libraries: Essays Presented to N.R. Ker*, ed. M.B. Parkes and A.G. Watson (London, 1978), pp. 145–61.

Richard H. Rouse, '*Florilegia* and Latin classical authors in twelfth- and thirteenth-century Orléans', *Viator*, 10 (1979), pp. 131–60.

Richard H. Rouse and Mary A. Rouse, '*Statim invenire*: schools, preachers, and new attitudes to the page', in Benson and Constable, pp. 201–25.

R.W. Southern, 'Aspects of the European tradition of historical writing, 1: The classical tradition from Einhard to Geoffrey of Monmouth', *Transactions of the Royal Historical Society*, 5th ser., 20 (1970), pp. 173–96.

—— 'Aspects of the European tradition of historical writing, 2: Hugh of St Victor and the idea of historical development', *Transactions of the Royal Historical Society*, 5th ser., 21 (1971), pp. 159–79.

—— 'Aspects of the European tradition of historical writing, 3: History as prophecy', *Transactions of the Royal Historical Society*, 5th ser., 22 (1972), pp. 159–80.

—— 'Aspects of the European tradition of historical writing, 4: The sense of the past', *Transactions of the Royal Historical Society*, 5th ser., 23 (1973), pp. 243–63.

G.M. Spiegel, *Romancing the Past: the Rise of Vernacular Prose Historiography in Thirteenth-Century France* (Berkeley, Los Angeles, and London, 1993).

CHAPTER 4: LAW, POLITICS, AND GOVERNMENT

Thomas Behrmann, 'The development of pragmatic literacy in the Lombard city communes', in *Pragmatic Literacy, East and West: 1200–1330*, ed. Richard Britnell (Woodbridge, 1997), pp. 25–41.

R.L. Benson, 'Political *renovatio*: two models from Roman antiquity', in Benson and Constable, pp. 339–86.

John F. Benton, 'Written records and the development of systematic feudal relations', in John F. Benton (ed. Thomas N. Bisson), *Culture, Power and Personality in Medieval France* (London and Rio Grande, OH, 1991), pp. 275–90.

Thomas N. Bisson, *The Fiscal Accounts of Catalonia under the Early Count-Kings (1151–1213)*, 2 vols (Berkeley, Los Angeles, and London, 1984). Vol. 1 contains the introduction and discussion of the administrative arrangements; vol. 2 edits the records, in Latin.

P. Brand, *The Origins of the English Legal Profession* (Oxford and Cambridge, MA, 1992).

James A. Brundage, *Medieval Canon Law* (London and New York, 1995).

Philippe Buc, '*Principes gentium dominantur eorum*: princely power between legitimacy and illegitimacy in twelfth-century exegesis', in *Cultures of Power: Lordship, Status, and Process in Twelfth-Century Europe*, ed. Thomas N. Bisson (Philadelphia, PA, 1995), pp. 310–28.

M. Burger, 'Sending, joining, writing, and speaking in the diocesan administration of thirteenth-century England', *Mediaeval Studies*, 55 (1993), pp. 151–82.

Joseph Canning, *A History of Medieval Political Thought, 300–1450* (London and New York, 1996).

Stanley Chodorow, *Christian Political Theory and Church Politics in the Mid-Twelfth Century: the Ecclesiology of Gratian's Decretum* (Berkeley, Los Angeles, and London, 1972). See also the review by Robert L. Benson in *Speculum*, 50 (1975), pp. 97–106.

——— 'Dishonest litigation in the church courts, 1140–98', in *Law, Church, and Society: Essays in Honor of Stephan Kuttner*, ed. Kenneth Pennington and Robert Somervile (Philadelphia, PA, 1977), pp. 187–206.

M.T. Clanchy, '*Moderni* in education and government in England', *Speculum*, 50 (1975), pp. 671–88.

Charles Duggan, *Twelfth-Century Decretal Collections and their Importance in English History*, University of London historical studies, 12 (London, 1963).

——— 'Papal judges delegate and the making of the "new law" in the twelfth century', in *Cultures of Power: Lordship, Status, and Process in Twelfth-Century Europe*, ed. Thomas N. Bisson (Philadelphia, PA, 1995), pp. 172–99 .

John H. van Engen, 'Observations on "De consecratione"', in *Proceedings of the Sixth International Congress of Medieval Canon Law: Berkeley, California, 28 July–2 August 1980*, ed. S. Kuttner and K. Pennington, Monumenta iuris canonici, series C: subsidia 7 (Vatican City, 1985), pp. 309–20.

C. Warren Hollister and John W. Baldwin, 'The rise of administrative kingship: Henry I and Philip Augustus', *American Historical Review*, 83 (1978), pp. 867–905.

*Donald J. Kagay, ed., *The Usatges of Barcelona: the Fundamental Law of Catalonia* (Philadelphia, PA, 1994).

Stephan Kuttner, 'The revival of jurisprudence', in Benson and Constable, pp. 299–323.

Cary J. Nederman, *Medieval Aristotelianism and its Limits: Classical Traditions in Moral and Political Philosophy, 12th–15th Centuries* (Aldershot and Brookfield, VT, 1997):

——— 'The physiological significance of the organic metaphor in John of Salisbury's *Policraticus*', ch. VI [reprinted from *History of Political Thought*, 8 (1987), pp. 211–23].

——— 'A duty to kill: John of Salisbury's theory of tyrannicide', ch. VII [reprinted from *Review of Politics*, 50 (1988), pp. 365–89].

J.T. Noonan, 'Gratian slept here: the changing identity of the father of the systematic study of canon law', *Traditio*, 35 (1979), pp. 145–79.

Knut Wolfgang Nörr, 'Institutional foundations of the new jurisprudence', in Benson and Constable, pp. 324–38.

W.M. Ormrod and János Barta, 'The feudal structure and the beginnings of state finance', in *Economic Systems and State Finance*, ed. Richard Bonney (Oxford, 1995), pp. 53–79.

Zvi Razi and Richard M. Smith, 'The origins of the English manorial court rolls as a written record: a puzzle', in *Medieval Society and the Manor Court*, ed. Z. Razi and R.M. Smith (Oxford, 1996), pp. 36–68.

I.S. Robinson, *Authority and Resistance in the Investiture Contest* (Manchester, 1978).

O.F. Robinson, T.D. Fergus, and W.M. Gordon, eds, *European Legal History: Sources and Institutions*, 2nd edn (London, Dublin, and Edinburgh, 1994).

Hiroshi Takayama, *The Administration of the Norman Kingdom of Sicily* (Leiden, New York, and Köln, 1993).

W. Ullmann, 'The significance of Innocent III's decretal, *Vergentis*', in *Études d'histoire du droit canonique dédiées à Gabriel le Bras* (Paris, 1965), pp. 729–41 [reprinted in W. Ullmann, *The Papacy and Political Ideas in the Middle Ages* (London, 1976), ch. 5].

H. Vollrath, 'Ideal and reality in twelfth-century Germany', in *England and Germany in the High Middle Ages*, ed. A. Haverkamp and H. Vollrath (London, 1996), pp. 93–104.

W.L. Warren, *The Governance of Norman and Angevin England, 1086–1272* (London, 1987).

C. Wickham, 'Lineages of western European taxation, 1000–1200', in *Actes: Col·loqui corona, municipis i fiscalitat a la baixa edat mitjana*, ed. M. Sánchez and A. Furió (Lleida, 1997), pp. 25–42.

Helene Wieruszowski, 'Roger II of Sicily, *Rex-Tyrannus*, in twelfth-century political thought', *Speculum*, 38 (1963), pp. 46–78 [reprinted in Helene Wieruszowski, *Politics and Culture in Medieval Spain and Italy*, Storie e letteratura: raccolta di Studi e Testi, 121 (Rome, 1971), pp. 51–97].

*F. de Zulueta and P. Stein, *The Teaching of Roman Law in England around 1200*, Selden Society, supplementary ser., 8 (London, 1990).

CHAPTER 5: INTELLECTUAL TRANSITIONS: PHILOSOPHY AND THEOLOGY, HUMANISM AND INDIVIDUALISM.

A.S. Abulafia, *Christians and Jews in the Twelfth-Century Renaissance* (London and New York, 1995).

Milton V. Anastos, 'Some aspects of Byzantine influence on Latin thought', in *Twelfth-Century Europe and the Foundations of Modern Society*, ed. Marshall Clagett, Gaines Post, and Robert Reynolds (Madison, WI, 1961), pp. 131–87.

Sverre Bagge, 'The autobiography of Abelard and medieval individualism', *Journal of Medieval History*, 19 (1993), pp. 327–50.

John W. Baldwin, *Masters, Princes, and Merchants: the Social Views of Peter the Chanter and his Circle*, 2 vols (Princeton, NJ, 1970).

John F. Benton, *Culture, Power and Personality in Medieval France*, ed. Thomas N. Bisson (London and Rio Grande, OH, 1991):

—— 'The personality of Guibert de Nogent', pp. 293–312 [reprinted from *Psychoanalytical Review*, 57 (1971), pp. 563–86].

—— 'Individualism and conformity in medieval western Europe', pp. 313–26 [reprinted from *Individualism and Conformity in Classical Islam*, ed. Amin Banani and Speros Vryonis, jr. (Wiesbaden, 1977), pp. 145–58].

—— 'Consciousness of self and perceptions of individuality', pp. 327–56 [reprinted from Benson and Constable, pp. 263–95].

John Boswell, *Christianity, Social Tolerance, and Homosexuality: Gay People in Western Europe from the Beginning of the Christian Era to the Fourteenth Century* (Chicago and London, 1980).

Leonard E. Boyle, 'The inter-conciliar period, 1179–1215, and the beginnings of pastoral manuals', in *Miscellanea Rolando Bandinelli, Papa Alessandro III*, ed. Filippo Liotta (Siena, 1986), pp. 43–56.

Caroline Walker Bynum, 'Did the twelfth century discover the individual?', *Journal of Ecclesiastical History*, 31 (1980), pp. 1–17 [reprinted in expanded form in Caroline Walker Bynum, *Jesus as Mother: Studies in the Spirituality of the High Middle Ages* (Berkeley, Los Angeles, and London, 1982), pp. 82–109].

Jeremy Cohen, 'The mentality of the medieval Jewish apostate: Peter Alfonsi, Hermann of Cologne, and Pablo Christiani', in *Jewish Apostasy in the Modern World*, ed. Todd M. Endelman (New York and London, 1987), pp. 20–47.

Marcia L. Colish, *Peter Lombard*, Brill's studies in intellectual history, 41, 2 vols (Leiden, New York, and Köln, 1994).

Giles Constable, *Letters and Letter Collections*, Typologie des sources du moyen âge occidental, Fasc. 17 A–II (Turnhout, 1976).

K. Danziger, 'The historical formation of selves', in *Self and Identity: Fundamental Issues*, ed. Richard D. Ashmore and Lee Jussim, Rutgers series on self and social identity, 1 (New York and Oxford, 1997), pp. 137–59.

Peter Dronke, ed., *A History of Twelfth-Century Philosophy* (Cambridge, 1988).

G.R. Evans, *Alan of Lille: the Frontiers of Theology in the Later Twelfth Century* (Cambridge, 1983).

—— *Old Arts and New Theology: the Beginnings of Theology as an Academic Discipline* (Oxford, 1980).

—— 'Alan of Lille and the threshold of theology', *Analecta Cisterciensia*, 36 (1980), pp. 129–47.

—— 'The borrowed meaning: grammar, logic, and the problem of theological language in C12 schools', *Downside Review*, 96 (1978), pp. 165–75.

—— 'The uncompleted *Heptateuch* of Thierry of Chartres', *History of Universities*, 3 (1983), pp. 1–13.

Chris D. Ferguson, 'Autobiography as therapy: Guibert de Nogent, Peter Abelard, and the making of medieval autobiography', *Journal of Medieval and Renaissance Studies*, 13 (1983), pp. 187–212.

Donald K. Frank, 'Abelard as imitator of Christ', *Viator*, 1 (1970), pp. 107–13.

N. Golb, 'Notes on the conversion of European Christians to Judaism in the eleventh century', *Journal of Jewish Studies*, 16 (1965), pp. 69–74.

Robert W. Hanning, *The Individual in Twelfth-Century Romance* (New Haven and London, 1977).

Julian Haseldine, 'Understanding the language of *amicitia*: the friendship circle of Peter of Celle (c. 1115–1183)', *Journal of Medieval History*, 20 (1994), pp. 237–60.

Thomas Head, '"Monastic" and "scholastic" theology: a change of paradigm?', in *Paradigms in Medieval Thought Applications in Medieval Disciplines*, ed. N. van Deusen and A.E. Ford, Mediaeval studies, 3 (Lewiston, NY, 1990), pp. 127–41.

J. Kritzeck, *Peter the Venerable and Islam* (Princeton, NJ, 1964).

Jean Leclerq, 'The renewal of theology', in Benson and Constable, pp. 68–87.

D.E. Luscombe, *The School of Peter Abelard: the Influence of Abelard's Thought in the Early Scholastic Period*, Cambridge studies in medieval life and thought, 2nd ser., 14 (Cambridge, 1969).

John Marenbon, *Early Medieval Philosophy (480–1150): an Introduction* (London, Boston, Melbourne and Henley, 1983).

—— *Later Medieval Philosophy (1150–1350): an Introduction* (London and New York, 1987).

—— 'The twelfth century', in *Routledge History of Philosophy, vol. III: Medieval Philosophy*, ed. John Marenbon (London and New York, 1998), pp. 150–87.

Colin Morris, *The Discovery of the Individual, 1050–1200* (London, 1972; reprinted Toronto, Buffalo, and London, 1987).

—— 'Individualism in twelfth century religion: some further reflections', *Journal of Ecclesiastical History*, 31 (1980), pp. 195–206.

Cary J. Nederman, *Medieval Aristotelianism and its Limits: Classical Traditions in Moral and Political Philosophy, 12th–15th Centuries* (Aldershot and Brookfield, VT, 1997):

—— 'Aristotelian ethics before the *Nicomachean Ethics*: alternative sources of Aristotle's concept of virtue in the twelfth century', ch. I [reprinted from *Parergon*, new ser., 7 (1989), pp. 55–75].

—— 'Aristotelianism and the origins of "political science" in the twelfth century', ch. II [reprinted from *Journal of the History of Ideas*, 52 (1991), pp. 179–94].

—— 'Nature, ethics, and the doctrine of "*habitus*": Aristotelian moral psychology in the twelfth century', ch. III [reprinted from *Traditio*, 45 (1989–90), pp. 87–110].

—— 'Knowledge, virtue and the path to wisdom: the unexamined Aristotelianism of John of Salisbury's *Metalogicon*', ch. IX [reprinted from *Mediaeval Studies*, 51 (1989), pp. 268–86].

G.W. Olsen, 'Twelfth-century humanism reconsidered: the case of St. Bernard', *Studi medievali*, 3rd ser., 31 (1990), pp. 27–53.

Jaroslav Pelikan, *The Christian Tradition; a History of the Development of Doctrine, 3: the Growth of Medieval Theology (600–1300)* (Chicago and London, 1978).

G. Post, 'Philosophantes and philosophi in Roman and canon law', *Archives d'histoire doctrinale et littéraire du moyen âge*, 19 (1954), pp. 135–8.

F. Robb, 'The fourth Lateran Council's definition of Trinitarian orthodoxy', *Journal of Ecclesiastical History*, 48 (1997), pp. 22–43.

Beryl Smalley, *The Study of the Bible in the Middle Ages*, 3rd edn (Oxford, 1983).

Martin Stevens, 'The performing self in twelfth-century culture', *Viator*, 9 (1978), pp. 193–218.

Tina Stiefel, *The Intellectual Revolution in Twelfth-Century Europe* (London and Sydney, 1985).

—— 'Science, reason and faith in the twelfth century: the cosmologists' attack on tradition', *Journal of European Studies*, 6 (1976), pp. 1–16.

—— 'The heresy of science: a twelfth-century conceptual revolution', *Isis*, 68 (1977), pp. 347–62.

Brian Stock, *Myth and Science in the Twelfth Century: a Study of Bernard Silvester* (Princeton, NJ, 1972).

F. Wade, 'Abelard and individuality', in *Die Metaphysik im Mittelalter: ihr Ursprung und ihre Bedeutung*, ed. P. Wilpert, Miscellanea Mediaevalia, 2 (Berlin, 1963), pp. 165–71.

Winthrop Wetherbee, *Platonism and Poetry in the Twelfth Century: the Literary Influence of the School of Chartres* (Princeton, NJ, 1972).

Ulrike Wiethaus, 'In search of medieval women's friendships: Hildegard of Bingen's letters to her female contemporaries', in *Maps of Flesh and Light: the Religious Experience of Medieval Women Mystics*, ed. Ulrike Wiethaus (Syracuse, NY, 1993), pp. 93–111, 174–7.

CHAPTER 6: THE ARTS, VERNACULAR LITERATURE, AND MUSIC

John W. Baldwin, 'The image of the jongleur in northern France around 1200', *Speculum*, 77 (1997), pp. 635–63.

John F. Benton, 'The court of Champagne as a literary center', *Speculum*, 36 (1961), pp. 551–91 [reprinted in John F. Benton (ed. Thomas N. Bisson), *Culture, Power and Personality in Medieval France* (London and Rio Grande, OH, 1991), pp. 1–43].

Herbert Bloch, 'The new fascination with ancient Rome', in Benson and Constable, pp. 615–36.

Jean Bony, *French Gothic Architecture of the 12th and 13th Centuries* (Berkeley, Los Angeles, and London, 1983).

Karen M. Broadhurst, 'Henry II of England and Eleanor of Aquitaine: patrons of literature in French?', *Viator*, 27 (1996), pp. 53–84.

Walter Cahn, *Romanesque Manuscripts: the Twelfth Century*, 2 vols (London, 1996).

M. Cothren, 'Cistercian tile mosaic pavements in Yorkshire: context and sources', in *Studies in Cistercian Art and Architecture*, 1, ed. M.P. Lillich, Cistercian studies series, 66 (Kalamazoo, MI, 1982), pp. 112–29.

B.E. Crawford, ed., *St Magnus Cathedral, and Orkney's Twelfth-Century Renaissance* (Aberdeen, 1988).

Richard Crocker and David Hiley, eds, *The Early Middle Ages to 1300*, New Oxford history of music (2nd edn), 2 (Oxford, 1990).

C.R. Dodwell, *The Pictorial Arts of the West, 800–1200* (New Haven and London, 1993).

Peter Dronke, 'Profane elements in literature', in Benson and Constable, pp. 569–92.

Beverly J. Evans, 'Music, text, and social context: reexamining thirteenth-century styles', in *Contexts: Style and Values in Medieval Art and Literature*, ed. Daniel Poirion and Nancy Freeman Regalado, *Yale French Studies*, special issue (New Haven and London, 1991), pp. 183–95.

Paula Lieber Gerson, ed., *Abbot Suger and Saint-Denis: a Symposium* (New York, 1986).

Natasa Golub, *Twelfth-Century Cistercian Manuscripts: the Sitticum Collection* (Ljubljana and London, 1996).

G.B. Guest, *Bible moralisée: codex Vindobonensis 2554, Vienna, Österreichische National-bibliothek* (London, 1995).

Ruth E. Harvey, 'Joglars and the professional status of the early troubadours', *Medium Ævum*, 62 (1993), pp. 221–41.

Denis Hollier, ed., *A New History of French Literature* (Cambridge, MA, and London, 1989).

C. Stephen Jaeger, 'Patrons and the beginnings of courtly romance', in *The Medieval opus: Imitation, Rewriting, and Transmission in the French Tradition. Proceedings of the Symposium held at the Institute for Research in the Humanities, October 6–7 1995, The University of Wisconsin-Madison*, ed. Douglas Kelly, Faux titre, 116 (Amsterdam and Atlanta, GA, 1996), pp. 45–58.

Ernst Kitzinger, *The Art of Byzantium and the Medieval West: Selected Studies*, ed. W. Eugene Kleinbauer, (Bloomington, IN, and London, 1976):

—— 'The first mosaic decoration of Salerno cathedral', pp. 271–89 [reprinted from *Jahrbuch der Österreichischen Byzantinistik*, 21 (1972), pp. 149–62].

—— 'World map and Fortune's wheel: a medieval mosaic floor in Turin', pp. 327–56 [reprinted from *Proceedings of the American Philosophical Society*, 117/5 (1973), pp. 343–73].

—— 'The Byzantine contribution to western art of the twelfth and thirteenth centuries', pp. 357–88 [reprinted from *Dumbarton Oaks Papers*, 20 (1966), pp. 25–47, 265–6].

—— 'Mosaic decoration in Sicily under Roger II and the classical Byzantine system of church decoration', in *Italian Church Decoration of the Middle Ages and Early Renaissance: Functions, Forms and Regional Traditions*, ed. William Tronzo, Villa Spelman Colloquia, 1 (Bologna, 1989), pp. 147–65.

—— 'The arts as aspects of a Renaissance: Rome and Italy', in Benson and Constable, pp. 637–70.

—— 'The Gregorian reform and the visual arts: a problem of method', *Transactions of the Royal Historical Society*, 5th ser., 22 (1972), pp. 87–102.

Hans Erich Kubach, *Romanesque Architecture* (London, 1988).

B. Kühnel, *Crusader Art of the Twelfth Century: a Geographical, an Historical, or an Art Historical Notion?* (Berlin, 1994).

Peter Lasko, *Ars Sacra, 800–1200* (Harmondsworth, 1972).

Sarah Macready and F.H. Thompson, eds, *Art and Patronage in the English Romanesque*, Society of Antiquaries of London: Occasional Paper (new ser.), 8 (London, 1986).

Per Nykrog, 'The rise of literary fiction', in Benson and Constable, pp. 593–612.

Christopher Page, *The Owl and the Nightingale: Musical Life and Ideas in France, 1100–1300* (London, 1989).

Elizabeth C. Parker and Charles T. Little, *The Cloisters Cross: its Art and Meaning* (London, 1994).

Michael Richter, 'Lingua latina – sacra seu vulgaris?', in *The Bible and Medieval Culture*, ed. W. Lourdaux and D. Verhelst, Mediaevalia lovaniensia, ser. I, studia VII (Louvain, 1979), pp. 16–34.

Conrad Rudolph, *Artistic Change at St-Denis: Abbot Suger's Program and the Early Twelfth-Century Controversy over Art* (Princeton, NJ, 1990).

Willibald Sauerländer, 'Architecture and the figurative arts: the north', in Benson and Constable, pp. 671–710.

Ian Short, 'Patrons and polyglots: French literature in twelfth-century England', *Anglo-Norman Studies*, 14 (1991), pp. 229–49.

Leo Treitler, 'Oral, written, and literate process in the transmission of medieval music', *Speculum*, 56 (1981), pp. 471–91.

P. Williamson, *Gothic Sculpture, 1140–1300* (New Haven and London, 1995).

Alois Wolf, 'Rewriting chansons de geste for a Middle High German public', in *The Medieval* opus: *Imitation, Rewriting, and Transmission in the French Tradition. Proceedings of the Symposium held at the Institute for Research in the Humanities, October 6–7 1995, The University of Wisconsin-Madison*, ed. Douglas Kelly, Faux titre, 116 (Amsterdam and Atlanta, GA, 1996), pp. 369–86.

L.M. Wright, 'Misconceptions concerning the troubadours, trouvères and minstrels', *Music and Letters*, 48 (1967), pp. 35–9.

Roger Wright, 'Translation between Latin and Romance in the Early Middle Ages', in *Translation Theory and Practice in the Middle Ages*, ed. Jeanette Beer, Studies in medieval culture, 38 (Kalamazoo, MI, 1997), pp. 7–32.

George Zarnecki, Janet Holt, and Tristram Holland, eds, *English Romanesque Art, 1066–1200: Hayward Gallery, London, 5 April–8 July 1984* (London, 1984).

CHAPTER 7: A RENAISSANCE FOR WOMEN?

Material discussing the authenticity of the letters of Abelard and Heloise is marked with #.

Richard Abels and Ellen Harrison, 'The participation of women in Languedocian Catharism', *Mediaeval Studies*, 41 (1979), pp. 215–51.

Gillian T.W. Ahlgren, 'Visions and rhetorical strategy in the letters of Hildegard of Bingen', in *Dear Sister: Medieval Women and the Epistolary Genre*, ed. Karen Charewatuk and Ulrike Wiethaus (Philadelphia, PA, 1993), pp. 46–63.

John F. Benton, *Culture, Power and Personality in Medieval France*, ed. Thomas N. Bisson, (London and Rio Grande, OH, 1991):

—— 'Clio and Venus: a historical view of medieval love', pp. 99–121 [reprinted from *The Meaning of Courtly Love*, ed. F.X. Newman (Albany, NY, 1968), pp. 19–42].

—— 'Trotula, women's problems, and the professionalization of medicine in the middle ages', pp. 363–86 [reprinted from *Bulletin of the History of Medicine*, 59 (1985), pp. 30–53].

#—— 'Fraud, fiction and borrowing in the correspondence of Abelard and Heloise', pp. 417–53 [reprinted from *Pierre Abélard – Pierre le Vénérable*, Colloques internationaux du Centre nationale de la recherche scientifique, 546 (Paris, 1975), pp. 471–506].

#—— 'A reconsideration of the authenticity of the correspondence of Abelard and Heloise', pp. 475–86 [reprinted from *Petrus Abaelardus: Person, Werke, und Wirkung*, ed. Rudolf Thomas, Trierer theologischen Studien, 38 (1980), pp. 41–52] .

#—— 'The correspondence of Abelard and Heloise', pp. 487–512 [reprinted from *Fälschungen im Mittelalter: Internationaler Kongress der Monumenta Germaniae Historica, München, 16.–19. September 1986*, Monumenta Germaniae Historica, Schriften 33, 6 vols (Hamburg, 1988–90), 5, pp. 95–120].

*Meg Bogin, *The Women Troubadours* (New York and London, 1976).

Caroline Walker Bynum, 'Jesus as mother and abbot as mother: some themes in twelfth-century Cistercian writing', in Caroline Walker Bynum, *Jesus as Mother: Studies in the Spirituality of the High Middle Ages* (Berkeley, Los Angeles, and London, 1982), pp. 110–69.

Madeline H. Caviness, 'Anchoress, abbess, and queen: donors and patrons or intercessors and matrons', in *The Cultural Patronage of Medieval Women*, ed. June Hall McCash (Athens, GA, and London, 1996), pp. 105–54.

#Peter Dronke, *Abelard and Heloise in Medieval Testimonies*, W.P. Ker Lecture, 26 (Glasgow, 1976).

Georges Duby, 'Women and power', in *Cultures of Power: Lordship, Status, and Process in Twelfth-Century Europe*, ed. Thomas N. Bisson (Philadelphia, PA, 1995), pp. 69–85.

Joan M. Ferrante, 'The education of women in the middle ages in theory, fact, and fantasy', in *Beyond Their Sex: Learned Women of the European Past*, ed. P.H. Labalme (New York and London, 1984), pp. 9–42.

Lois L. Huneycutt, '"Proclaiming her dignity abroad": the literary and artistic network of Matilda of Scotland, queen of England 1100–1118', in *The Cultural Patronage of Medieval Women*, ed. June Hall McCash (Athens, GA, and London, 1996), pp. 155–74.

Karen K. Jambeck, 'The *Fables* of Marie de France: a mirror of princes', in *In Quest of Marie de France, a Twelfth-Century Poet*, ed. Chantal A. Maréchal (Lewiston, NY,

Queenston, Ont., and Lampeter, 1992), pp. 59–106.

Patricia A. Kazarow, 'Text and context in Hildegard of Bingen's *Ordo virtutum*', in *Maps of Flesh and Light: the Religious Experience of Medieval Women Mystics*, ed. Ulrike Wiethaus (Syracuse, NY, 1993), pp. 127–51, 179–82.

Christiane Klapisch-Zuber, ed., *A History of Women in the West: II, Silences of the Middle Ages* (Cambridge, MA, and London, 1992).

Glenda McLeod, '"Wholly guilty, wholly innocent": self-definition in Héloïse's letters to Abélard', in *Dear Sister: Medieval Women and the Epistolary Genre*, ed. Karen Charewatuk and Ulrike Wiethaus (Philadelphia, PA, 1993), pp. 64–86.

Jo Ann McNamara, 'The *Herrenfrage*: the restructuring of the gender system, 1050–1150', in *Medieval Masculinities: Regarding Men in the Middle Ages*, ed. Clare A. Lees, Medieval cultures, 7 (Minneapolis, MN, and London, 1994), pp. 3–29.

Barbara Newman, *From Virile Woman to Woman Christ: Studies in Medieval Religion and Literature* (Philadelphia, PA, 1995):

—— *Sister of Wisdom: St Hildegard's Theology of the Feminine* (Aldershot, 1987).

—— 'Flaws in the golden bowl: gender and spiritual formation in the twelfth century', pp. 19–45, 252–62 [reprinted from *Traditio*, 45 (1989–90), pp. 111–46].

#—— 'Authority, authenticity, and the repression of Heloise', pp. 46–75, 262–9 [reprinted from *Journal of Medieval and Renaissance Studies*, 22 (1992), pp. 121–57].

Harriet Speigel, 'The woman's voice in the *Fables* of Marie de France', in *In Quest of Marie de France, a Twelfth-Century Poet*, ed. Chantal A. Maréchal (Lewiston, NY, Queenston, Ont., and Lampeter, 1992), pp. 45–58.

Katharina M. Wilson, ed., *Medieval Women Writers* (Manchester, 1984).

Biographies

M.T. Clanchy, *Abelard: a Medieval Life* (Oxford and Cambridge, MA, 1997).

Anne L. Clark, *Elisabeth of Schönau, a Twelfth-Century Visionary* (Philadelphia, PA, 1992)

John H. van Engen, *Rupert of Deutz* (Berkeley, Los Angeles, and London, 1983).

V.I.J. Flint, 'Honorius Augustodunensis', in *Authors of the Middle Ages, vol. 2, nos 5–6* (Aldershot, 1995), pp. 89–183 [also published separately].

Hans Liebeschütz, *Mediaeval Humanism in the Life and Writings of John of Salisbury*, Studies of the Warburg Institute, 17 (London, 1950).

Constant J. Mews, 'Peter Abelard', in *Authors of the Middle Ages, vol. 2, nos 5–6* (Aldershot, 1995), pp. 1–88 [also published separately].

Wolfgang P. Müller, *Huguccio: the Life, Works, and Thought of a Twelfth-Century Jurist*, Studies in medieval and early modern canon law, 3 (Washington, DC, 1994).

R.W. Southern, *Saint Anselm: a Portrait in a Landscape* (Cambridge, 1990).

Michael Wilks, ed., *The World of John of Salisbury*, Studies in church history: subsidia 3 (Oxford, 1994).

Translated Texts

KNOWN AUTHORS

Peter Abelard, *Peter Abelard's Ethics*, ed. D.E. Luscombe (Oxford, 1971).

——ˆ*A Dialogue of a Philosopher with a Jew and a Christian*, ed. Pierre J. Payer, Pontifical Institute of Mediaeval Studies: Mediaeval sources in translation, 20 (Toronto, 1979).

Betty Radice, ed., *The Letters of Abelard and Heloise* (Harmondsworth, 1974).

Alan of Lille *Anticlaudianus, or the Good and Perfect Man*, trans. James J. Sheridan (Toronto, 1973).

Anselm, *Anselm of Canterbury* (ed. Jasper Hopkins and Herbert Richardson), 4 vols (London, Toronto, and New York, 1974–6). The first three volumes contain translations of Anselm's works, including the *Monologion* and *Proslogion* in vol. 1, and *Why God became a Man* in vol. 3.

Anselm, *The prayers and meditations of Saint Anselm*, trans. Benedicta Ward (Harmondsworth, 1973).

Geoffrey of Monmouth, *History of the Kings of Britain*, trans. Lewis Thorpe (Harmondsworth, 1966).

Gratian, *Gratian: The Treatise on Laws (Decretum DD.1-20) with the Ordinary Gloss*, trans. Augustine Thompson and James Gordley, Studies in medieval and early modern canon law, 2 (Washington, DC, 1993).

Guibert of Noget, *A Monk's Confessions: the Memoirs of Guibert of Nogent*, trans. Paul J. Archambault (University Park, PA, 1996).

Hildegard of Bingen, *Scivias*, trans. Mother Columba Hart and Jane Bishop (New York, 1990).

—— *The Book of the Rewards of Life (Liber vitae meritorum)*, trans. Bruce W. Hozecki (New York and Oxford, 1994).

—— *Saint Hildegard of Bingen: Symphonia. A Critical Edition of the Symphonia armonie celestium revelationum [Symphony of the Harmony of Celestial Revelations]*, ed. Barbara Newman (Ithaca, GA, and London, 1988).

Hugh of St Victor, *The Didascalicon of Hugh of St Victor*, trans. Jerome Taylor, (New York, 1961).

Jocelin of Brakelond, *Chronicle of the Abbey of Bury St Edmunds*, trans. Diana Greenway and Jane Sayers (Oxford, 1989).

John of Salisbury, *The Letters of John of Salisbury, vol. 1: The Early Letters (1153–1161)*, ed. W.J. Millor and H.E. Butler, rev. C.N.L. Brooke (2nd edn, Oxford, 1986).

—— *The Letters of John of Salisbury, vol. 2: The Later Letters (1163–1180)*, ed. W.J. Millor and C.N.L. Brooke (Oxford, 1979).

—— *The Metalogicon of John of Salisbury: a Twelfth-Century Defense of the Verbal and Logical Arts of the Trivium*, trans. Daniel D. MacGarry (Gloucester, MA, 1971).

—— *Policraticus: Of the Frivolities of Courtiers and the Footprints of Philosophers*, ed. and trans. Cary J. Nederman (Cambridge, 1990).

Marie de France, *The Lais of Marie de France*, trans. Robert Hanning and Joan Ferrante (Durham, NC, 1978).

Richard fitzNeal, *The Course of the Exchequer by Richard, son of Nigel, Treasurer of England and Bishop of London*, trans. Charles Johnson (London, etc., 1950).

Suger, *On the Abbey Church of St-Denis and its Art Treasures*, trans. Erwin Panofsky (Princeton, NJ, 1946).

A. Dalzell, ed., *'Introductiones dictandi' by Transmundus*, Pontifical Institute of Mediaeval Studies: Studies and texts, 123 (Toronto, 1995).

William of Malmesbury, *The Historia Novella of William of Malmesbury*, trans. K.R. Potter (London, etc., 1955).

ANONYMOUS AUTHORS AND GENERAL BOOKS

Rita Hamilton and Janet Perry, trans., *The Poem of the Cid* (Manchester, 1975; Harmondsworth, 1984).

Norman Kretzmann and Eleonore Stump, eds, *The Cambridge Translations of Medieval Philosophical Texts, vol. 1: Logic and the Philosophy of Language* (Cambridge, 1988). Sections 2–7 contain translations of extracts from works from the years c.1100–1275.

Pauline Matarasso, *The Cistercian World: Monastic Writings of the Twelfth Century* (Harmondsworth, 1993). Includes extracts from Aelred of Rievaulx, *On Spiritual Friendship*.

A.J. Minnis and A.B. Scott, eds, *Medieval Literary Theory and Criticism, c. 1100–c. 1375: the Commentary Tradition* (rev. edn, Oxford, 1991). A wide-ranging series of extracts, including the prologue to Abelard's *Sic et non* at pp. 87–100.

Bernard O'Donoghue, ed., *The Courtly Love Tradition* (Manchester, 1982).

Index

Works are indexed under author, where known, otherwise by title. Except in rare cases where a surname is appropriate, individuals are indexed by Christian names.